# CHRISTIANITY
# AND THE AGE
# OF THE EARTH

# CHRISTIANITY AND THE AGE OF THE EARTH

DAVIS A. YOUNG
Associate Professor of Geology, Calvin College

**ZONDERVAN**
**PUBLISHING HOUSE**   OF THE ZONDERVAN CORPORATION
GRAND RAPIDS, MICHIGAN 49506

CHRISTIANITY AND THE AGE OF THE EARTH
Copyright © 1982 by The Zondervan Corporation
Grand Rapids, Michigan

First printing March 1982

**Library of Congress Cataloging in Publication Data**
Young, Davis A.
    Christianity and the age of the earth.

    Includes bibliographies and index.
    1. Bible and geology. 2. Earth—Age.
3. Catastrophes (Geology) I. Title.
BS657.Y67          231.7'65          81-16266
ISBN 0-310-44591-4                   AACR2

Edited by Ben Chapman
Designed by Martha Bentley
*Printed in the United States of America*

## TO MY MOTHER

"She speaks with wisdom,
and faithful instruction
is on her tongue."
*Proverbs 31:26*

# Contents

# Preface

Human beings are fascinated by the spectacular, the bizarre, and the mysterious. We are intrigued by stories of flying saucers, the Loch Ness monster, Bigfoot-Sasquatch, and the Bermuda triangle. Thoughts of vast conspiracies to murder national leaders or to alter foreign governments stimulate our curiosity. The monumental catastrophic explanations of world history by Immanuel Velikovsky had great popular appeal.

Evangelical Christians share this fascination for such topics. Perhaps curiosity about and belief in bizarre and unusual occurrences comes more easily for the Christian. We do, after all, believe in the Virgin Birth and the Resurrection. One fascinating matter that is perennially popular in evangelical circles concerns the origins and history of the Earth. It is common among Christians to believe that the Earth is very young and has experienced a brief, violent, catastrophic history dominated by two events: a miraculous creation and a global flood. Many Christian scientists have been arguing that the Earth's geological features can be explained in terms of this short, catastrophic history. Vast numbers of Christian laymen have been intrigued by this Christian catastrophism, and much literature on the subject exists today. This Christian catastrophist literature claims that the interpretations of Earth history held by the geological community are incorrect, and that the Earth is not an ancient planet at all but was created only a few thousands of years ago.

In view of the literature advancing biblical catastrophism, the interest of Christian laymen, and attempts to introduce the catastrophist view of Earth history into public school curricula, the Christian community should seriously consider this issue of the age of the Earth. Does the biblical and scientific evidence support the idea that the Earth is extremely young or does the evidence indicate otherwise? Has the Earth experienced a brief sudden catastrophic history dominated by a single global flood or has its history been vastly longer and somewhat less spectacular? In this book I seek to examine some of the evidence of nature that relates to the age of the Earth.

Often, geological evidences have been put forward by Christian scientists in support of the idea that the Earth is only a few thousands of years old; this book will show that the evidence from the science of geology does not at all support the idea of a young Earth. The evidence, in fact, destroys that view. In an earlier work, *Creation and the Flood,* I dealt with the biblical evidence regarding the age of the Earth, and showed that the Bible does not compel the Christian to believe in a young Earth.

Although I am opposing an idea that is common and on the surface sounds biblical, the reader must not draw the conclusion that I am opposing Christianity or attacking the Bible or even opposing the idea that the Flood was global in nature. I write as one who is firmly committed to the infallibility and inerrancy of Scripture and in full agreement with historic Christianity. I simply believe that the young-Earth view is unscientific and not necessarily biblical. I believe that continued promotion of such ideas will in the long run damage the credibility of Christianity and thus hinder our evangelistic and apologetic efforts.

I regret the fact that in this book I must call those with whose views I disagree, "creationists," because I am a creationist, and I believe the biblical record of creation. Unfortunately, however, those who advocate the creation of the world in seven literal days only a few thousand years ago have come to be known generally as creationists. Hence, the reader should not draw the conclusion that I am opposed to creation simply because I use the term "creationist." I would like to say only that my understanding of creation as taught in Scripture differs from that of those whom I term "creationists."

The text has profited from the reviews and comments of a number of people. My wife has provided a number of stylistic suggestions, which I trust improve the flow of thought. Nearly the entire manuscript has been read by Dr. Robert Manweiler, formerly a physicist at Calvin College and now at Valparaiso University, and by Dr. Clarence Menninga, a geologist at Calvin College. Their incisive comments were very helpful. I would also thank Jan Woudenberg who so faithfully and diligently typed the manuscript. Chapter 10 is a modified version of an article, "Flood Geology is Uniformitarian!" that appeared in the *Journal of the American Scientific Affiliation.*

*Davis A. Young*
*Grand Rapids, Michigan*

# PART ONE

# CHURCH HISTORY
# AND THE
# AGE OF THE EARTH

# —1—
# THE AGE of the EARTH in CHRISTIAN THOUGHT to the SEVENTEENTH CENTURY

MORE THAN A CENTURY ago the geologist and ecclesiastical journalist Hugh Miller, predicted that soon the ideas of a group he called "anti-geologists" would be as obsolete as those of the astronomers who upheld the geocentric orthodoxy of Ptolemy against the heliocentric idea of Galileo. According to Miller, it would soon be plain to all that the concept of a young Earth destroyed by a single, global flood (antigeology) was a bizarre relic. The time was at hand when the history of the Earth through long geologic ages would be found "more worthy of its Divine Author than that which would huddle the whole into a few literal days, and convert the incalculably ancient universe which we inhabit into a hastily run-up erection of yesterday."[1]

Miller's prediction, quite surprisingly, has failed; the age of the Earth is still a controversial issue within the Christian community, particularly in the United States. Scores of books, pamphlets, and articles have recently been written by Christians who are still convinced that the world is only a few thousand years old. Nonetheless, other Christians are convinced, with Miller, that a long geological history is consistent with the inspired account of creation in Genesis. Such sharp divergence of opinion on this question is recent, for until the end of the eighteenth century, Christians were virtually unanimous in the belief that the Earth was about six thousand years old according to the teaching of Scripture.

However, increased scientific study during the eighteenth and nineteenth centuries brought pressures to bear upon Christian thinkers to reevaluate the question of the age of the Earth. Accumulating evidence from nature pointed in the direction of the vast antiquity of the Earth and forced theologians to take a much harder, more penetrating look at the biblical record than ever before. Many new exegetical insights were developed as a result of the impetus provided by a scientific investigation of nature, but not all Christians have agreed.

The present controversy over the age of the Earth within evangelical Christendom is both biblical and scientific. Those who argue that the Earth is only a few thousand years old generally maintain that the six days of creation (Gen. 1) must be taken as six literal, ordinary, twenty-four-hour days. They also maintain that the Flood covered the entire globe and did a tremendous amount of geological work. There are other Christians who believe that the Earth is extremely old, and have not felt the necessity of maintaining the literalness of the six days, but have instead interpreted the days in various other ways.[2] Genesis does not necessarily require us to believe that the Flood covered the entire globe; the Flood could have been a very large local inundation. The various exegetical considerations concerning the Flood have been discussed repeatedly by many writers, and thus will not be discussed very much in this book.[3]

The controversy also involves science. Christians who believe that the Earth is very ancient are generally persuaded by scientific arguments that such is the case. On the other hand, many Christians, who might be considered the modern equivalents of Miller's "anti-geologists," are persuaded that the scientific evidence does not support the antiquity of the Earth at all. These men, who have been variously termed "mature creationists," "recent creationists," "Flood geologists," "Flood catastrophists," "biblical neo-catastrophists," or "strict creationists," have put forward a large number of scientific arguments in favor of a young Earth. Because there have been relatively few attempts to refute these arguments, this book examines the scientific arguments given to support a young-Earth view to see if they are valid.

However, in order that we may see the present controversy in somewhat clearer perspective, it will be helpful for us to consider briefly the history of the matter of the age of the Earth within the Christian church. The first part of the book is an historical sketch dealing with Christian thought on the age of the Earth. The second part will discuss specific scientific arguments that have been put forward in support of the young-Earth theory.

## Greek Views

The early church provided us with much valuable material on the interpretation of the creation account. Many profound thoughts were expressed about Genesis by the church fathers. Christians today can still be edified by the sermons on the hexameron (the creation of the universe in six days) by Basil or Ambrose, and challenged to deeper thought by the ideas of Origen or Augustine. In spite of the valuable nature of their contributions, the early Christian writers were not pressed to dig as deeply into ᵑesis 1 as more recent Christians have been because they did not have to ᵑgainst the background of the scientific investigation of the Earth. ℰⱼ      ᵗt to say that there was no study of the Earth at all in the times of the early church. Although their main scientific interests were in astronomy and geometry, the Greeks did inquire into the nature of earthquakes, volcanoes, rivers, fossils, and other geological phenomena. It has been suggested that the Greeks had even developed a fairly elaborate theory of marine transgressions onto the land in order to account for the existence of fossils far removed from present coastlines.[4]

The earliest of the Greeks known to have commented on the existence of fossils was Xenophanes (6th cent. B.C.), some of whose ideas have been preserved in the work of Hippolytus (A.D. 170–236) who wrote that

Xenophanes is of opinion that there had been a mixture of the earth with the sea, and that in process of time it was disengaged from the moisture, alleging that he could produce such proofs as the following: that in the midst of earth, and in mountains, shells are discovered; and also in Syracuse he affirms was found in the quarries the print of a fish and of seals, and in Paros an image of a laurel in the bottom of a stone, and in Melita parts of all sorts of marine animals. And he says that these were generated when all things originally were embedded in mud, and that an impression of them was dried in the mud, but that all men had perished when the earth, being precipitated into the sea, was converted into mud; then, again, that it originated generation, and that this overthrow occurred to all worlds.[5]

Xenophanes explained the existence of fossils in terms of flooding of the land by the sea, although he may have been influenced in his thinking by the Greek legend of Deucalion's flood. No indication of how much time Xenophanes thought was involved in the process is found in the existing literature from classical times, but the idea of marine transgression became firmly embedded in Greek thought.

Herodotus (5th cent. B.C.), astute observer that he was, also was well aware of the existence of fossils and of various geological processes. His travels in Egypt led him to hypothesize about the history of the Nile River. He believed that the Nile valley was originally a gulf much like the Red Sea and that the valley had gradually silted up over the course of time.

Suppose, now, that the Nile should change its course and flow into this gulf— the Red Sea—what is to prevent it from being silted up by the stream within, say, twenty thousand years? Personally I think even ten thousand would be enough. That being so, surely in the vast stretch of time which has passed before I was born, a much bigger gulf than this could have been turned into dry land by the silt brought down by the Nile—for the Nile is a great river and does, in fact, work great changes.[6]

The existence of fossil shells in the hills and salt in the soil supported his idea that the Nile valley had once been under the sea. There is also some evidence that information about Nile delta geography obtained from Egyptian records played a part in Herodotus' calculations. Herodotus' estimate appears to be the earliest effort to quantify a geological process; he believed that several thousands of years were required for the silting of the

Nile and this time clearly exceeds the 5500 year age of the Earth accepted by the early Christians.

Xanthus of Sardis (5th cent. B.C.) is recorded by Strabo as also having taught the former occupancy of land by the sea.

> . . . far from the sea, in Armenia, Matiene, and Lower Phrygia, he himself had often seen, in many places, stones in the shape of a bivalve, shells of the pecten order, impressions of scallop-shells, and a salt-marsh, and therefore was persuaded that these plains were once sea.[7]

Aristotle (384–22 B.C.) contributed more than all other Greeks to knowledge of the earth sciences. His views on the nature of earthquakes and volcanoes and of different kinds of exhalations from the earth, spelled out in considerable detail in *Meteorologica,* exerted tremendous influence on geological thinking in the Western world until well after the Middle Ages. Like his predecessors Xenophanes, Xanthus, and Herodotus, he, too, believed that the sea had once been where land now is.

> The same parts of the earth are not always moist or dry, but change their character according to the appearance or failure of rivers. So also mainland and sea change places and one area does not remain earth, another sea, for all time, but sea replaces what was once dry land, and where there is now sea there is at another time land. This process must, however, be supposed to take place in an orderly cycle . . . But these changes escape our observation because the whole natural process of the earth's growth takes place by slow degrees and over periods of time which are vast compared to the length of our life, and whole peoples are destroyed and perish before they can record the process from beginning to end.[8]

Aristotle believed that all rivers came into being and then eventually disappeared because the universe is eternal and thus plenty of time is available for such continuing changes to occur.

> It is therefore clear that as time is infinite and the universe eternal that neither Tanais nor Nile always flowed but the place whence they flow was once dry: for their action has an end whereas time has none. And the same may be said with truth about other rivers. But if rivers come into being and perish and if the same parts of the earth are not always moist, the sea also must necessarily change correspondingly. And if in places the sea recedes while in others it encroaches, then evidently the same parts of the earth as a whole are not always sea, nor always mainland, but in process of time all change.[9]

Although these and other Greek thinkers saw evidences of geological change that seemed to extend well into the past they were unable to develop any convincing means for estimating the amount of time that such changes might have implied. Even Herodotus' calculation was only an educated guess. Moreover, no other lines of evidence for the antiquity of the Earth were worked out at all, so it is little wonder that early Christians were unimpressed by Greek earth science. Such efforts must have appeared to them as so much wild speculating.

The chief sources for the idea of the antiquity of the Earth in early Christian times were not derived from science but stemmed rather from philosophy and the historical records of the Egyptians, Chaldeans, and other Middle Eastern peoples. The idea of the eternity of the world was a philosophical speculation widely held by Greek thinkers. The early Christians quite rightly opposed the eternity of the world; they believed in the creation of the world by God and the eternity of God alone. Moreover, the historical records of other peoples were regarded by the Christians as rather unreliable in comparison with the divinely inspired biblical records. For example, Theophilus of Antioch (A.D. 115–81) condemned

> the empty labor and trifling of these authors, because there have neither been twenty thousand times ten thousand years from the flood to the present time, as Plato said, affirming that there had been so many years; nor yet 15 times 10,375 years, as we have already mentioned Apollonius the Egyptian gave out; nor is the world uncreated. . . .[10]

Then, too, Julius Africanus (c. A.D. 200–45) took issue with others as follows:

> The Egyptians, indeed, with their boastful notions of their own antiquity, have put forth a sort of account of it by the hand of their astrologers in cycles and myriads of years; which some of those who have had the repute of studying such subjects profoundly have in a summary way called lunar years; and inclining no less than others to the mythical, they think they fall in with the eight or nine thousands of years which the Egyptian priests in Plato falsely reckon up to Solon . . . why should I speak of the three myriad years of the Phoenicians, or of the follies of the Chaldeans, their forty-eight myriads?[11]

## Christian Reaction to Greek Science

If the Greeks did not develop any particularly impressive evidence for the antiquity of the Earth from their study of the phenomena of nature, they at least tried to study the Earth. Early Christians were not very interested in investigation of the Earth; they evidently were not given to any natural scientific study. To be sure, the opportunity for leisurely investigation of nature was not present during the early centuries of Christian history, but even if it had been one may doubt how enthusiastically Christians would have pursued scientific inquiry. While Christian apologists were often willing to use genuine scientific knowledge in their defense of the faith, they frequently displayed deep suspicion toward scientific investigation. The study of nature was strongly bound up with philosophy in Greek culture and was therefore suspect.

For example, Basil (4th cent.), in his sermons on the hexameron, showed considerable acquaintance with Greek thought on science. He even accepted the classic four elements of Greek science as well as the sphericity of the Earth, but nonetheless he was somewhat wary of Greek science for it had clearly not led the Greeks to a true knowledge of God. Moreover, he was aware that on a given topic of study there might be a large number of conflicting viewpoints and so he viewed the whole primitive scientific enterprise as rather speculative and unfruitful and as not leading to sound knowledge as did Scripture. He felt that attempts to investigate the Earth were of little value.

> These same thoughts, let us also recommend to ourselves concerning the earth, not to be curious about what its substance is; nor to wear ourselves out by reasoning, seeking its very foundation . . . Therefore, I urge you to abandon these questions and not to inquire upon what foundation it stands. If you do that, the mind will become dizzy, with the reasoning going on to no definite end.[12]

Others, like Lactantius (A.D. 260–330) and Augustine (354–430), were openly sceptical of the sphericity of the Earth, a fact that had been established long before the appearance of Christ, and were decidedly hostile to the inferences drawn by the Greeks that there might actually be people living on the other side of the globe. Lactantius, for example, said:

> How is it with those who imagine that there are antipodes opposite to our footsteps? Do they say anything to the purpose? Or is there any one so senseless as to believe that there are men whose footsteps are higher than their heads? or that the things which with us are in a recumbent position, with them hang in an inverted direction? that the crops and trees grow downwards? that the rains, and snow, and hail fall upwards to the earth. And does any one wonder that hanging gardens are mentioned among the seven wonders of the world, when philosophers make hanging fields, and seas, and cities, and mountains? . . . I should be able to prove by many arguments that it is impossible for the heaven to be lower than the earth, were it not that this book must now be concluded. . . .[13]

And in the Epitome of his Divine Institutes, he said still more confidently:

> About the antipodes also one can neither hear nor speak without laughter. It is asserted as something serious, that we should believe that there are men who have their feet opposite to ours. The ravings of Anaxagoras are more tolerable, who said that snow was black.[14]

Augustine used reason and Scripture rather than sarcasm in his criticism of the theory of the antipodes:

> But as to the fable that there are Antipodes, that is to say, men on the opposite side of the earth, where the sun rises when it sets to us, men who walk with their feet opposite ours, that is on no ground credible. And, indeed, it is not affirmed that this has been learned by historical knowledge, but by scientific conjecture, on the ground that the earth is suspended within the concavity of the sky, and that it has as much room on the one side of it as on the other; hence they say that the part which is beneath must also be inhabited. But they do not follow that the other side of the earth is bare of water; nor even, though it be bare, does it immediately follow that it is peopled. For Scripture, which proves the truth of its historical statements by the accomplishment of its prophecies, gives no false information; and it is too absurd to say, that some men might have taken ship and traversed the whole wide ocean, and crossed from this side of the world to the

other, and that thus even the inhabitants of that distant region are descended from that one first man. Wherefore let us seek if we can find the city of God that sojourns on earth among those human races who are catalogued as having been divided into seventy-two nations and as many languages.[15]

Fortunately, however, other early Christians were more open-minded toward learning and the fruits of learning, including scientific work. Commenting on astronomy, Clement of Alexandria (A.D. 153–217) said:

And by astronomy, again, raised from the earth in his mind, he is elevated along with heaven, and will revolve with its revolution; studying ever divine things, and their harmony with each other; from which Abraham starting, ascended to the knowledge of Him who created them.[16]

And also,

The same holds also of astronomy. For treating of the description of the celestial objects, about the form of the universe, and the revolution of the heavens, and the motion of the stars, leading the soul nearer to the creative power, it teaches to quickness in perceiving the seasons of the year, the changes of the air, and the appearance of the stars; since also navigation and husbandry derive from this much benefit, as architecture and building from geometry. This branch of learning, too, makes the soul in the highest degree observant, capable of perceiving the true and detecting the false, of discovering correspondences and proportions, so as to hunt out for similarity in things dissimilar; and conducts us to the discovery of length without breadth, and superficial extent without thickness, and an indivisible point, and transports to intellectual objects from those of sense.[17]

Nonetheless the rule was that Christians tended to shy away from the investigation of nature and were skeptical of many conclusions about nature drawn by the Greeks. Moreover, the Greeks had not really drawn out abundant, conclusive, compelling evidence for the antiquity of the world from the phenomena of nature. Thus early Christian thinkers grappled with Genesis without any external pressure from the realm of science, and so they often did not probe as deeply as they might otherwise have and they often did not press onward to logical conclusions of positions they tentatively elicited from the text. We need not wonder that the early fathers did not fully work out the theology of creation, for they had not fully worked out other dogmas either. As Kuyper[18] has pointed out, the church was still in a state of relative theological naïveté.

## The Early Christian View of the Earth's Age

The virtually unanimous opinion among the early Christians until the time of Augustine was that human history from the creation of Adam to the birth of Christ had lasted approximately fifty-five hundred years. It is also very probable that the age of the world was regarded as the same number of years, for the writings of the church fathers generally do not reveal any sharp distinction between the initial creation and the creation of man. The widespread conviction existed that the present world order would last for six thousand years. Upon completion of the six thousand years, Christ would return to establish His kingdom of righteousness and peace. The early Christian thinkers thus fully expected the millennium to be ushered in around A.D. 500.

These beliefs were based on three lines of evidence. The first line derived from the fact that God had created the world in six days as recorded in Genesis one. In general, the church fathers regarded the days of creation as ordinary days corresponding to our existing sun-measured, solar days. Yet they did not shy away from regarding the days in a more figurative or allegorical sense either. Virtually all of them were struck by Psalm 90:4, "For a thousand years in your sight are like a day that has just gone by, or like a watch in the night," and by 2 Peter 3:8, "With the Lord a day is like a thousand years, and a thousand years are like a day." They had no difficulty whatever in transferring the days of creation into thousand-year periods on the basis of these texts. They had no difficulty in viewing the days figuratively as millennia as well as ordinary days. For them the concept of day was much broader than merely an ordinary, solar day. But the interesting feature of this patristic view is that the equation of days and millennia was not applied to the creation week but rather to subsequent history. They did not believe that the creation had taken place over six millennia but that the totality of human *history* would occupy six thousand years, a millennium of history for each of the six days of creation. Why this connection between creation and history was made is obscure. No reason for it is given by the fathers; it was simply assumed and taught. We meet first with this opinion in the epistle of Barnabas[19] and subsequently in the writings of Irenaeus (120–202).[20] Hippolytus,[21] Methodius (260–312),[22] Lactantius,[23] John of Damascus,[24] and others. Although many early theologians may have misinterpreted and misapplied Psalm 90:4 and 2 Peter 3:8, it is clear that they had little difficulty in making a connection between the six days of creation and long periods of time.

The church fathers also suggested that the world was less than six thousand years old at the time of Christ because of the chronology of the genealogical accounts of Genesis 5 and 11 and other chronological information in Scripture. Appeal was frequently made to such chronological data in an effort to demonstrate the antiquity and greater reliability of the Mosaic revelation as over against Greek or pagan thought in men like Homer, Hesiod, or Plato. Justin Martyr (110–65) and Tatian (110–72), in fact, frequently accused the Greeks of having plagiarized from the Old Testament.

The appeals to chronology were most fully worked out first by Theophilus of Antioch and subsequently by Clement of Alexandria, Julius Africanus, Eusebius (c. 265–340), and Augustine. In *Ad Autolycus* Theophilus[25] calculated that from the creation of the world to the onset of the flood was 2242 years, to Abraham 3278 years, to the Babylonian captivity 4954 years, and to the time of his own writing 5698 years. Thus he would have placed creation at 5529 B.C.

Theophilus, in his brief commentary on the hexameron,[26] clearly regarded the days of creation as types. For example, he regarded the first three days as a type of the Trinity and the fourth day as a type of man. Nonetheless he also definitely thought of the creation days as ordinary solar days for he attempted to date various events and people from the beginning of the creation of the world, and not just from the creation of Adam.

Clement of Alexandria freely applied allegorical interpretations to the days of creation.[27] Whether or not he also regarded the days literally is unclear, but he certainly regarded human history as of short duration. His calculations from chronological data in Scripture led him to conclude that 2148 years and four days had elapsed between the creation of Adam and the Flood, and that approximately 5590 years had elapsed between Adam's creation and the birth of Christ.

The most extensive calculations were those of Julius Africanus. In his *Chronography* Julius elaborately worked out calculations based on both Scripture and secular history and concluded that from Adam to the Flood was 2262 years, and that from Adam to the Advent of the Lord was 5531 years.[28]

Augustine also maintained that less than six thousand years had passed in the history of the world.[29] In the context of his argument, he was speaking against the vast antiquities claimed for kingdoms like Assyria, Persian, and Macedonia by heathen writers. Thus it may be that Augustine was thinking in terms of human history being less than six thousand years in duration. Augustine's allegorical ideas about the days of creation may have led him to think that the date of creation could have been earlier than this, but there is no evidence that such is the case, and we need to remember that Augustine's views on creation were not completely consistent. Elsewhere[30] Augustine noted that according to copies of Scripture available to him 2262 years had elapsed between the time of Adam and the deluge, but according to the Hebrew text, 1656 years.

A third line of argument in support of a short history for the Earth was provided by Hippolytus.[31] When Hippolytus asked the question as to how we know that the Lord appeared in the year fifty-five hundred he did not make the obvious appeal to the genealogies and other chronological data in the Bible, nor did he at this point lean heavily on the supposed equation between days of creation and millennia of history. Instead he argued on symbolic grounds. He saw that numbers throughout Scripture were not just literal numbers but also were symbols of spiritual realities. For example, he referred to Exodus 25:10, a text that states the dimensions of the ark of the covenant. The ark is seen to be $2\frac{1}{2} \times 1\frac{1}{2} \times 1\frac{1}{2}$ cubits in size. These three figures when added yield a sum of $5\frac{1}{2}$ cubits, and so it was plain to Hippolytus that the $5\frac{1}{2}$ cubits are a symbol of the five-and-a-half millennia of history that had elapsed prior to the coming of Christ. But appeal was also made to Revelation 17:10, which says that the seven horns on the beast are seven kings, "five have fallen, one is, the other has not yet come." Hippolytus completely ignored the reference to kings and saw the numbers as referring to millennia. From his perspective, five millennia had gone, he was living in the middle of the sixth, and the seventh was for him wholly future. Hippolytus also believed that John 19:14 gives a hint as to the age of the world. Here it is recorded that at the trial of Jesus it was about the sixth hour, that is, noon or halfway through the day. Since one day is as a thousand years, half a day equals five hundred years. So it is plain that the end of Christ's life history was in the middle of another millennium.

In order to arrive at the conclusion that the world was approximately fifty-five hundred years old at the time of Christ it was necessary to hold to a strictly literal view of the genealogies of Genesis 5 and 11. It does not seem to have occurred to any of the early Christians that there might be gaps or omissions in those genealogies of Scripture. Hence they felt perfectly justified in summing the ages of the patriarchs in, say, Genesis 5, in order to obtain the number of years between Adam and the Flood. The calculations worked out from these genealogies by Theophilus, Julius, and others were based on the Septuagint rather than the Hebrew text, so that the sums obtained for the time that had elapsed between Adam and Abraham were greater by several hundred years than they would have been had the Hebrew text been followed.

It was also generally necessary that the days of creation (Gen. 1) be regarded as ordinary days if one were to hold that the Earth was only fifty-five hundred years old. We find absolutely no one arguing that the world is tens of thousands of years old on the grounds that the six days are used figuratively for indefinite periods of time. Not even Origen (185–254),[32] who came closest to holding the great antiquity of the Earth, maintained such a view. In fact, Origen argued for a succession of worlds rather than a very ancient existing world. Many of the church fathers plainly regarded the six days as ordinary days. Basil explicitly spoke of the day as a twenty-four-hour period.[33]

Several patristic theologians, however, regarded the six days of creation as unique, somewhat peculiar, and so had difficulty in regarding them only as literal days. Thus we find allegorical interpretations in profusion. Of course, much else in Scripture was also treated allegorically. There are hints of the idea that the six days were not a real succession, but that everything had been created simultaneously. Augustine hinted at such a view. Hilary of Poitiers (c. 300–67) supposedly held such a view according to Luther, but a close examination of what Hilary said indicates that he was establishing the point that God had a single plan prior to creation rather than that He created all things at once.[34] What Hilary denied was that God created the earth, then thought out the next step, then created the waters, thought out the next step, and so on. Augustine, however, did depart from the idea that the six days were ordinary days. His views on the subject are the most thoroughly worked out of any of the early Christians.

Augustine initiated the view that the first three days were not ordinary days. He said that these days could not have been ordinary days because they were not marked by the rising and setting of the sun.[35] Furthermore he said "what kind of days these were is difficult or impossible to conceive."[36] He also maintained that the events described in the first two verses of the Bible were not a part of the six days. He spoke of the heavens as some kind of intellectual creature, not co-eternal with God, but still a partaker of eternity, surpassing all the rolling change of time.[37] Thus he opened the door for an understanding of Genesis 1 that would allow for an Earth that is much older than six thousand years and began to develop one of the major emphases of the restitution hypothesis, which appeared nearly fourteen hundred years after his time.

Also of extreme importance in Augustine's writing was his contention that the seventh day of creation week still continues. He said that the seventh day has no evening and morning because God sanctified it to everlasting continuance.[38] This view likely did not originate with Augustine, however. Anastasius[39] indicated that men like Irenaeus and Justin taught that the seventh day was different in character because it is not recorded that there were morning and evening. According to Anastasius, they held that, because of lack of that expression, the consummation was to take place before the seventh day was finished. Whether this referred to the seventh day itself or simply to the seventh millennium corresponding to that day we cannot tell, but the uniqueness of the seventh day of creation week was clearly recognized. Augustine, however, does seem to have maintained its continuing existence. Despite the idea that the seventh day continues, no thought was really given to the idea that the other six days might also be long time periods, and this is doubly intriguing because of the ready connection between the day and the millennium. Despite anticipations of internal biblical evidence suggestive of the antiquity of the Earth in the creation account the church fathers failed to carry through the logic of their insights.

## The Medieval Church

Churchmen continued to think about the meaning of Genesis and creation, and numerous studies of creation and the hexameron appeared, written by men such as the Venerable Bede (8th cent.), St. Bonaventure (1221–74), Albertus Magnus (c. 1193–1280), and Thomas Aquinas (c. 1225–74). These works were strongly influenced by the thinking of the Fathers and relatively little new material that is of significance regarding the question of the age of the Earth appeared.

## Reformation and Post-Reformation Views

During and after the Reformation there was increased interest in deriving the age of the Earth from biblical considerations. Biblical chronology became a highly refined science as scholars eventually sought to determine not only the year in which creation had taken place, but also the season, and in some cases, the month, week, day, and hour. The results of these more modern determinations of the Earth's antiquity differed significantly from those of the church fathers in that the chronological calculations were based not on the Septuagint but on the more accurate Hebrew text. As a result the typical date for the creation of the Earth was approximately fifteen hundred years later than the date held by the fathers. Moreover, we find a strong tendency to abandon some of the more allegorical and figurative interpretations of the days of Genesis adopted by many of the church fathers, and a heavy dependence on the strictly literal view of the days.

Martin Luther (1483–1546), for example, completely rejected Augustine's approach to Genesis 1 and insisted on a strictly literal exegesis of the six days.[40] Luther insisted that the Earth was not yet six thousand years old, and was of the opinion that the creation had occurred in the spring. Others of the Lutheran wing of the Reformation who agreed with him were Philip Melanchthon (1497–1560) and John Gerhard (1582–1637). On the other hand, Calvisius (1556–1615) calculated that the creation had occurred in 3944 B.C., but concluded that the creation took place in the autumn.

John Calvin (1509–65) in his *Institutes of the Christian Religion* assumed that the world had not yet seen its six thousandth year. For example, Calvin stated:

> We must not be moved by the profane jeer, that it is strange how it did not sooner occur to the Deity to create the heavens and the earth, instead of idly allowing an infinite period to pass away, during which thousands of generations might have existed, while the present world is drawing to a close before it has completed its six thousandth year.[41]

Other Calvinists concurred regarding the age of the Earth, and men like Zanchius (1516–90), Voetius (1589–1676), Maresius (1599–1673), and Francis Turretin (1623–87), who, years after the death of Galileo, was still insisting from Scripture that the Earth was fixed and the Sun moved around it, believed that the creation had taken place in the autumn.

Roman Catholic thinkers like Francisco Suarez (1548–1617) and Thomas Cajetan (1469–1534) also held to a recent creation, and Petavius (1583–1652) fixed the date of creation at 3984 B.C. In the British Isles the famous Archbishop of Armagh James Ussher (1581–1656) proposed the date of 4004 B.C. as the time of creation, while Bishop Lightfoot of Cambridge went a bit further and suggested that the creation had occurred toward the end of October in 4004 B.C. and that Adam had been created at nine o'clock in the morning on October 23!

Our modern tendency is to regard such date setting with considerable amusement and incredulity. We tend to think of men like Ussher and Lightfoot as obscurantist fanatics. Yet we need to keep in mind that these men were in a line of accepted scholarship and that in their attempts to date the creation they were carefully using the best tools and methods available to them. We must not judge them harshly in terms of our own modern knowledge and outlook.

One slightly different point of view was presented by Bishop Simon Patrick (1626–1707) regarding the interpretation of Genesis. He suggested ideas that were reminiscent of some of those of Augustine. Patrick wrote:

> How long all things continued in mere confusion after the chaos was created, before light was extracted from it, we are not told. It might have been, for any thing that is here revealed, a great while; and all that time the mighty Spirit was making such motions in it, as prepared, disposed, and ripened every part of it for such productions as were to appear successively in such spaces of time as are here afterwards mentioned by Moses. . . .[42]

Patrick also suggested that the sixth day may have required a considerable amount of time in order to accomplish everything that is recorded as having occurred on that day. These ideas, however, had no impact on theology in terms of calling into question the idea that the Earth was only about six thousand years old.

It cannot be denied, in spite of frequent interpretations of Genesis 1 that departed from the rigidly literal, that the almost universal view of the Christian world until the eighteenth century was that the Earth was only a few thousand years old. Not until the development of modern scientific investigation of the Earth itself would this view be called into question within the church.

# —2—
# GEOLOGICAL
# INVESTIGATIONS
# to 1750

NATURAL PHILOSOPHERS FROM THE Renaissance to 1750 did not in any way regard the commonly accepted six thousand years of Earth history as restrictive to their scientific studies. They, too, believed that the dates obtained by the theologians for the age of the Earth were the fruits of careful scholarship using the best sacred and secular information available. Moreover, they developed no clear evidence to challenge such dates. Discoveries in the realm of science could be fitted quite neatly into a short Earth history without any embarrassment. However, during these years the foundations were being laid which would eventually lead to serious questioning of the accepted opinion about the age of the Earth. Advances in the study of fossils and rock strata were both necessary before such a challenge would come about. The Earth would not be seen to be very old until it was recognized that there had been several successions of animal and plant populations through time and that these populations had become fossilized in slowly deposited sediments that hardened into rock strata. Before these discoveries were made it was first necessary that the nature of both fossils and rock stratification be clearly understood. Advances in understanding in both these areas were made by 1750.

## The Nature of Fossils

Today we characteristically think of fossils as the remains of once-living plants and animals or parts thereof that were entombed in mud, sand, or clay, and eventually hardened into rock along with the enclosing material. However, there was little agreement on this point until nearly the middle of the eighteenth century. To be sure, some scholars thought of fossils as once-living things just as the classical Greeks had. Many who so believed felt that these objects were the remains of the creatures that had perished in the Noachian Deluge. Others found it difficult to account for the distribution of fossils in terms of the Flood, and so spoke of the interchanges between land and sea. Curiously, a great many able scholars were not convinced that fossils were organic at all. A wide variety of explanations were put forward to account for them. Fossils were variously regarded as sports or jokes of nature, as the works of God or perhaps the devil created directly in place in the rocks for a variety of inscrutable purposes, as the discards of divine dry runs at the creation of an organic world before God finally pronounced the present creation of animals and plants very good, as productions of various celestial influences, of fermenting vapors or plastic virtues in rocks, or of some subterranean fluid charged with the seminal principles of animals or plants.

Difficult as it is for us to comprehend such explanations today, we need to realize that a few centuries ago the very definition of a fossil created confusion.[1] Fossils to naturalists of, say, the sixteenth century, were any objects that were dug out of the Earth and included all manner of things, whether true fossils, minerals, crystals, rocks, concretions, ores, and so on. Given the state of knowledge of the Earth sciences, it was not always easy to distinguish among the various objects that came from the Earth. There are indeed many geological objects that superficially resemble organisms without being true fossils. For example, concretions can resemble all sorts of fossilized vegetables, ear lobes, bananas, and so on. Other concretions with mineral coatings can look a lot like the shells of turtles. Dendrites are branching, tree-like coatings of manganese oxides on rock surfaces; their arborescent pattern gives them a striking resemblance to plants. Geodes resemble eggs. So we need not wonder that if many inorganic rock materials look like living things, then true fossils could be regarded no differently and be seen simply as another expression of some force in nature that causes rocks to resemble organic materials.

The confusion was further compounded because of philosophical influences. Neo-Platonism held that there was no sharp distinction between living things and non-living things. Even the Earth itself was held to be in some sense alive. And so it should not be particularly surprising if we find the Earth studded with objects that look like living things. The nearly alive Earth created productions that mimicked life. Not only that, but many non-living things display some of the characteristics of living things. For example, stalactites and stalagmites in caves can actually be seen to be growing. Mineral crystals also exhibit the phenomenon of growth. There was even a belief in male and female stones, and in some cases it was thought that stones could give birth to new stones, when, for example, a hollow concretion was broken open and a much smaller stone was found inside the hollow. Thus powers of reproduction were not uncommonly attributed to the rocks. All of nature was seen as replete with all sorts of examples of organic processes and analogies. There was no need to rely on any elaborate explanation of fossils in terms of once living organisms that died, were buried, hardened, and so on. The living nature of the Earth was sufficient to produce the shapes of these figured stones.

Yet another powerful philosophical influence was that of Aristotle. In his *Meteorologica*, Aristotle had stressed the importance of vapors or exhalations in terrestrial phenomena.[2] Even a variety of stones were explained in terms of the actions of wet or dry vapors. Avicenna (980–1037), the great Arab scientist, modified and developed Aristotle's theory of exhalations, and proposed that rocks were produced by two processes, congelation and conglutination.[3] At the heart of Avicenna's theory was the idea of a congealing petrifying virtue, a fluid that had the capacity of transforming liquid into solid. The stalactites in caves were obvious examples of the operations of such a petrifying virtue. One could plainly see the dripping water turning into stone. So, too, were the hard deposits formed by hot springs. In later times, such virtues were viewed as operative in all of nature. So, then, the action of petrifying virtue in people produces gallstones, and the action of petrifying virtue in the atmosphere produced meteoritic stones falling from the sky. Fossils, it was maintained, could be explained in terms of the action of such a petrifying virtue on the seeds of animals or plants that had fallen down cracks and become trapped inside rocks where they then grew into petrified shapes resembling mature adults. Again, seemingly sensible explanations of the origins of fossils were available as alternatives to the modern explanation.

Besides the availability of acceptable nonorganic explanations, there were insurmountable difficulties associated with the idea that the so-called "formed stones" were the buried remains of once living organisms. Even when the neo-Platonic and Aristotelian influences gradually diminished toward the end of the seventeenth century and into the eighteenth century, these difficulties remained. They found expression in the work of some of the ablest natural philosophers of the times. One problem, for example, was the fact that many true fossils are not composed of the same material as modern animals, but rather are composed of the same material as the surrounding rock. This was the problem of the stoniness of fossils, and found its expression in the work of Martin Lister (c. 1638–1712), an outstanding student and collector of fossils, author of several books on fossil shells, and member of the Royal Society of London. Lister knew fossils so well that he even recognized the fact that only certain kinds of fossils were found in certain rock strata. But he was not convinced they were once alive. Lister pointed out that

> Iron-stone Cockles are all iron stone; Lime or Marble, all limestone or marble; sparre or Christalline-Shells, all sparre, etc., and that they were never any part of an animal.[4]

If a fossil shell was truly once a shell then why wasn't it composed of the exact material as a modern shell?

Other difficulties were expressed ably by John Ray (1627–1705), one of the finer naturalists of his time. In his great work, *Three Physico-Theological Discourses,*[5] Ray summarized in considerable detail the arguments both for and against the organic origin of fossils and quoted extensively from other experts. Ray was torn in both directions, and really could not make up his mind too convincingly. He believed that fossils are probably organic, and yet he felt very keenly the arguments against such a hypothesis. Indeed he felt it so keenly that he was inclined to reject the organic origin of at least some fossils that plainly are the remains of animals. There were two main stumbling blocks for Ray and many others. First, Ray was well aware of the fact that although the fossils bore a strong resemblance to modern living organisms they were generally not identical. Most fossils were not representatives of living species. If these fossils were truly once alive they must have been groups of creatures that are now totally extinct. But people in Ray's time simply were not prepared to accept the idea of extinction, for they believed in the plenitude of creation. It could not be seen how God, having pronounced the world very good, could permit any of His creatures to vanish from the face of the earth. Then, too, why was it that God took such extraordinary pains to see to it that nothing completely vanished from the Earth during the Flood? If two of each kind of animal were on the ark, then plainly God did not want any extinctions of species to occur. So the idea of extinction was not palatable to Ray. Nonetheless he suggested that perhaps we do not fully know all the types of living things that are on the Earth. It may well be that in the depths of the oceans there are as yet undiscovered creatures. Maybe some of these are the same as what we actually see embedded in the rocks. If such were true, fossils would be organic and yet there would be no problem of extinction. Ray's conjecture is certainly a correct one for several organisms have been discovered to be living today after they first became known from the fossil record. In spite of this way out of accounting for the differences between fossils and known living organisms, Ray still could not quite bring himself to accept the organic origin of the *cornua ammonis,* a type of extinct cephalopod, and some other fossil remains. Despite the fact that these objects resembled the modern nautilus, they just weren't similar enough, and Ray evidently did not think that modern representatives would be found in the sea. Up to this time, his view has been substantiated by the facts.[6]

Ray's second difficulty concerned the position of fossils. Fossils were found not only lying around loose on the surface close to the shorelines in relatively unconsolidated sediments, but they also were being found embedded in hard rock deep in quarries and in the highest mountains far removed both vertically and horizontally from the nearest ocean. If fossils were to be regarded as organic, one had to face the problem of accounting for the position of fossils. How did they ever get to be way up in the mountains far from the sea? One current explanation was the Genesis Flood, but Ray and many others did not see how a flood of less than a year's duration could possibly account for the observed distribution of rocks and fossils. If the Flood did not account for the fossils, then perhaps great earthquakes had lifted former sea beds to their present elevations as proposed by Robert Hooke. Without question, earthquakes had raised sea floors in historical times, but certainly not to the elevations found in mountainous regions. Besides that, no historical records of any earthquakes of such obviously enormous magnitude existed. Surely earthquakes capable of lifting the sea floor to heights of several thousands of feet would have been recorded by mankind; but they were not. As far as Ray was concerned, no known mechanism adequately accounted for the position of the fossils if they were treated as organic.[7] The letters of John Ray seem to indicate that he realized the serious implications of the organic origin of fossils for the Earth's history. He sensed that the Earth's history might have to be expanded backward in time from the commonly accepted six thousand years in order to account for the existence of fossil remains in the mountain tops, a step he was not ready to take.[8] Ray's views on fossils thus remained at something of a stalemate.

Views purporting the inorganic origins of fossils gradually faded from acceptance by the early eighteenth century as study of fossils continued and philosophical objections vanished. The last capable naturalist to advocate an inorganic origin was Johann Beringer, a professor in the University of Würzburg in Germany. Beringer loved to collect and sketch fossils, but was nonetheless convinced that they were simply curious shapes produced by nature. His published work, *Lithographiae Wirceburgiensis* (1726) contained drawings and descriptions of all manner of objects dug from local quarries including many genuine fossils, but also images of birds sitting in their nests, purely imaginary animals, and Hebrew letters including the name of God. Such extremely odd discoveries simply confirmed Beringer's belief that fossils were not buried organisms but only sports of nature. Beringer finally realized that he had been the victim of a cruel hoax when one day he discovered a rock with his own likeness and name on it. The perpetrators of the hoax, jealous of Beringer's reputation, had baked and carved fake fossils and planted them in Beringer's favorite collecting localities, and their creations became increasingly imaginative the longer their scheme went undetected. Beringer spent the rest of his life attempting to recall all the published copies of his book. It is probable that this tragicomic episode provided the death blow for the inorganic origin of fossils as a viable option among educated people.

## Diluvial Theories

A growing number of natural philosophers during the seventeenth and early eighteenth centuries accepted the organic origin of fossils and believed that they had found suitable explanations to account for their position in stratified rocks high in mountainous terrains. The Noachian Deluge emerged for a time as the most widely held explanation. The Book of

Genesis spoke of a great watery cataclysm that engulfed the Earth and destroyed all living things; hence it was sensible to assume that the Flood was responsible for all the dead plants and animals entombed in the rocks. This general point of view can be traced back to the time of the church fathers. Tertullian had spoken of the fossils in mountains as demonstrating a time when the globe was overrun by all waters, but it is not really clear whether or not he was talking about the Deluge.[9] There are hints that Chrysostom and Augustine thought of the Flood as responsible for many fossils, and Martin Luther is said to have attributed the origin of fossils to the agency of the Flood. During the seventeenth and eighteenth centuries such men as Jacobus Grandius, John Harris, John Hutchinson, Patrick Cockburn, and Alexander Catcott wrote in defense of some brand of Flood theory.

The most persuasive and influential expositions of Deluge theories were those which sought to explain the history of the Earth in terms of a combination of biblical information and the known laws of physics. Renè Descartes, for example, had sought to apply the laws of mechanics to the development of the Earth. Strongly influenced by this Cartesian view of the Earth, Thomas Burnet (1635–1715), an English theologian, tried to elaborate a history of the planet's development from the creation to the final consummation by melding the Bible and Descartes. The role of the Flood was elaborated in great detail. Burnet's work had a great impact on other writers who sought to develop Flood theories in terms of Scripture and the later Newtonian physics. Among these other views of the Earth were those of John Woodward and William Whiston.

Burnet's monumental work, entitled *The Theory of the Earth Containing an Account of the Original of the Earth, and of all the General Changes which it hath already Undergone, or is to Undergo till the Consummation of all Things,* first appeared in 1681. *The Sacred Theory of the Earth,* as it is usually known, cannot be considered as a genuine scientific work, even though it is about the Earth. Burnet's theory of the Earth was not built up through painstaking observation of the phenomena of nature; rather the theory was worked out through a combination of reasoning and Scripture.

> This Theory being chiefly Philosophical, Reason is to be our first Guide; and where that falls short, or any other just occasion offers itself, we may receive further light and confirmation from the Sacred writings. Both these are to be lookt upon as of Divine Original, God is the Author of both; He that made the Scripture made also our faculties, and 'twere a reflection upon the Divine Veracity, for the one or the other to be false when right us'd. We might therefore be careful and tender of opposing these to one another, because that is, in effect, to oppose God to himself. As for Antiquity and the Testimonies of the Ancients, we only make general reflections upon them, for illustration rather than proof of what we propose. . . .[10]

There was little recognition of the necessity for scientific observation, and Burnet even noted that the ancients in their contemplation of the Earth (many of the Greeks did try to theorize from geological observation) had never arrived at knowledge of what he is proposing. Only occasionally did Burnet mention some casual observations when they fell in line with his theory.

Burnet argued from Scripture that there had been a universal Deluge, and he calculated that about eight times the volume of the present ocean would have been necessary to cover all the land areas of Earth.[11] Where did all this water come from? It will not do, said Burnet, to argue that God created all that water specifically for the purpose of the Flood and then annihilated it when the Flood was over. We should not rely on a miracle to get us out of a difficulty. Rather, this extra water was built into the planet right from the beginning.[12] When Earth came from its chaotic condition, it was a perfectly smooth sphere with no irregularities. A differentiation of materials occurred with an oily fluid separating out on top of a watery sphere, which in turn surrounded the interior of the Earth. The oily fluid collected earthy particles and became the hardened, smooth crust. Hence in early times the land actually rested above a subterranean abyss or sphere of waters.[13] That this was so, Scripture supports, as in Psalm 24:2, "For he founded it upon the seas and established it upon the waters." This primitive Earth, suited for paradise, was idyllic. It was perpetually summer.[14] However, the lack of changing seasons caused the Earth to dry out gradually from the heat of the sun. Not only was the Earth gradually shrinking and desiccating, but the abyss was also starting to vaporize owing to the heat penetrating the crust. This vaporization created additional pressure on the underside of the crust.[15] At length in God's providence the time was ripe for the Flood, which was accomplished by the severe fragmenting of the crust and foundering of the crustal slabs into the abyss at all sorts of angles, thus accounting for mountains and lowlands. The sudden shock of the collapse of the crust caused tremendous outward surges of the abyssal waters, thus temporarily inundating the land.[16] This, according to Burnet, is the true meaning of the expression in Genesis 7:11, "On that day all the springs of the great deep burst forth."

When the Flood was over the waters gradually receded back into the channels of the sea, but also back into the vast subterranean caverns created by the collapses of the crust. That these caverns exist was abundantly plain to Burnet because of the existence of caves, volcanoes, and earthquakes. Moreover, the Mediterranean and Caspian Seas, having no significant surface outlets, would overflow if they were not connected to the oceans by means of underground passageways.[17]

Although Burnet's work never actually mentioned fossils, his Flood theory prompted considerable reaction and stimulated efforts to develop theories that did account for fossils. Among these efforts was the classic book of John Woodward (1665–1722), Professor of Physics at Gresham College, London, *An Essay towards a Natural History of the Earth* (1695). Burnet's theory had hardly been built up inductively from observations of the phenomena of the Earth. Woodward, on the other hand, was convinced that the only sound way to a true philosophy of the Earth was by means of careful observation.[18] The introduction to Woodward's work repeatedly stresses the importance of observation and takes pains to point out how careful he had been in carrying out observations of the Earth.[19] His observations led him to the realization that his own country and other areas that he had visited were all characterized by stratification of rock layers. Through correspondence with friends and other scholars he further learned that his own country was not unique in regard to the stratification of rocks.[20] Moreover, he also observed that the strata were very frequently fossiliferous.[21] Woodward then sought to account for the phenomena of stratification and fossilization. He argued convincingly that fossils were really the remains of organisms and discounted the inorganic theories.[22] Likewise he saw weaknesses in the idea that the sea and land had changed places.[23] Instead he invoked the existence of a global deluge. It was Woodward's contention that during the Flood, the prediluvian world was effectively dissolved, not in the chemical sense, but all rock and soil were completely disaggregated and became a thick slurry. All living things on the surface of the Earth were caught up and destroyed by this particle-charged flood.[24] As the flood waters diminished and disappeared the materials in suspension in the waters including the bodies of plants and animals gradually settled out in accordance with their specific gravity.[25] Thus, according to Woodward we find that fossils in certain strata typically are characterized by the same general specific gravity as the rocks which enclose them.[26] Now to be sure Woodward did make some measurements of the specific gravities of fossil shells and rocks and to that extent based his theory on observation, but it is quite plain that even here he began to be rather speculative; he was influenced by his knowledge of physics and did not base his views on observations, for it is perfectly plain that stratified rock layers were not laid down in order of decreasing specific gravity. Relatively low density rocks very commonly lie underneath those with heavier densities, and there is no definite progressive change in specific gravity from the bottom to the top of a stack of layered sedimentary rocks.

In the same vein as the two preceding books was William Whiston's (1667–1752) *A New Theory of the Earth* published in 1697. Whiston's credentials were impressive inasmuch as he was Newton's successor in mathematics at Cambridge. His theory contained much physics and astronomy, and, in that sense, is more of a scientific book than is Burnet's. Nevertheless Whiston's theory of the Earth is no more geological than is Burnet's. The theory was not worked out from geological observations to the degree that Woodward's was, but was a combination of Newtonian physics and Scripture superimposed on the Earth and supported by an occasional fact.

Whiston was highly favorable towards Archbishop Ussher's chronology of the Earth. He modified it slightly and concluded that the Earth had been created in 4010 B.C.[27] The original chaos of Genesis 1:2 from which the organized planet developed was the atmosphere of a comet.[28] The Earth then was originally a comet permanently captured by the sun. At first the Earth, said Whiston, did not rotate daily on its axis but had only an annual motion, so that from a given point on the planet's surface there was only one interchange of light and dark in a year.[29] Thus one of Whiston's more intriguing contentions was that the six days of creation were each one year in length. This is why his date for the creation is six years earlier than that of Ussher.

At the time of the fall of Adam, the Earth tilted on its axis to its present position; it began to rotate, and departed from a circular to an elliptical orbit about the sun.[30] The repetition of seasons and ordinary solar days thus began at the time of the fall of Adam. This state of affairs continued until the Deluge when another comet approached the planet. The comet triggered the onset of drenching rains, which covered the planet.[31] Life on the surface was destroyed and various life-forms settled out of the flood-waters in accordance with their specific gravity.[32] Thus, like Woodward, Whiston attributed fossil remains in mountains to the action of the Flood.

A curious aspect of Whiston's theory is his notion that the six days of creation were each one year in length because at that time there was no daily rotation of the Earth on its axis, but only an annual revolution about the sun. Whiston argued at great length from Scripture in defense of this view. In so doing he anticipated some of the arguments that reappeared in the day-age theory of the nineteenth century. First Whiston argued against taking the six days literally by noting that Genesis 2:4 spoke of the six days as "the day that the LORD God made the earth and heavens."[33] Second, he attempted to show the equivalence of days and years through such references as 1 Kings 2:11, "The days that David reigned over Israel were forty years," or Genesis 5:5, "All the days that Adam lived were nine hundred and thirty years," and particularly in the prophetic writings like Daniel 9:24ff., where the seventy weeks are weeks not of days but of years.[34] Third, Whiston argued that the various Levitical sabbaticals suggested a connection between days and years.[35] He also said that the events of the six days could not have taken place in twenty-four hours. He felt that the runoff of the waters from the emerging dry lands on day three would require much more than twenty-four hours, especially if subsequent growth of vegetation was to occur also. And too many events occurred on the sixth day to take place in twenty-four hours.[36] So here we have a catastrophic flood theory presented in terms of a very recent creation, yet anticipating the day-age view of Genesis 1 that subsequently was developed in defense of the idea that the Earth was extremely old.

In a considerably different vein flood "geology" found an enthusiastic advocate in the German naturalist, J. J. Scheuchzer (1672–1733). Scheuchzer cleverly attacked the inorganic view of fossils in a treatise entitled *The Fishes' Complaint and Vindication* (1708). In this work the argument was placed in the mouths of fossil fishes who complained about the unreasonableness of being treated as mere freaks of nature and insisted on being regarded as true fishes that had once lived and been stranded during the recession of the flood waters. The fish claimed to have been cosufferers with man in the Flood, and asked for the dignity of being recognized as such. As the climax to his flood theory Scheuchzer argued that some large vertebrae he had found were the remains of one of the sinners who had died in the Flood. Some time after the publication of his book, Scheuchzer learned that the bones belonged to a fishlike creature (subsequently known as *Ichthyosaurus*) rather than to a human being. Scheuchzer's sinner disappeared.

Despite this defeat Scheuchzer was still persuaded of his flood theory and sought for evidence of human remains to prove the occurrence of the Flood. Eighteen years after the appearance of *The Fishes' Complaint* some stone workers uncovered an entire fossilized skeleton and shipped it to Scheuchzer. After its reconstruction Scheuchzer was persuaded that here at last was the *homo diluvii testis,* the human witness of the flood, a notorious sinner, and a giant at that, who had perished in the Noachian Deluge. In 1726 he issued a treatise on the drowned man. It was not until 1787, to save Scheuchzer from any further embarrassment, that it was disclosed that the flood man was in reality a giant extinct salamander!

## Other Views on Fossils and Rock Strata

Some individuals were fully persuaded that fossils were indeed buried organisms but had not been formed during the Noachian Deluge. Leonardo da Vinci's (1452–1519) notebooks contain thoughts on fossils that suggest that he did not believe that the Flood was capable of accounting for the distribution of fossil shells, and Girolamo Fracastoro (1478–1553) held basically the same idea. Bernard Palissy (1510–89), was a self-taught man who had not read widely in the works of known authorities on nature and was not acquainted with the scholarly Latin of his day. Thus, for his views on nature, Palissy relied relatively little on established opinions and more on his own observations. As a ceramist, Palissy was necessarily much interested in the properties of soils and clays, and while studying them in nature he became quite aware of many geological phenomena, including fossils. His own observations convinced him that fossils were not sports of nature, but once living creatures. He did not, however, believe that the Flood had provided enough time for the effects he observed, and he thought that fossils were much too far from the sea and too far above sea level to be accounted for in terms of the Flood. It was his belief that fossils had once lived in lakes.

Robert Hooke (1635–1703) also regarded fossils as organic but rejected the flood theory. He has given us the most comprehensive discussion of fossils from this point of view to appear before 1750, in the form of *Lectures and Discourses of Earthquakes and Subterraneous Eruptions*

(1668). Hooke is better known for his researches in physics (Hooke's law), but nonetheless he made very important contributions to geology in spite of his acceptance of the traditional age of the Earth and his Aristotelian views of rock formation. Hooke was a meticulous observer who first applied the newly invented microscope to the study of geological materials. His comparative microscopic investigations of slices of fossil woods and modern living woods strongly influenced his attitudes regarding the true character of fossils. His work on earthquakes begins with a thorough description of many fossils and an elaborate argumentation over how to account for these "figured Bodies."[37] Hooke thought it very "difficult to imagine that Nature formed all these curious Bodies for no other End, than only to play the Mimick in the Mineral Kingdom, and only to imitate what she had done for some more noble End, and in a greater Perfection in the Vegetable and Animal Kingdoms. . . ."[38] He also thought it strange that nature should mimic only certain kinds of creatures.

> If there by the apish Tricks of Nature, Why does it not imitate several other of its own Works? Why do we not dig out of Mines everlasting Vegetables, as Grass for instance, or Roses of the same Substance, Figure, Colour, Smell? etc. Were it not that the Shells of Fishes are made of a kind of stony Substances which is not apt to corrupt and decay. Whereas, Plants and other animal Substances, even Bones, Horns, Teeth and Claws are more liable to the universal Menstruum of Time. 'Tis probable therefore, that the fixedness of their Substance has preserved them in their pristine Form, and not that a new plastick Principle has newly generated them.[39]

Hooke acknowledged that the two greatest difficulties with the organic view in the minds of his contemporaries were the composition of the fossils, namely, that they are composed of various kinds of stone, clay, marble, and so on, and the fact that fossils were buried in places far from the sea.[40] In a series of eleven elaborately developed propositions, Hooke showed how he thought these two main objections could be dispensed with.[41] He argued how buried remains of once living organisms might gradually be converted into stone through some kind of petrifying process.[42] In his discussion it is clear he had not yet fully escaped the thinking of Aristotle and Avicenna. He appealed to the stone-making processes observable in caves as an example of how a fluid might transform a fossil into stone. Also he suggested that exhalations or vapors given off by subterraneous earthquakes or eruptions might have caused buried objects to turn into stone.[43] As for how the fossils are found in their present positions either far above or far below sea level, Hooke again appealed to the action of earthquakes, and reported numerous descriptions of the action of historically known volcanic eruptions and earthquakes in elevating the sea floor, raising mountains, burying animals in volcanic ash, forming islands and so on.[44] And Hooke was greatly impressed by the fact that it is the mountainous areas that have the most earthquake activity. Thus he saw the existence of fossiliferous mountains as a result of continued earthquake activity in the past. He was very sceptical of the idea that the Noachian Deluge could be responsible for all fossiliferous rocks although he attributed some action to the Flood. In Hooke's mind, the Flood of Noah was nowhere near long enough to permit the production of all the shells as well as the very great thickness of fossil shell deposits. As evidence for his great earthquakes, Hooke appealed to the classical poets of Greek and Rome with their stories of the wars of the gods[45] as well as to Plato's account of the sinking of Atlantis.[46] He suggested that these are romantic descriptions of great Earth upheavals. The fact that no written eyewitness records of such earthquakes exist, Hooke believed was an indication that the great catastrophes occurred before the invention of writing, but he was sure that these upheavals occurred after the first creation, which he says was a world smooth all over and covered with water. Under the influence of the traditional six thousand-year-old Earth view, Hooke could not yet distinguish between an earlier geological history and a subsequent human history.

Without question, the most important geological thinking and writing before 1750 was done by Niels Steensen (1638–86), a Danish Lutheran who converted to Roman Catholicism, and who later in life abandoned his scientific work for the life of a theologian. Steensen, generally known as Steno, was, like Hooke, a very meticulous observer of nature. He began his career as an anatomist, and his early research led to his discovery of the duct of the parotid gland, which provides the mouth with most of its saliva. During the days of his tenure in Florence, a great shark was dragged ashore and Steno was given the opportunity to dissect the shark's head. Among other things, Steno paid very careful attention to the shark's teeth and noted that they strongly resembled the well-known natural curiosities known as glossopetrae ("tongue-stones"). Steno carefully established the identity between glossopetrae and shark teeth, and as a result became very much interested in the problem of fossilization and the determination of useful criteria which could serve to distinguish between objects in rock that had been buried in the rock and those that had developed in place in the rock. The product of Steno's very detailed reasoning was a brief but very concentrated work entitled *De Solido intra Solidum naturaliter Contento Dissertationis Prodromus*. The *Prodromus* (forerunner) was published in 1669, just a year after Hooke's work on earthquakes had appeared, but the final dissertation never appeared because Steno abandoned his scientific work.

The *Prodromus* presents very careful reasoning about the geometrical interrelationships between such geological objects as fossils, mineral crystals, rock fragments, and rock strata. Steno argued persuasively that fossils must be of organic origin, but he also worked out carefully the most fundamental principles of the science of stratigraphy. Although Woodward's *Essay* later stressed the importance of stratification, that work did not develop the significance of strata nearly so far as did Steno. Steno established the principle that sedimentary rock layers were deposited in an essentially horizontal manner on the subjacent sea or lake bed surface, as are modern river, lake, or beach deposits,[47] so that it became necessary to explain why it is that many rock layers have been severely tilted on edge. Steno also demonstrated that the strata are not simply deposited en masse, but rather as a succession, one layer oftentimes hardening before deposition of the next layer on top of it.[48] This would be particularly the case where pebbles derived by erosion of a given layer are incorporated into the layer next above it. This successive deposition of strata came to be known as the law or principle of superposition. He unwittingly began the development of a geological time scale by distinguishing between primary and secondary rocks.[49] Primary rocks were those crystalline rocks at the bottoms of mountains. Secondary rocks were the stratified rocks lying on top of them. Moreover, Steno generally believed that fossils and the enclosing rock layers were produced by flooding rivers, torrents, the sea, or storms.[50] In places Steno noted that horizontal layers lay on top of the truncated edges of other tilted layers. From the geometry he correctly surmised that the truncated layers had been deposited, hardened, tilted, eroded, and then covered by later layers of sediment. Steno worked out the relative sequence of geological events in the Tuscany region of Italy by applying his stratigraphic principles.[51] This is the first known exercise in applying principles of historical geology to the rock record. Steno noted that historical records had generally left no accounting of the upheavals of strata which obviously had taken place in the past.[52] As a man of his times, Steno did not fully follow through on the ideas he derived inductively from his study of strata and fossils but assumed that his conclusions fit into the framework of a six thousand-year history and a universal deluge. Although Steno's impact was not felt for nearly another century, he had solidly established the fundamental principles of historical geology and stratigraphy on the basis of which Earth history would later be worked out and which would make abundantly clear the vast antiquity of the Earth, a discovery that would have greatly surprised him.

By the time that the eighteenth century was well under way, the age of the Earth was still generally regarded at about six thousand years on the basis of literal interpretation of Scripture and known historical records. Geological studies had not yet disclosed any clearly damaging evidence to that accepted opinion, but the stage had been set for the discovery of the antiquity of the planet. By 1750 the true nature of fossils as the remains of buried organisms was almost unanimously accepted by scientists. Naturalists were now very much aware of the Earth's stratification and were becoming more aware of sequence in stratification. Some people like John Ray had begun to wonder if the Earth might not be older than was generally believed. Edmund Halley (1656–1722) in 1715 had even begun to suggest the possibility of calculating the age of the Earth by determining the amount of salt in the ocean and measuring the rate at which it was added to the ocean. But these were just faint glimmers of things to come.

During the latter half of the eighteenth century investigators built on the foundations laid by men like Steno. By the early nineteenth century the conclusion became inescapable: the Earth was vastly older than six thousand years.

# —3—
# THE DEVELOPING AWARENESS and ACCEPTANCE of the EARTH'S ANTIQUITY

## New Developments in Stratigraphy and Historical Geology

Steno's methods of reasoning about the geological history of rocks from their geometrical relationships began to influence other European naturalists more strongly during the eighteenth century. In 1751, Jean Etienne Guettard (1715–86) was studying rocks and landforms in central France and gradually became aware that the features he was looking at were volcanic in nature. To his amazement, he recognized that there were actually extinct volcanoes in his own native land. In his day the summit craters were pleasant grassy areas in which sheep could safely graze, and villages and houses had been built near the volcanoes with no evident thought of danger. Not only that but there was evidence that the Romans had used the local volcanic rock for various purposes. Clearly the volcanic activity predated the Roman occupation of Gaul, and in fact Guettard could find no mention at all of volcanic activity in France among the written records. As a result Guettard began to wonder if these extinct volcanoes might not have been active prior to the advent of people in France. Like Hooke and Steno before him, Guettard was beginning to uncover evidence of presumably spectacular geological events for which there were no convincing written records. Was there indeed a geological history that preceded human history?

Guettard's investigations were carried still farther by Nicholas Desmarest (1735–1815). Not only did Desmarest reinvestigate the volcanic region of central France more thoroughly than had Guettard, but he also examined several other active and extinct volcanic terrains throughout Europe. Through his careful studies of several superimposed lava flows Desmarest reached the conclusion that there had actually been a long series of eruptions spaced out over a considerable time. In fact he had recognized that some lava flows had stream channels carved into them, and that the former stream channels were subsequently filled in by later flows. This arrangement implied an extensive period of erosion to form the stream channel prior to the eruption of the next lava flow. Elsewhere beds of sediments could be found lying in between lava flows, implying a lapse of time between flows to permit sedimentation. Moreover, the volcanic activity clearly postdated older events represented by the existence of granite and various other rocks. Desmarest suspected from what he saw that Earth history might well be more extensive than was customarily thought to be the case.

About the same time several naturalists were recognizing the extensive lateral continuity of many rock formations, and noted that in local areas certain formations typically occurred in a well-defined vertical succession. Such observations by men like Lehmann, Arduino, and Werner on the distribution of rock strata led to the development of a geological time scale and growing awareness of the Earth's antiquity.

Johann Lehmann (d. 1767) in Germany and Giovanni Arduino (1714–95) in Italy were both involved in study of the strata in mountains. Both men generally recognized that the oldest, bottom rocks in a mountainous region were typically crystalline, and often massive rather than stratified, such as granite, schist, and gneiss. These rocks, termed primary or primitive, were devoid of any organic remains and frequently contained metallic ores. These primitive rocks were typically severely contorted. Lying on top of these rocks were thick piles of stratified, tilted, and folded rocks such as limestone, coal, shale, and sandstone that contained fragments or pebbles of the primary rocks. These in turn were typically partially covered by more loosely consolidated strata that contained the remains of relatively modern forms of life such as mammals and deciduous trees. These kinds of materials were generally present as horizontal layers and rarely tilted on edge. Such younger rocks were designated as tertiary rocks.

Lehmann believed that the primary rocks may have dated back to creation and that the secondary rocks could be attributed to the Flood. Arduino, however, was not sure that all primary rocks actually formed at the same time, nor did he attribute secondary rocks to the Flood. He suggested that the strata might be explicable in terms of ordinary processes like erosion and marine deposition of sediment over a long period of time, but he did not speculate on how much time.

The importance of stratification in rocks was further emphasized by Abraham Gottlob Werner (1749–1817), perhaps the most influential geologist of his time. After intensive study of the rock strata in the vicinity of Freiberg, Saxony, Werner concluded that they are always arrayed in the same unvarying vertical succession, and, although he had never studied rocks in other parts of the world, that his succession of strata was of worldwide validity. It was Werner's contention that this presumably universally valid stratigraphic succession had been deposited from a primeval universal ocean. The primary or primitive rocks, of a crystalline nature, were said to have precipitated chemically from the primeval ocean, while the more obviously sedimentary rocks were deposited mechanically. Moreover, the inclined positions of rock strata were generally regarded as the original position in which the rocks were either precipitated or deposited.

Werner's stratigraphic succession consisted of primitive rocks, that is, crystalline rocks like granite, gneiss, and schist (rocks that today would be regarded as igneous and metamorphic rocks),[1] which were chemical precipitates from the now defunct universal ocean and formed the substratum on top of which the other rocks were deposited. Above the primitive rocks were the so-called transition rocks, composed of graywacke and slate, a combination of mechanical deposits and chemical precipitates. Transition rocks were found to contain fossils of simple forms of life as well as some primitive fish forms. Above the transition rocks were the Flötzgebirge, or stratified rocks. This series, essentially the equivalent of the secondary and tertiary of other geologists, consisted predominantly of well-layered sandstones, limestones, shales, and other clearly sedimentary rocks that Werner would have considered as mechanically deposited rocks, as well as some basalt lava flows that Werner insisted were chemically precipitated. The Flötz rocks frequently contained abundant fossils of more advanced forms of life, including mammals and trees. These in turn were covered over by alluvial materials, consisting of unconsolidated gravels and sands in essentially horizontal position and containing remains of life forms very similar to those in existence today. Werner's fifth stratigraphic category was the volcanic category, in which local lava flows and ash deposits were produced by modern volcanoes. Werner considered volcanic activity a very recent phenomenon triggered by the burning of subterranean coal deposits. He was not influenced by the work of Desmarest and Guettard on the nature of ancient volcanism.[2]

As a very capable teacher in an influential position in the Mining Academy at Freiberg, Werner founded a school of geology known as Neptunism. Werner was called a Neptunist because of his heavy reliance on the universal ocean as an agent in the production of stratified rocks. Werner's students, often excelling even Werner in their zeal for his system, taught Neptunist doctrines regarding rock strata and their sequential development far and wide over Europe. Even though geologists, because of continuing study of rock outcrops, recognized that Werner's stratigraphic sequence needed to be modified severely, the Neptunist school did a great service to geological study by its continued stress on the fact that so many rocks are stratified and that this stratification did develop in a time sequence.

Thus by the end of the eighteenth century it was generally recognized that there was considerable regularity to the positions of individual strata or groups of strata in a stratigraphic sequence. Then, too, there was a growing awareness that different kinds of fossils were found in different strata and in different localities as Lister had observed in the seventeenth century. It remained for William Smith (1769–1839), a British engineer, to demonstrate just how intimate is the connection between types of fossils and the regularity of strata.

During the 1790s while laying plans for a system of coal-transporting canals in England, Smith paid very close attention to rock structure. He came to recognize that the English countryside was underlain by a thick series of very gently tilted strata that were arranged in unvarying order like a tilted stack of papers. Smith realized that each group of layers could be traced continuously for many miles across the countryside where the edge of that group was truncated by the Earth's surface. He also noted that each group of layers lay above and below the same strata everywhere it cropped out. He discovered that each group of strata in the sequence contained a characteristic suite of fossils that differed from those in the strata above and below. Thus each group of layers he found could be identified by means of its fossil content. Smith eventually developed the ability to predict what kind of rocks and what kind of fossils could be expected to occur in distant hills, and he came to know the characteristics of both the rocks and fossils so well that, to the amazement of his friends, he could tell them exactly where their specimens had been collected.

In time Smith developed a card showing a complete table of English formations on which these rock strata were named and described. He had actually been demonstrating the extreme regularity of individual strata within the so-called category of secondary rocks. The regularity of strata that Smith disclosed thus permitted further development and refinement of the geological time scale, so that the secondary could be subdivided into several smaller units. The formations he had been working on were eventually attributed to the Carboniferous through Cretaceous geological time periods. His efforts led eventually to the publication in 1815 of an excellent geological map of much of England, and laid the basis for continued stratigraphic work.

Smith was strictly a practical geologist and did not indulge in theories about whether the strata had been laid down in a catastrophic deluge or over long periods of time. Other geologists, however, began to realize that the extreme regularity of strata over great distances was difficult to reconcile with the action of a global flood. Still more difficult, however, was the fact that fossil remains were restricted in regular manner to certain strata. It was felt that surely a global flood would have produced a much more chaotic, mixed array of fossils than what was actually observed. Many geologists began to realize that the strata could not have been produced in a one-year deluge, but had no form over a long period of time by deposition in a succession of ancient seas, rivers, and floods. Students of the Earth were having an increasingly hard time envisioning the regularity of strata and the successions of organic worlds hinted at by the fossils in terms of a six thousand-year-old Earth.

## More "Theories of the Earth"

The eighteenth century had its share of dedicated men like Guettard and Smith who painstakingly collected geological facts in the field and then left it to other men to work out the meaning of those facts. Fortunately, however, the eighteenth century also produced men of synthetic genius and vivid imagination who tried to paint the whole canvas. Two such outstanding individuals were the colorful, flamboyant Georges Louis Leclerc, Comte de Buffon (1707–88), one of the most brilliant Frenchmen of his time, and the colorless, dry Scot, James Hutton (1726–97).

Buffon was very much in the line of earlier speculative thinkers like Burnet, Liebniz, and Whiston. Like these predecessors he was interested in trying to develop a theory of Earth history that could take advantage of the very latest knowledge from the realm of physics. Buffon's work is basically the last of those global speculations and thus represents the end of an era regarding speculations on Earth history, yet it broke new ground in its daring attempt to calculate the age of the Earth, an age which turned out to be significantly greater than six thousand years.

Buffon was an ardent naturalist who on occasion corresponded with Thomas Jefferson about whether American or European natural history was more interesting. Buffon had suggested that American life forms were rather puny compared with European forms, thus prompting Jefferson to have the skeleton of a bull moose shipped to Buffon! The Comte was acquainted with much of the geological evidence of the Earth's antiquity that had been developed up to his day, and he became persuaded that the Earth was really quite old. Buffon was also a thoroughly convinced Newtonian who sought to work out a theory of the Earth's origin and history in terms of Newtonian principles. Buffon, somewhat reminiscent of Whiston, suggested that the Earth originated when a comet closely approached the sun and tore off a chunk of solar material.[3] This solar glob was flung out into space where the incandescent mass gradually cooled through successive states until it was eventually habitable. Buffon was especially interested in how long it would take a molten globe the size of the Earth to cool down to a temperature at which life could be sustained.[4] His own interest in this question had been spurred by the fact that Newton had attempted just such a calculation. Newton arrived at a figure of fifty thousand years for the cooling of the Earth, but since that greatly exceeded the allowable six thousand years he figured that something must have been wrong with his computations. Buffon, however, had more confidence in Newton's work than Newton himself, so he conducted a series of experiments utilizing a group of spheres of varying sizes and materials. He heated the spheres until they reached white heat and then permitted them to cool.

The time elapsed until the surface of the globes could be touched was measured as was the amount of time that elapsed until the interior had also cooled off.[5] Armed with a lot of experimental data he then extrapolated for a body the size of the Earth. In *Epochs* he stated that 74,832 years had been required for the cooling of the Earth from white heat to its present condition, and that 93,291 more years would pass before the Earth froze over and life would be eliminated. Privately Buffon believed that the Earth was a great deal older than he had allowed in print, but Buffon suspected that his conclusions regarding the age of the Earth would create a furor (an earlier work had been censored), so he attempted to show how they were not really out of accord with Genesis at all.[6] He maintained that the days of creation should really be taken as long time periods and not as ordinary solar days. And as he outlined his scheme of Earth history, he did so quite deliberately in terms of seven successive epochs to match the seven days of Genesis 1:1–2:3. Buffon's was one of the earliest efforts to quantify the age of the Earth on "scientific" grounds.

Of a very different nature was the work of James Hutton. Hutton's work lacked the daring, vivid imagination that Buffon brought to his task, but was nonetheless probably much sounder than Buffon's effort. Hutton was, unlike Buffon, not interested in applying the principles of physics in a speculative manner to the history of the Earth. Instead Hutton's theory was rather a suggestion of basic ways in which the Earth probably operates or in which we ought to approach the study of Earth history on the basis of continued observation of rocks and modern geological processes over a period of several years. Without question there were speculative elements to Hutton's thinking, but his thought was undoubtedly based on an attempt to infer inductively from the facts of nature how nature operates and has operated. Hutton's ideas were laid out in a monumental, somewhat tedious work entitled simply *The Theory of the Earth,* published in 1795.

In the *Theory* Hutton reasoned cogently and at sometimes excruciating length from the present day behavior of nature and the characteristics of rocks and strata to construct his theory, unlike Burnet and Whiston whose theories were imposed on geological phenomena. He applied the principles worked out by predecessors like Steno and Arduino more consistently. He felt it was unnecessary to invoke processes to explain rock strata and mountains other than ordinary everyday processes like erosion and sedimentation whose effects we can readily observe.[7] Hutton argued, as had others, but in much more detail, that rock strata are composed of mineral particles of exactly the same characteristics and constitution as are those on beaches or sea floors or river beds.[8] Thus it must be, he said, that rock strata were formed on ancient sea beds as loose unconsolidated gravel and sand layers that were eventually fused into rock and elevated by the internal heat of the Earth.[9] Moreover, everywhere that there are presently mountains we can see plainly that they are in the process of decay and destruction by the erosive forces of wind, rain, and rivers. We can see that the gravels and sands produced by erosion are gradually being carried down to the sea in streams.[10] Hence, may we not infer, he asked, that just as modern beach and sea sediments are derived by the erosion of present day mountains, so, too, the strata now composing those mountains were derived from elevated beach deposits that in turn had been derived in a previous cycle of erosion from no longer existing mountains?[11] Hutton believed he could see in rock strata evidences of cycle after cycle of erosion, deposition, and uplift to form mountains. He was convinced of the cyclic nature of these processes because, like Steno, he saw and understood the meaning of the numerous unconformities[12] visible in rock outcrops. He recognized that these unconformities were ancient erosional surfaces cut into the bevelled edges of tilted strata and subsequently buried underneath new strata. Hutton likewise was convinced that the primitive or primary schists and gneisses in the cores of mountains did not really date back to creation, as Lehmann had suggested, but really were very old sedimentary rock layers that had been altered into their present crystalline condition by extremes of heat within the depths of the Earth.[13] He thus became the first person to enunciate the principle of metamorphism. Hutton thought he could see in rocks evidences of cycles of mountain-building, erosion, and sedimentation stretching far back into the indefinite past and concluded in his famous, controversial statement that he could see in the course of nature "no vestige of a beginning, no prospect of an end."[14] To those who were still rigidly insistent on sticking to the traditional interpretation of Mosaic history, this statement sounded like atheistic blasphemy.[15] Hutton was accused of holding to the eternity of the Earth, but such was far from his intent. He was simply confessing on the basis of his observations that Earth processes seemed to reach far back in time and that he was unable to see in the rocks where these processes had not been operative. He simply could not find the primeval, created rocks. Hutton's system was hardly atheistic, anti-Christian, or antibiblical. He did not even discuss how his views fit in or didn't fit in with Scripture, but merely explained what he thought the evidence of the rocks was telling him.

## Theological Accommodation to the Antiquity of the Earth

Hutton's approach to geology was considerably different from that of Werner in several ways. Hutton had stressed the very important role that heat plays in the development of the Earth. For example, he urged that many crystalline rocks such as granite and basalt were in reality the products of crystallization of very intensely hot molten rock either underground or on the surface; they were not at all derived by crystallization from an ocean. He likewise maintained, quite incorrectly, that great heat was necessary in order to convert loose sediments into hardened sedimentary rocks under pressure. He further suggested that heat was the important agent that permitted the elevation of large portions of the Earth above the seabeds. In contrast Werner and his Neptunist school downplayed the importance of volcanic or plutonic[16] action and stressed the role of water. Rocks were precipitated or deposited from water and aqueous solutions helped harden loose sediment into rock. Thus during the end of the eighteenth and the beginning of the nineteenth centuries intensive controversy raged between two opposing geological camps, the Neptunists and the Volcanists, the supporters of Werner and the supporters of Hutton. Perhaps the most intensely debated issue was that Hutton had not even bothered to try to correlate his scheme of geology in any way with the Genesis account. Such ignoring of Scripture was tantamount to blasphemy and many regarded Hutton's views as atheistic. Moreover, the fact that Hutton had not been able to see any vestige of a beginning in the rocks was misinterpreted by his opponents as a heretical denial of the doctrine of creation. Others were simply afraid of the possibility of the limitless antiquity of the Earth opened up by Hutton's method of looking at the earth.

Hutton's views were bitterly attacked by Richard Kirwan,[17] and more gently opposed by Jean Andrè Deluc. Deluc, a Swiss Calvinist, tried to refute Hutton on Wernerian grounds in a series of letters and ultimately in his *An Elementary Treatise on Geology* (1809).[18] He sought to show that the Neptunist system was actually the true system of geology because it could be squared with a basically literal interpretation of Scripture. Genesis 1 mentions the "great deep" upon which the Spirit of God moved and this was conveniently taken as the universal ocean of Werner, and furthermore the sequence of rocks with their changing life-forms represented by the fossils fit nicely with the successive creations of the six days. Yet interestingly, even though Deluc was troubled by the vast antiquity that had been opened up by Hutton, he, too, recognized that the geological record required more time to develop than was allowed by the traditional six literal days of creation. And so we find Deluc advocating a more figurative usage of the six days, as in his comment that he had spent most of his life in showing "the conformity of geological monuments with the sublime account of that series of operations which took place during the *Six Days,* or periods of time, recorded by the inspired penman."[19] Even Hutton's geological opponents were beginning to concede that the Earth was more ancient than a strictly literal interpretation of the Bible would allow.

Hutton, of course, had his defenders. The chief of these was John Playfair (1748–1819), a Scottish professor of mathematics in the University of Edinburgh. Playfair was also an ordained minister of the Church of Scotland. He had served in pastorates for about a decade before joining the university. He not only supported Hutton's geology but defended Hutton against the charges of atheism. In his classic *Illustration of the Huttonian Theory of the Earth* (1802), Playfair correctly maintained that to say that we see "no mark, either of a beginning or an end, is very different from affirming, that the world had no beginning, and will have no end."[20] Of course, Hutton had nowhere asserted, and certainly did not believe, the latter. Likewise, said Playfair, if Hutton were atheistic in his views he would have represented the world as the "result of necessity or change"[21] rather than continually admiring "the instances of wise and beneficent design manifested in the structure, or economy of the world."[22] Playfair also defended Hutton's ideas respecting the antiquity of the Earth. He observed that others thought that the high antiquity ascribed by Hutton's theory to the Earth was inconsistent with the Scriptural chronology. But

> this objection would no doubt be of weight, if the high antiquity in question were not restricted merely to the globe of the earth, but were also extended to the human race. That the origin of mankind does not go back beyond six or seven thousand years, is a position so involved in the narrative of the Mosaic books, that any thing inconsistent with it, would no doubt stand in opposition to the testimony of those ancient records. On this subject, however, geology is silent. . . .
>
> On the other hand, the authority of the Sacred Books seems to be but little interested in what regards the mere antiquity of the earth itself; nor does it appear that their language is to be understood literally concerning the *age* of that body, and more than concerning its *figure* or its *motion*. The theory of Dr. Hutton stands here precisely on the same footing with the system of Copernicus. . . .[23]

No specific attempt at harmonization is presented by Playfair who was content simply to deny that Scripture fixed the age of the Earth.

Amidst all the vigorous attacks and counterattacks launched by both churchmen and geologists, another important development occurred in 1804 when a hitherto obscure, young clergyman of the Church of Scotland, Thomas Chalmers (1780–1847), announced to this audience that

> There is a prejudice against the speculation of the geologist which I am anxious to remove. It has been said that they nurture infidel propensities. By referring the origin of the globe to a higher antiquity than is assigned to it by the writings of Moses, it has been said that geology undermines our faith in the inspiration of the Bible, and in all the animating prospects of immortality which it unfolds. This is a false alarm. The writings of Moses do not fix the antiquity of the globe. If they fix anything at all, it is only the antiquity of the species.[24]

Chalmers' explanation of how to harmonize the biblical account with the geological record had its origins in the thinking of Augustine and a handful of subsequent theologians like Episcopius and Bishop Patrick. The key point developed by Chalmers was that the creation of the heaven and the Earth was not a part of the six days but preceded them. The creation of the heaven and Earth was said to have taken place in the beginning, but when that beginning was is not recorded. Thus one could quite nicely fit all the geological activity exposed in the rock record into this presumably vast stretch of time prior to the six days, which Chalmers maintained were truly ordinary days of recreating the Earth from the chaotic condition that followed the initial creation. Chalmers' theory, the first modern expression of the gap, restitution, ruin-reconstruction theory as it is variously named, gradually gained considerable favor, but this theory was not the only attempt at reconciling Genesis with the growing conviction of geologists regarding the high antiquity of the planet.

The figurative interpretation of the six days also received impetus as a result of the catastrophism of Georges Cuvier (1768–1832), a great French comparative anatomist and vertebrate paleontologist. Cuvier and his associate, Alexandre Brongniart (1770–1847), spent a number of years at the very beginning of the nineteenth century studying the complex vertebrate faunas in the tertiary strata of the Paris basin. Cuvier, like William Smith in England, recognized the fact that individual strata or groups of strata were characterized by wholly unique faunas. Faunas appeared to have lived for awhile and then were replaced by wholly new faunas whose fossils were found in successively younger rock strata. Cuvier recognized a whole series of faunal replacements. He could not reconcile the observed distribution with the action of a single universal flood and instead proposed that the fossil evidence was consistent with the idea that there had been a series of global catastrophes or revolutions of which the Deluge was the latest.[25] He suggested that the fauna of an area would live for a while, and then be eradicated in a great catastrophe. This extinction of the fauna would then be followed by a wholly new and different fauna. This fauna in turn would be catastrophically destroyed and replaced by a new fauna, and so on. Cuvier believed that this succession of revolutions required a long period of time,[26] and that the final revolution, which brought the continents into their present conditions, occurred only a few thousand years ago at the time of the Flood.[27]

Cuvier's catastrophism was eagerly adopted in England by James Parkinson (1755–1824) whose *Organic Remains of a Former World* (1804–11) presented a synthesis of Cuvierianism and Moses in which the days of Genesis were treated as vast periods of time. The emergence of this alternative harmonization stimulated Chalmers to put forward his own harmonization yet more vigorously. He felt strongly that the six days were literal days and to make them into periods was to take liberties with the text. Geology must thus fit into the vastness of time that presumably existed before the six days.

William Buckland (1784–1856), an English clergyman and Oxford professor, also adopted the Cuvierian catastrophism but modified it by seeking for geological evidence of a Flood more short-lived and universal than Cuvier's. Few geologists were any longer attributing the entire stratigraphic record to the Flood as had John Woodward, but rather they were looking at the most recent, surficial deposits as evidences of the Flood. Abundant deposits of surficial gravels existed through Europe as did large isolated boulders that had quite obviously been transported great distances from their original sources. These phenomena were attributed to the action of great tidal waves of the Noachian Deluge. To this presumed evidence for the Flood Buckland added evidence from caves and large fissures. Numerous discoveries of large collections of fossil mammals had been made in a number of caves and fissures. Many of these mammals were very similar to modern day animals and many of them, such as rhinoceros, hippopotamus, and elephant, were no longer living in Europe. Thus, in his great classic *Reliquiae Diluvianae* (1823), Buckland marshalled the evidence for the Flood. But as the Flood was removed from being the sole explanation of geological history to the last in a series of catastrophes, Buckland, like Cuvier, believed that the Earth very likely had a long history prior to the Flood so that the world was much older than six thousand years. As a geologist and an ordained minister, Buckland was quite naturally interested in harmonizing revelation with the discoveries of his science. In his famous Bridgewater Treatise, *Geology and Mineralogy with Reference to Natural Theology* (1837), Buckland adopted the restitution theory put forward by Chalmers a few years earlier.

In that work we find Buckland defending both Scripture and geology, and attempting to harmonize them.

> It may seem just a matter of surprise, that many learned and religious men should regard with jealousy and suspicion the study of any natural phenomena, which abound with proofs of some of the highest attributes of the Deity; and should receive with distrust, or total incredulity, the announcement of conclusions, which the geologist deduces from careful and patient investigation of the facts which it is his province to explore. These doubts and difficulties result from the disclosures made by geology, respecting the lapse of very long periods of time, before the creation of man. Minds which have been long accustomed to date the origin of the universe, as well as that of the human race, from an era of about six thousand years ago, receive reluctantly any information, which if true, demands some new modification of their present ideas of cosmogony; and, as in this respect, Geology has shared the fate of other infant sciences, in being for a while considered hostile to revealed religion; so like them, when fully understood, it will be found a potent and consistent auxiliary to it, exalting our conviction of the Power, and Wisdom, and Goodness of the Creator.[28]

In Buckland's view, it was no longer possible to argue that the Earth was only six thousand years old.

> The truth is, that all observers, however various may be their speculations, respecting the secondary causes by which geological phenomena have been brought about, are now agreed in admitting the lapse of very long periods of time to have been an essential condition to the production of these phenomena.[29]

He rejected other harmonizations, especially the ideas that all rock strata could be attributed to the Deluge or to the time between the creation of man and the onset of the Deluge.

> Some have attempted to ascribe the formation of all the stratified rocks to the effects of the Mosaic Deluge; an opinion which is irreconcilable with the enormous thickness and almost infinite subdivisions of these strata, and with the numerous and regular successions which they contain of the remains of animals and vegetables, differing more and more widely from existing species, as the strata in which we find them are placed at greater depths. The fact that a large

proportion of these remains belong to extinct genera, and almost all of them to extinct species, that lived and multiplied and died on or near the spots where they are now found, shows that the strata in which they occur were deposited slowly and gradually, during long periods of time, and at widely distant intervals. These extinct animals and vegetables could therefore have formed no part of the creation with which we are immediately connected.[30]

Buckland disagreed with Chalmers who said that the days of creation could not be taken as long periods of time. They certainly can, he said, but doing so does not give us the needed harmonization, since, he felt, the order of events revealed by geology does not agree with that of Moses, especially as regards the relative time of appearance of vegetation. Instead, the Book of Genesis expresses

an undefined period of time, which was antecedent to the last great change that affected the surface of the earth, and to the creation of its present animal and vegetable inhabitants; during which period a long series of operations and revolutions may have been going on; which, as they are wholly unconnected with the history of the human race, are passed over in silence by the sacred historian, whose only concern with them was barely to state, that the matter of the universe is not eternal and self-existent, but was originally created by the power of the Almighty.[31]

And moreover,

This first evening may be considered as the termination of the indefinite time which followed the primeval creation announced in the first verse, and as the commencement of the first of the six succeeding days, in which the earth was to be fitted up, and peopled in a manner fit for the reception of mankind. We have in this second verse, a distinct mention of earth and waters, as already existing, and involved in darkness; their condition also is described as a state of confusion and emptiness, *(tohu bohu),* words which are usually interpreted by the vague and indefinite Greek term, "chaos," and which may be geologically considered as designating the wreck and ruins of a former world.[32]

He rejected the fallen angel hypothesis of Episcopius but still noted that if that idea were valid it would further suggest that some kind of natural interval occurred between verses one and three.

## The Rise of Uniformitarianism

While the catastrophism of Cuvier and Buckland was popular in Europe between 1810 and 1830, a trend toward uniformitarianism, foreshadowed by Hutton, was developing. Uniformitarianism was essentially the doctrine that the past history of the Earth could be adequately explained in terms of causes that can presently be observed to be in operation on the globe without having recourse to supernatural explanations or causes that had ceased to operate. In the minds of uniformitarians it was unnecessary to invoke spectacular one-time catastrophes to account for geological phenomena when the processes we see around us could account for them quite nicely if allowed to operate over a long period of time. Both John Fleming and George Poulett Scrope argued for such a viewpoint. Fleming (1785–1857), a Scottish biologist and minister of the Free Church of Scotland, opposed the popular Bucklandian diluvialism on the grounds that it was both unscientific and unbiblical in many respects. Fleming believed that the gravels and cave deposits of Buckland could not be explained solely in terms of one great event, but that the animal extinctions recorded by the fossil bones and the deposition of gravels themselves could only be explained by processes acting gradually over a long time. Scrope (1797–1876), an English geologist and member of Parliament, likewise believed from his study of river valleys and volcanic activity in central France that currently existing processes acting over long periods of time could explain geological phenomena much better than the current catastrophic explanations. After these anticipations, the uniformitarian viewpoint reached its climax with the publication in 1830 of the first edition of the monumental *Principles of Geology* of Charles Lyell (1797–1875).

As a student of Buckland, Lyell began his geological career as a catastrophist, and he was certainly already in agreement with Cuvier and Buckland that geological evidence required that Earth history be in excess of six thousand years. However, he later came to the conclusion that global catastrophes were unnecessary and that even the surficial gravels and boulders might be explained in terms of several local floods. The *Principles* showed in great detail how a variety of geological phenomena could be explained in terms of modern day processes such as river and marine erosion and deposition acting at essentially the same rates as now over a long period of time. Lyell suggested that instead of invoking Cuvierian catastrophes of which we have no experience, we ought rather to rely on processes we can observe or reasonably infer to have operated from the evidence of the rocks. Being sensitive to religious concerns, Lyell had no intention of denying the existence of Noah's Flood; rather he believed it was not a global catastrophe, as Buckland had said, but an extensive inundation in the Middle East that had relatively little geological effect of a global nature. Following Fleming he suggested that the Flood might have been relatively tranquil. Lyell's uniformitarian approach appeared to require even much greater stretches of time than was called for by catastrophism.

The work of Louis Agassiz (1807–73) on glaciation did much to overthrow catastrophist theories and to further uniformitarian thinking. A native of Switzerland, Agassiz had noted that glacially produced features like erratic boulders, scratches and grooves on rocks, smoothed, polished rock outcroppings, and moraines[33] existed in regions several miles removed from the nearest active Alpine glaciers. From this distribution of glacial features he postulated that glaciation had been much more extensive in Alpine regions in the past. Later on Agassiz recognized the same kinds of features all over northern Europe and northern North America and proposed the existence of gigantic ice sheets that had covered much of those continents. Lyell and even Buckland came to recognize that many of the surficial, "diluvial" phenomena heretofore attributed to the Deluge had, in reality, been caused by the action of such extinct ice sheets. Thus the ice age replaced the Flood as a causative agent, and with the disappearance of diluvial catastrophism it became clearer to active geologists that the world had probably had a very long slow history more explicable in terms of observable processes like glaciation, erosion, deposition, and the like, rather than one that could be explained in terms of a few very sudden, ancient global catastrophes.

There continued to be much reaction against the developing trends in geology. A torrent of books and pamphlets were published on "Scriptural" geology and Flood geology, all designed to uphold the traditional point of view on the age and history of the world.[34] The "heretical" and "infidel" tendencies of geology were roundly condemned by some churchmen, few of whom had any real knowledge of geology. Those who had geological knowledge were now largely convinced that the Earth was very old. Exactly how old no one knew, nor was there any way of knowing the Earth's age given the current state of knowledge, but the Earth seemed far greater than six thousand years old.

A great number of those who were contributing to the study of the Earth and to the new view of the Earth's antiquity were outspoken Christian men who were concerned to uphold Scripture and the Christian faith. They had absolutely no intention of denying the faith. Among such Christian naturalists as John Playfair, William Buckland, Adam Sedgwick,[35] William Conybeare,[36] and John Fleming, we find genuine efforts to defend the creation narrative. Soon not only geologists and ministers, but also a large number of professional theologians and biblical scholars began to recognize that the traditional exegesis of Genesis 1 might not be fully consistent with all the internal biblical evidence. The latter two-thirds of the nineteenth century thus became the age of harmonization and a time when theologians generally adopted either the restitution theory or the day-age theory of Genesis 1.

# —4—
# THE AGE
# of HARMONIZATION

THE LATTER TWO-THIRDS of the nineteenth century saw the rise of a number of men of achievement in the sciences and theology who were persuaded that scientific evidence had established that the Earth was very old. During this time theories were developed in great detail that sought to show how the biblical data were consistent with the findings of geology.[1] Having been forced to look anew at the biblical accounts, experts in the original languages were persuaded that there was indeed no real conflict at all between nature and Scripture. Few had rejected the Bible or reverted to calling Genesis a myth in order to explain away difficulties. It was recognized that the traditional exegesis of Genesis 1 was not the only one that adequately satisfied the data. During this period relatively few hostile denunciations of the science of geology came from the Christian community, and relatively few works on Flood geology appeared in print.

## The Restitution Theory

The restitution theory, first proposed by Thomas Chalmers and later advocated by William Buckland, advanced the thought that the long periods of time required by geology could adequately be accounted for by assuming that the first two verses of Genesis 1 described a condition that lasted an indeterminate amount of time and preceded the six days of creation. In England the restitution theory received one of its ablest treatments at the hands of John Pye Smith (1774–1851), a highly respected biblical scholar, in *On the Relation between the Holy Scriptures and Certain Parts of Geological Science* (1840). Smith with Chalmers held that the date of creation was not revealed in the Mosaic account, that the events of the geological record could be applied to Genesis 1:1, that recently, as suggested by verse two, the Earth was brought into a state of disorganiza-

55

tion or ruin, i.e., the Earth *became* waste and void (not *"was"*), and that God subsequently adjusted the surface of the Earth to its presently existing condition over a period of six natural days. Smith, however, added an intriguing twist to the theory in that he held that the condition of chaos and darkness from which the Earth was recreated actually was of restricted extent, and, in fact, applied only to a region between the Caucasus Mountains and the Caspian Sea south to the Persian Gulf and the Indian Ocean. Outside of this area, over most of the Earth, life and sunshine continued to exist and the condition expressed by verse two did not apply. The six days referred to the restoration or recreation of that localized area in which man was to be placed at the end of creation.

Another very stimulating work striving for a harmonization of Scripture and scientific discovery was *The Bible and Astronomy* by J. H. Kurtz (1809–90), Professor of Church History in the University of Dorpat. The book appeared in 1842 and enjoyed success through several editions. Like previous adherents of the restitution theory Kurtz believed that Genesis 1:1 was prior to the six days' work. The desolation and waste of verse two was not an original desolation, argued Kurtz, but possibly a state of ruination of a previously existing creation of God.[2] Kurtz was intrigued by the evidence in Scripture of the fall of angels, and he maintained that this coincided with the production of the Earth's ruined state.[3] The following six days were days of restitution. Thus far, Kurtz's view is the classic restitution theory, but his view of the six days is unique.

Kurtz maintained that the account of the six days was not poetry or philosophy, but an account of events that had been handed down by tradition and incorporated into the Pentateuch by Moses. The originator of the tradition of Genesis 1 did not compose it on his own, because he had neither been present at creation nor would he be able to understand the creation by intuitive insight. Even Adam in his state of moral and intellectual perfection before the Fall could not have penetrated the creation by intuition.[4] Instead the account was given to the first recipient, whether Adam or Enoch, or one of the other early patriarchs, by divine revelation in a prophetic vision.[5] God revealed to the original seer a series of successive scenarios of the creation. The days were thus "prophetic days," according to Kurtz. This does not mean that it took six days for the visions to occur, but rather that the events occurred in six prophetic days. A prophetic day is not necessarily an ordinary day, but is of indeterminate length, said Kurtz, and in order to determine just how long these prophetic days were, we would need to consider how the term day is used in its immediate context.[6] Kurtz was convinced that these prophetic days of restitution were natural days because they were marked by recurring periods of light and dark. But again, this did not necessarily mean twenty-four hours, since other planets, for example, have regular periods of recurring light and dark that differ from the terrestrial twenty-four hours. Despite Kurtz's restitution hypothesis and his insistence on six ordinary days for the restitution, he has had considerable influence on a popular rival view, the day-age hypothesis.

In the United States the restitution theory was extensively advocated in *The Religion of Geology* (1851) by Edward Hitchcock (1793–1864), president of Amherst College. Hitchcock was not only an excellent geologist who did much of the pioneering geological work in New England, but he was also a professional theologian, and thus well qualified to attempt the harmonization of his book. Nevertheless there are no relatively novel aspects to Hitchcock's version of the restitution theory.

One of the most influential harmonizations from the point of view of the restitution hypothesis is found in *Earth's Earliest Ages* by G. H. Pember. This work had considerable influence on the author of the first edition of the Scofield Reference Bible. Pember laid great stress on the fall of Satan and the wicked angels during the primeval history of the Earth prior to the six days. This fall of the spirits is connected with a great global catastrophe to which may be attributed the remains of the geological time periods. Thus the six days have nothing to do with the geological record, but are seen as days of restoration of the Earth from the great catastrophe that occurred at the time of Satan's fall.

## The Day-Age Theory

Now if the restitution theory had its thousands, the day-age theory may have had its tens of thousands. The day-age view had its origins in the harmonizing attempts of William Whiston, Comte de Buffon, Jean Andrè Deluc, and James Parkinson. The essential point of the theory is that the six days of creation either should not be or cannot be regarded as ordinary days determined by the rotation of the Earth with respect to the sun or another light source but should be considered as time periods of indeterminate length. If these days are truly of indeterminate length then we may legitimately equate the vast amounts of time required for the geological history of the Earth with the six days. If the six days really are long periods of time then the question arises as to whether or not the sequence of events in Genesis 1 really coincides with the sequence of events as disclosed by geological inqury. Advocates of the day-age hypothesis frequently were enamored of pointing out that there is indeed general agreement between the two sequences. Interestingly, however, the sequences proposed by different authors were as varied as their interpretations of the creation story.

The ablest defenders of the day-age theory were geologists. Excellent defenses of the day-age view were presented by Benjamin Silliman (1779–1864) of Yale in a supplement to an American edition of Bakewell's *Introduction to Geology*[7] (1833), James Dwight Dana[8] (1813–95) of Yale, Arnold Guyot[9] (1807–84) of Princeton, and J. William Dawson[10] (1820–99) of McGill. Without question these four men were among the best North American geologists of the nineteenth century. The most eloquent and gracious exposition of the day-age view, however, was that of the great Scottish churchman, journalist, and geologist, Hugh Miller (1802–56), in *The Testimony of the Rocks* (1857). Miller, Guyot, and Dawson were also influenced by Kurtz and regarded the first chapter of Genesis as a prophetic vision in which more phenomenal, or optical, language was used. That is, Genesis 1 does not present absolute physical truth but presents the phenomena as they appeared to the observer. For example, the sun and moon are referred to in the language of appearance and not absolute fact, for the sun and moon in terms of absolute physical truth are far outside of the expanse of the sky. Miller expressed great admiration for the many able spokesmen for the restitution view like Chalmers and Buckland, but was unable to accept that harmonization, for to him it was quite evident from the geological record that there had never been a sudden break from an initial pristine world to a desolate chaos plunged in darkness and covered with the deep. All the geological evidence indicated to Miller a continuity between the past and the time of the appearance of man.

Although geologists defended the day-age hypothesis, many Bible expositors and theologians gave support to the notion that the days of creation were not ordinary days but indeterminate periods. Such excellent German commentators as Franz Delitzsch[11] (1813–90) and John Peter Lange[12] (1802–84) favored this view. In the United States an outstanding contribution was made by Tayler Lewis (1802–77) of the Reformed Church in his *Six Days of Creation* (1855) and notes to Lange's *Commentary on Genesis*. Lewis' writings without question provide the most exhaustive exegetical study of Genesis 1 from the point of view that the days cannot possibly be twenty-four-hour days. What makes Lewis' work all the more compelling is his desire *not* to be influenced by current scientific findings. In Scotland the great expositor Alexander Maclaren[13] (1826–1910) viewed the six days as long time periods. Many excellent works in systematic theology also adopted variations of the day-age theory. Among these were the theologies of the American Presbyterians Charles Hodge[14] (1797–1878) and William G. T. Shedd[15] (1820–94), the Scottish Free Church theologian James Orr[16] (1844–1913), Baptist theologian A. H. Strong[17] (1836–1921), and Methodist John Miley[18] (1813–95).

Several exegetical arguments that the days were protracted time periods appear repeatedly in the writings of these men. First, it was observed that in Scripture, the Hebrew word for "day" (יוֹם) frequently denotes a long period of time rather than an ordinary day. In fact, at least once in the creation account itself (Gen. 2:4) the word "day" refers to the entire period of creation. Further, the word "day" is used in several different senses in Genesis 1, so that it cannot be dogmatically asserted that the six days must be treated as ordinary days.

Second, it was argued in the line of Augustine that at least the first three days cannot be treated as ordinary days inasmuch as the sun, in relation to which Earth's rotation is utilized as a chronometer, was not even yet in existence, at least in respect to its being a time measurer. Not until day four were the heavenly bodies made to serve for signs and seasons and for days and years.

Several writers also pointed out that the events depicted in the six days are not of such a nature as to have occurred within twenty-four hours. This is particularly the case with respect to day six, which includes the creation of animals, the creation of Adam, the planting of the garden, man's being placed in the garden, his observation and naming of the animals, his deepening loneliness, his deep sleep, and the creation of Eve. It was said to be difficult to conceive of all of this occurring in one ordinary day. Lewis, in a similar vein, pointed out that the events of many of the six days, as with the vegetation of day three, describe natural growths according to the nature of the created thing, and that these growths cannot be viewed as taking only one ordinary day.[19]

The fourth major argument generally put forward by advocates of the day-age hypothesis is that the seventh day, the day of God's rest, is still going on and is therefore a long period of time. The fact that it does not say of the seventh day, as it does of the other six, that "there was evening and there was morning—the seventh day," was viewed as one clear indication that the seventh day was never terminated. Further, New Testament passages such as Hebrews 4 gave further credence to the continuing existence of God's Sabbath. If the seventh day was a long period of time then it is also clear, according to the argument, that the preceding six days might also legitimately be treated as long periods of time of indeterminate length.

## Biblical Genealogies

Another major theological advance was made with the appearance of the paper, *Primeval Chronology*,[20] of William Henry Green (1825–1900), Professor of Old Testament at Princeton Theological Seminary. Green addressed himself to the antiquity of man in light of the genealogies of Genesis 5 and 11. Green showed that it was impossible to obtain dates for various biblical events like creation, the creation of Adam, or the Flood just by adding up the ages of the patriarchs given in these chapters. Using several other genealogies in Scripture, and especially comparing the corresponding genealogies of 1 Chronicles 6 and Ezra 7, he showed conclusively that gaps and omissions are commonplace in biblical genealogy. Inasmuch as this is the case elsewhere in Scripture then we have no way of knowing whether or not there may have also been deliberate omissions in the genealogies of Genesis 5 and 11. If there have been omissions then we cannot calculate the age of man; man may be much older than the six thousand years traditionally allowed. B. B. Warfield[21] (1851–1921), also of Princeton Seminary, maintained that there was no theological significance to the question of the antiquity of man.

# —5—
# THE
# TWENTIETH
# CENTURY

FOR THE MOST PART Christian scholars in the western world made peace with the idea of the Earth's antiquity. They became comfortable with the idea that Genesis 1 could be interpreted in alternative ways that would allow for a world created in more than six literal days only a few thousand years ago. They also became more comfortable with the idea that even man himself might have been on the Earth for more than six thousand years. Christians generally did not abandon their Christianity or even their faith in an infallible Bible as a result of the discoveries of geology regarding the age of the Earth. There were few hostile attacks on Christianity coming from geologists, for many of the great geologists of the nineteenth century were Christian men determined to uphold Scripture in spite of the apparent discrepancies between nature and Scripture.

While Christians were becoming accustomed to the idea of the Earth's antiquity, new scientific developments were gradually permitting the definition of exactly how old the Earth may be. People like Cuvier and Buckland surmised that the Earth was very old, but no one had the means for calculating the age of the Earth reliably. Many discussions of the age of the Earth provided calculations suggesting the relative lengths of the various geological time periods in the form of ratios, and most geologists assumed that the Earth was probably millions of years old. Expressions like "inconceivably vast" were commonplace.

Throughout the nineteenth century various estimates of the age of the Earth were made. Charles Lyell suggested that at least 240 million years had elapsed since the beginning of the Cambrian period by basing his calculations on the rates of paleontological extinction.[1] John Goodchild proposed an age well in excess of a billion years.[2] Charles Darwin (1809–82) attempted estimates on the basis of rates of erosion.[3] John

Phillips (1800–74) calculated an age of 96 million years for the Earth on the basis of a combination of data involving the thicknesses of strata, rates of sedimentary deposition, and rates of erosion.[4] Toward the turn of the century John Joly (1857–1933) suggested, as had Edmund Halley centuries earlier, that the sodium content of the sea could be used to estimate the Earth's age. His actual calculations showed that the Earth might be 90 million years old.[5] William Thomson (1824–1907), better known as Lord Kelvin, issued a series of several papers during the latter half of the nineteenth century dealing with the subject of the age of the Earth. Early in his career he calculated that the Earth might be 400 million years old on the basis of rates of heat loss from a gradually cooling Earth, but by the end of his career he had revised downward his estimate for the maximum possible age of the Earth. Analyzing in detail all possible sources of energy that might contribute to heating and cooling of the Earth since its origin, Kelvin concluded that the Earth was no more than 20 million years in age.[6] The wide variation in ages suggested by these individuals indicates that there obviously was not widespread agreement, and that the various methods used for determination of the age of the Earth were fraught with untestable assumptions and pitfalls. At best all the methods seemed to be indicating an age that was on the order of a few millions of years.

In 1896 the phenomenon of radioactivity was discovered. As knowledge of radioactivity increased scientists found that radioactive elements spontaneously disintegrated into other elements at measurable rates that appeared not to vary with varying external conditions such as temperature or pressure. Furthermore, early evidence seemed to indicate that the rates of radioactive decay probably had not changed throughout geological time. Thus early in the twentieth century it was proposed that the decay of radioactive elements could be used in order to obtain absolute ages of rocks and minerals. The earliest age determinations, although somewhat crude, yielded ages for minerals of tens or hundreds of millions of years.[7] Understanding of radioactivity increased through the twentieth century. It was discovered that many chemical elements are characterized by variable forms of their atoms known as isotopes. The discovery of isotopes permitted scientists to distinguish the radioactive atoms from the nonradioactive atoms of a given element or to distinguish among different kinds of radioactive atoms of an element. As a result of the discovery of isotopes age determinations improved. Further improvements were also made because of improved analytical techniques and better understanding of the geological processes that affect the rocks and minerals in which radioactive elements are contained. A number of dating methods utilizing radioactive decay have been abandoned because they have been found too difficult or fraught with too many uncertainties, but at the same time several very reliable, well understood dating methods have been developed and are now routinely used in a number of laboratories around the world. Consequently thousands of radiometric dates of rocks and minerals are obtained each year by several radiometric methods, and these dates are routinely millions or even a few billion years.

While radiometric dating has not permitted a direct determination of the age of the Earth itself, various studies that carefully analyze the distribution of radioactive elements within the earth have been used to calculate a probable age for the Earth.[8] Likewise ages have been determined from numerous samples of meteorites,[9] and many lunar rocks have been dated.[10] Calculations have also been made suggesting the age of the Moon.[11] The radiometric evidence on the age of the Earth, the age of the meteorites, and the age of the Moon is remarkably consistent in pointing to about 4.5-4.7 billion years. This age is certainly far greater than anything William Buckland ever imagined, but it is almost universally accepted by both the non-Christian and Christian scientific community.

The vast antiquity of the Earth has continued to receive the support of many evangelical theologians and Christian scientists in the twentieth century. Regrettably not many leading geologists in our day have Christian convictions and so they no longer have a special interest in harmonizing Genesis and geology; indeed, many introductory geology textbooks are fond of belittling the biblical story of creation. Some theologians have adopted critical and purely naturalistic approaches to Scripture, and so are not concerned about harmonization either. Nonetheless, many truly evangelical scholars have still shown much support for the antiquity of the Earth and the integrity of the Bible as God's revelation, and have been eager to relate the discoveries of science to Genesis 1.

The day-age view, or some variation of it, has continued to enjoy support in this century. Among theologians such men as Nazarene Orton Wiley,[12] Episcopalian Francis Hall[13] (1857–1932), Lutheran Friedrich Bettex[14] (1837–1915), Roman Catholic Joseph Pohle[15] (1852–1922), and Presbyterian J. Oliver Buswell[16] (1895–1977) favored some variant of this view. Bernard Ramm[17] also leans in this direction, although he sees a very strong topical flavoring to Genesis 1. Robert Newman and Herman Eckelmann adopted a rather unusual version of the day-age view.[18] Among Christian scientists, both Russell Maatman[19] and the present writer[20] favor this view.

Several theologians like Herman Bavinck[21] (1854–1921), E. J. Young[22] (1907–68), Derek Kidner,[23] and R. L. Harris[24] have maintained that the days were not ordinary days without committing themselves to any theory of harmonization.

The restitution theory has fallen out of favor with most scholars. The theory was adopted in the first edition of the Scofield Reference Bible and has been strongly linked with dispensationalist thinking. With an increasing emphasis on fallen angels, judgments, and catastrophes and linkage with the idea of a gospel in the stars, the restitution theory has at times become rather bizarre as, for example, in the work of Reuben L. Katter![25] A very thorough recent defense of the biblical basis for the restitution theory has been put forward by Arthur Custance.[26]

One interesting development of the twentieth century has been the appearance of the "framework theory" of Genesis 1 advocated by such men as A. Noordtzij, Nicholas Ridderbos, and Meredith Kline.[27] The framework view also is consistent with the antiquity of the Earth because time considerations are completely removed from discussion. In the framework theory the days are not regarded chronologically, but symbolically like the numbered sequences of the visions in the Book of Revelation. The days are not to be viewed as so many periods of time, either shorter or longer. For example, attention is called to the fact that days four through six are essentially parallel to days one through three. Day one speaks of light, day four speaks of light bearers; day two speaks of waters and firmament, day five speaks of dwellers in the waters and the firmament; day three speaks of land, and day six speaks of dwellers on the land. This striking parallelism has led advocates of the framework view to regard the interest in Genesis 1 as topical rather than chronological. One benefit of the framework view is that it eliminates sequence and thus removes all possibility of conflict with the sequence of events proposed by geology. There is some tendency among evangelicals to adopt the strictly topical approach suggested by the framework hypothesis.

Several evangelical theologians have continued to defend the idea that the days of Genesis 1 are normal twenty-four-hour days and that the Earth was recently created. In the Lutheran tradition Frances Pieper[28] (1852–1931), John T. Mueller,[29] and H. C. Leupold[30] have argued for this view. In the Dutch Calvinist tradition Herman Hoeksema[31] (1886–1965) and Louis Berkhof[32] (1879–1950) were staunch proponents of the literal view of creation. Valentine Hepp (1879–1950) in his Stone lectures entitled *Calvinism and the Philosophy of Nature*[33] vigorously denounced efforts by Christians to find millions of years in Earth history; to him this was a compromise with evolutionism. Hepp called for a total rethinking of geology in terms of recent creation and a global flood.

### Reactionary Developments

What is astonishing about the twentieth century evangelical scene is a remarkable resurgence of belief among many Christian scientists in the crucial geological role of the Flood and in the idea that the Earth is extremely young. A host of biologists, physicists, chemists, geographers, and engineers (extremely few geologists and astronomers) have recently been insisting on a return to a belief in creation in six twenty-four-hour days only a few thousand years ago, an abandonment of all theories of harmonization, and wholehearted acceptance of a global deluge that accounted for the stratigraphic and paleontological record. There is in America today a movement within evangelicalism favoring recent creation and flood geology. This movement has strong support among Christians who are not engaged in scientific endeavors.

The Flood geology movement in America has gained tremendous

momentum throughout the twentieth century. Perhaps the sole spokesman for this point of view in the 1920s was George McCready Price who authored a number of works including *Common Sense Geology* and *The New Geology* (1923), espousing catastrophic geology and attacking standard geological theory.[34] In 1931 Byron Nelson wrote an interesting and very sympathetic history of the flood theory entitled *The Deluge Story in Stone.*[35] Harold Clark's *The New Diluvialism*[36] appeared in 1946, and Alfred Rehwinkel's *The Flood*[37] in 1951.

The movement received its strongest impetus with the publication in 1961 of *The Genesis Flood* by John Whitcomb and Henry Morris. There followed a long list of writings devoted to the Flood and to the young-Earth theory, including such books as D. M. Patten's *The Biblical Flood and the Ice Epoch*[38] (1966), Melvin Cook's *Prehistory and Earth Models*[39] (1966), Reginald Daly's *Earth's Most Challenging Mysteries*[40] (1972), a whole series of books by Henry Morris,[41] and a set of symposia entitled *Symposium on Creation.*[42] Six volumes in this latter series have already been published. Also of importance have been the formation of such organizations as the Creation Research Society, Creation Science Research Center, the Institute for Creation Research, and the Bible-Science Association. Since 1964 the Creation Research Society has published a quarterly journal containing articles devoted to catastrophism, flood geology, and the young Earth. Several anthologies of articles from this journal have been issued under the titles *Why Not Creation?*[43] (1970), *Studies in Special Creation*[44] (1971), and *Speak to the Earth*[45] (1975).

Of particular interest have been several articles written by creationists who claim to have uncovered valid scientific evidence that shows that the Earth is no more than a few thousand years old.

Before analyzing the scientific arguments put forward in defense of a young Earth (Part Two), an explanation of this remarkable resurgence of recent creationism should be given. Since the nineteenth century geology has become strongly linked with a doctrine of organic evolution that extends not only to lower animals and plants but to man himself. The biological mechanism of evolution has often been transformed by unbelieving scientists into an anti-Christian philosophy (evolutionism). The evolutionistic philosophies of the modern day take man out of the realm of being a creature directly responsible to God and place him in a realm where he is subject to blind forces and inherited instincts. Hence evolutionary philosophy is a threat to Christianity. It attacks Christianity at the heart of the gospel by denying that man needs to be saved by a supernatural redeemer and affirming the idea of racial self-improvement. Evolutionary theory has its strongest evidential supports in the paleontological record and in the vast stretches of time provided by geology. Creationists attempt to discredit not just paleontological theory but any evidence that would suggest enough time for evolution to occur. If the Earth is only six thousand years old, there is insufficient time for evolution, so, we destroy evolution and preserve Christianity (so the thinking runs). Without question a materialist evolutionary philosophy is hostile to Christianity and ought to be opposed by Christians. Likewise the doctrine of the evolution of man is unscriptural and should be opposed. Christians should not, however, attempt to disprove evolutionary theory by discrediting the antiquity of the Earth. Evolution and the antiquity of the Earth are two separate matters and while evolution falls if the antiquity of the Earth falls, it does not necessarily stand if the antiquity of the Earth stands.

Creationists have had a tendency to criticize early geologists as if they were opposed to Christianity and were developing their ideas in order to attack the truth of the gospel. It is, for example, frequently charged that the idea of evolution led to the geologic time scale and the "arrangement" of strata to fit a preconceived order of the evolution of life. Such charges simply ignore the historical facts. The great majority of pioneer geologists in the late eighteenth and early nineteenth centuries were Christian men who as we have seen were intent on upholding Scripture. Virtually all of them were opposed to Lamarck's or anybody else's theory of evolution. William Smith had absolutely no interest in evolution; Cuvier vigorously opposed it. Yet both of them discovered a progression or increasing general complexity of life forms in their successions of strata. The progression of life forms suggested evolution to some people, but evolutionary theory did not lead to juggling of strata to give a "right" order of fossils.

The charge has also been made, for example, by Reginald Daly,[46] that before 1830 and the publication of Charles Lyell's *Principles of Geology* practically everybody was a flood geologist, and that Lyell's uniformitarian and evolutionary philosophy changed the scene. Such contentions are totally false. Daly includes Silliman and Buckland with Whiston and Woodward as flood geologists, but there was a great difference! Both Silliman and Buckland explained only surficial deposits as flood deposits, and both thought the Earth very old; they were very different from Whiston and Woodward.

Moreover, Lyell had many critics long after he wrote the *Principles,* and it was not Lyell who destroyed Buckland's flood geology; it was the glacial theory of Louis Agassiz. By no means could Lyell be called an evolutionist until near the end of his life when he reluctantly adopted Darwin's theory. As a uniformitarian who said the Earth was always basically as it is now, Lyell was opposed for a long time to the idea that there had been progression of life forms. He even tended to ignore the paleontological evidence for progression of life, and maintained that there were no fossils of reptiles and mammals in the earliest rocks because their remains had not been preserved. Never did Lyell teach, as Daly says, that life forms evolved from primitive forms.

The facts are that the modern view that the Earth is extremely old was developed by Christian men who believed wholeheartedly in creation and the Flood and who were opposed to evolution. They came to their view, not because of a preconceived evolutionary philosophy, but because of their intimate knowledge of rocks gained over the years from thorough field study. The traditional ideas of a six thousand-year-old Earth and a global Flood simply could not account for what they saw.

# PART TWO

# SCIENTIFIC CONSIDERATIONS
# AND THE
# AGE OF THE EARTH

# —6—
# STRATIGRAPHY, SEDIMENTATION, and the FLOOD

IN THE LAST CHAPTER it was observed that many Christian scholars in the twentieth century are challenging the notion, widely accepted by both Christian and non-Christian scientists, that the Earth is extremely old, in fact on the order of 4.5 billion years old. Those who are making the challenge are doing so on several fronts. First, the challenge is being made philosophically. It is, for example, being argued that modern science is constructed on the basis of a uniformitarian philosophy, which at root is inherently godless and antiscriptural. In contrast, it is argued that we should do our science on the basis of a catastrophist philosophy, which, it is said, is a biblical way of viewing the world. We will discuss philosophically this challenge in chapter 10 and will show that those who are challenging the antiquity of the Earth are just as uniformitarian in their thinking as those whose views they are attacking.

The challenge is also being made in terms of biblical interpretation. It is simply stated that the Bible plainly teaches the creation of the Earth in purely miraculous fashion just a few thousand years ago, and that the six days of Genesis 1 must be taken in strictly literal fashion. In an earlier book, *Creation and the Flood,* I sought to answer some of those challenges.

Third, the challenge to the antiquity of the Earth is being presented in scientific terms. It is charged that the scientific evidence, which supposedly supports the antiquity of the Earth, is invalid. For example, it is maintained by virtually all young-Earth creationists that the results of radiometric dating are completely spurious and untrustworthy. On the other hand, it is maintained that there is valid scientific evidence that has been deliberately ignored by the scientific community, and that this evidence strongly argues for the young-Earth position. For example, it is said that the gradual decay in strength of the Earth's present magnetic field must be explained in terms of an Earth that is only a few thousands of years old.

In the next few chapters we will look at several of the supposed scientific arguments for a young-Earth as well as scientific arguments against the antiquity of the Earth to show that they are fallacious. We begin with a consideration of the stratigraphic record and its contained fossils. Historically speaking the growing understanding of the Earth's strata led early geologists to suspect that the Earth was fairly old. The view that was displaced was the view that the Earth's strata were largely deposited by the Noachian Deluge.

## Stratigraphy

One of the earliest arguments for the great antiquity of the Earth stemmed from the evidence contained within our planet's accumulations of sedimentary rock. Thick piles of layered, often fossil-bearing sedimentary rocks, such as sandstone, shale, and limestone, cover large portions of the continental land masses. A thickness of four to five thousand feet of layered sedimentary rocks is exposed in the walls of the Grand Canyon. Vast areas of Kansas, Nebraska, Iowa, Illinois, and other central and midwestern states are underlain by a thickness of about one mile of sedimentary rock that lies on top of older crystalline basement rocks. In mountainous regions, thicknesses of tens of thousands of feet of sedimentary rocks may be present. During the mountain building process these great piles of sedimentary rock have been highly deformed and contorted by folds and faults.

Before geology really developed into a full-fledged science during the early nineteenth century, there was considerable confusion over the nature and origin of stratified sedimentary rocks. A few individuals throughout history such as Xenophanes, Avicenna, Steno, and Woodward recognized through careful study of sedimentary rocks that they had formed by a mechanical accumulation of sediments, that is, soil, sand, gravel, and so on, in a fluid medium such as water. Many argued that the sediments had been deposited in the sea, while others thought the great Flood had been responsible. James Hutton, in his classic *Theory of the Earth,* published in 1795, more clearly than ever before stressed the idea that sedimentary rocks had been derived from accumulations on the sea floor of the products of weathering and erosion of preexisting rocks on land. He argued that sedimentary rocks are really formed from the destruction of older mountain systems and uplifted land areas undergoing active and continuous erosion. Although Hutton had numerous sharp critics, his basic thesis strongly influenced subsequent geological thinking.

Since Hutton's time, it has become more and more clearly recognized that sedimentation occurs not only on the sea floor but in a large variety of environments. Modern day sediments accumulate in rivers and stream valleys and floodplains, in deltas, in lakes, in desert basins. Sediments can be transported not only by running water but also by wind and glacial ice. Sediments produced in these modern environments have distinctive characteristics such that a desert deposit is readily distinguishable from a glacial deposit, and a deltaic deposit is distinguishable from a deep sea deposit. During the past one hundred and fifty years geologists have become increasingly proficient in recognizing the products of various geological environments in the sedimentary rock record. Geologists have learned to recognize former desert sediments such as fossil sand dunes in the sedimentary rock record. They can also distinguish former lacustrine (lake) sediments and former river deposits in the rock record. The evidence of sedimentary accumulation in ancient analogs of modern sedimentary environments is overwhelming and continually increasing.

This strong evidence of development of thick piles of sediment in ancient deserts, lakes, rivers, deltas, shores, seas, and basins of all types indicates that it must have taken a very long time to form the entire sedimentary rock record for the simple reason that the formation of deltas, glacial deposits, lakes, and so on, is a measurable process that takes considerable time. By comparing modern processes of sedimentation with the evidences in the sedimentary rock record, geologists have come to the conclusion that the Earth must be far older than was ever dreamed of only two hundred years ago. The physical evidence contained within sedimentary rocks is a powerful argument that the Earth is much older than just a few thousand years.

Not unexpectedly those who are insistent that the Earth is very young are not pleased with the approach to sedimentary rocks taken by modern geologists. There has been a prodigious effort by creationists to discredit the evidences that indicate the antiquity of sedimentary rock sequences. In addition, there has been a great deal of creationist literature that, while ignoring, discrediting, or explaining away the evidences for antiquity, focuses attention on several features in the sedimentary rocks that supposedly can be accounted for only in terms of very rapid or catastrophic deposition. The evidences of catastrophic deposition are then used as one supposed proof of the young-Earth position. The creationist argument typically follows these lines: (1) Modern geologists believe that sedimentary rocks must be interpreted in light of modern sedimentary processes. (2) Modern geologists believe that modern processes are all slow and that since no catastrophes occur today, none have ever occurred. (3) Sedimentary rocks actually show a number of features that can be accounted for only by very rapid catastrophic deposition. (4) The evidences of catastrophic deposition contradict modern geological theory and practice. (5) Therefore, creationists are right and modern geologists are wrong. (6) The only catastrophe of worldwide proportions that could account for the worldwide distribution of evidences for catastrophic deposition is the Noachian Flood. (7) Scripture indicates that the Flood affected the Earth only for one year, that it occurred only a few thousand years ago, and that it occurred only a few thousand years after the creation in six twenty-four-hour days. (8) Therefore, the Earth is only a few thousand years old.

In very general terms we can say that the premises of the arguments are faulty and therefore the conclusion is by no means certain. As regards premise (3), we will show that many sedimentary rocks around the world do indeed contain features that were produced by very rapid or catastrophic deposition. But the premise is misleading because it tells only a half truth; we must also insist that many sedimentary rocks around the world also contain features indicative of extremely slow rates of deposition. Our theory of the origin of sedimentary rocks must not ignore *either* of these features.

Regarding premise (2), it simply is not true that modern geology entertains the idea that modern-day geological processes are all slow. Neither is it true that modern geology rejects the idea that catastrophes occur today or that they occurred in the past.[1] Geologists certainly accept the idea that the *average* rates of sedimentary depositional processes over long stretches of time are quite low, and they also believe that most of the time, rates of sedimentation are slow. But it is also accepted that there may be brief, spasmodic episodes when rates of deposition may be extremely high, even catastrophic. We will look at some examples of modern catastrophic deposition later in this chapter.

Since premises (2) and (3) are incorrect, conclusion (4) does not follow. It is not true that the evidences of catastrophic deposition contradict modern geological theory and practice. Thus neither is conclusion (5) established, that the creationists are right and modern geologists are wrong.

We also need to note with regard to premise (6) that there exist other reasonable explanations besides a global flood that can explain the worldwide distribution of evidences for catastrophic deposition. Because of the incorrect premises, conclusion (8) is not established. Let us now look in greater detail at the creationist arguments about sedimentary rocks and attempt to evaluate them.

There are to be sure a number of features in sedimentary rocks that are suggestive of rapid or catastrophic deposition. Creationists have repeatedly called attention to the existence of fossil graveyards, the remarkable preservation of very delicate structures in many fossil forms, the dismemberment and contorted manner of burial of many fossils, the preservation of such sedimentary features as ripple marks and animal tracks, and the existence of fossil trees that penetrate through numerous strata (polystrate fossils). It is said that these phenomena argue for rapid, even catastrophic sediment deposition and burial, the global nature of the Noachian Flood, and ultimately establish the young-Earth position.

## Fossil Graveyards and Mass Mortality

Creationists have made much over the existence of fossil graveyards. Fossil graveyards are complex accumulations of tremendously large numbers of fossil flora and fauna of a great variety of species in a relatively restricted area of sedimentary rock. In many instances the numerous types of associated organisms were derived from differing ecological habitats. Whitcomb and Morris,[2] for example, discussed fossil deposits in Lincoln County, Wyoming, which contain a great abundance and variety of fossils including palm leaves, alligators, several types of fish, birds, mollusks, crustaceans, turtles, mammals, and insects. They also discussed the remarkable fossil beds near Florissant, Colorado, where well-preserved insects, mollusks, fish, birds, plants, including nuts and blossoms are found in profusion.

The claim is made by various creationist writers that uniformitarian geology cannot account for these deposits. Some catastrophe, it is said, must be responsible. For example, creationist Stuart Nevins argued in his discussion of an accumulation of vast numbers of fossil clams in Texas that "some catastrophe like the Flood seems to be a most reasonable explanation."[3] Now in order to make the argument favoring origin of fossil graveyards by the Flood more cogent, one must also show that such fossil graveyards are not being formed today. Such a demonstration has certainly been attempted. As to the Wyoming occurrence, Whitcomb and Morris comment as follows:

> It is not easy to imagine any kind of "uniform" process by which this conglomeration of modern and extinct fishes, birds, reptiles, mammals, insects and plants would have been piled together and preserved for posterity. Fish, no less than other creatures, do not naturally become entombed like this but are usually quickly devoured by other fish after dying.[4]

The inference is that the only way in which modern uniformitarian geologists believe that fossil fish are formed is by the very gradual accumulation of animals, dying one by one, and slowly sinking to the sea floor and ultimately being buried by very slowly sinking sediment. With regard to the Florissant deposits Whitcomb and Morris say the following:

> Again, one must realize the difficulty of trying to account for such phenomena on the basis of continuity with present processes. The general sort of explanation postulated for the Florissant deposits has to do with volcanic dust showers over a body of water, but no one can point to similar phenomena creating similar deposits today![5]

Now the argument of the creationists that the formation of fossils in general and of fossil graveyards in particular requires some kind of "rapid" or "catastrophic" burial process is valid in many instances, but, contrary to the impression given by creationists, geologists have long recognized that this is the case. The fact that a fossil requires rapid or catastrophic burial in order to have a chance of forming, however, by no means implies a global catastrophe. We may simply be talking of localized, brief catastrophes, and it must be stressed that such catastrophes as give rise to fossil deposits like the Florissant occurrence *are* occurring at the present time. These catastrophes are observable processes. Storms, earthquakes, tsunamis, volcanic eruptions, floods, mudslides and the like are all examples of modern-day, brief, local catastrophes which may be responsible for much fossil formation and preservation.

Let us consider some examples of constantly recurring, modern-day phenomena that result in mass killings of animals and plants and thus are fully capable of producing more fossil graveyards. For a thorough discussion of this subject, the reader should consult the excellent review paper on mass mortality in the sea by Margaretha Brongersma-Sanders.[6] The appendix to her paper gives a detailed tabulation of numerous examples of modern mass mortalities from different causes.

One very important cause of mass mortality in the world today is the phenomenon of waterbloom. Waterbloom is essentially an explosive production of planktonic organisms in seawater. The sea becomes so full of plankton that the water is discolored. The famous red tides (Alabama's Crimson Tide!) seen around the world from time to time are caused by waterbloom. Excessive plankton in the sea can either be poisonous so that virtually all sea life in the vicinity of the red water is killed or in other instances the excessive plankton kills animals by diminishing the oxygen supply. Fish by the millions are found floating on the surface or are washed up on shore during noxious waterblooms. Millions of dead creatures such as shrimp, oysters, seals, penguins, turtles, crabs, and barnacles have been dredged from the seafloor. All shellfish are generally killed. Birds are poisoned after eating the poisoned fish, and even domesticated animals like cows, cats, and chickens die from feeding on dead animals on the beaches or drinking the poisoned water. It is thus not difficult to envisage quite a variety of poisoned animals lying on the sea floor. Their bodies will not decay or be eaten for a long time, because all potential scavengers are killed, too. All it takes to bury this great mass of animals is a sudden disturbance of sea floor sediment by a storm or an earthquake, and perhaps even the temporarily heightened sedimentation rate of planktonic organisms, e.g., diatoms, can bury the animals. In some places the bottom sediment is soft enough that dead bodies can easily nestle into it and be preserved from later scavenger attack. Mass mortality by waterbloom is commonplace, and even today the potential exists for forming great numbers of fossil graveyards, which could be explained without recourse to a global flood.

But there are also many other causes of mass mortality. Brongersma-Sanders gave numerous examples of mass destruction by volcanic eruption. Great varieties of plants and animals have been entombed in falling volcanic ash, or in fluidized ash (volcanic mudslides), or in flowing lava. Others have been killed by heat as lava entered the sea. Great numbers of fish have suffocated in ash-laden streams. One may recall the plight of the salmon during the 1980 eruptions of Mount St. Helens in Washington. Others have been killed by the shocks associated with eruption. Whitcomb and Morris suggested that fossilization by volcanic ash-falls over bodies of water is not observable today and is therefore inconsistent with modern uniformitarian geology. This simply is not true. The 1912 Katmai, Alaska, eruption created great quantities of ash falling over streams and land. A great variety of plants and animals, including insects have been well preserved in the ash.[7] The eruption of Krakatoa in 1883 ejected ash that blanketed everything in the vicinity and smothered all animal life. Ash from Mt. Vesuvius has destroyed animals in the Gulf of Naples. Volcanic activity, like waterbloom, is also responsible for many local modern-day fossil graveyards. Thus there is no reason to assume that such was not also the case in the past. A global-Flood catastrophe is not the only possible explanation for phenomena such as the Florissant beds.

Earthquakes, particularly those located under the sea, have killed life in catastrophic proportions. Shock waves from the earthquakes have killed tremendous numbers of organisms, especially fish. Local rapid uplift of the seabed above sea level has killed all bottom dwelling organisms such as barnacles, clams, snails, starfish, urchins, sponges, anemones, and others. Poisonous gases and flood waves associated with earthquakes have also destroyed organisms in other localities. One must also realize that earthquakes can be responsible for temporarily rapid sedimentation. Sea-floor sediment can be briefly stirred up by the shock of earthquakes and rapidly bury the dead or dying organisms killed by the shock. Major earthquakes are a common occurrence today, particularly around the rim of the Pacific Ocean basin. Several examples of mass kills triggered by earthquakes have been recorded from Alaska, Japan, Chile, Mexico, and Peru, and others were recorded from the Mediterranean area, which is also an active earthquake region.

Mass mortalities in modern times have been also caused by changes in salinity of seawater or lakewater. There are several records of fish kills where lakes or lagoons have become excessively salty owing to too rapid evaporation, where seawater was suddenly washed into relatively fresh water, or where fresh water springs entered into seawater.

Severe temperature changes have also been responsible for great catastrophic mortalities. Such mortalities are typically associated with unusually cold spells or severe winters. Great varieties of fish, crustaceans, turtles, pelicans, manatees, eels, squids, and other animals have been killed in great numbers in various places by extreme cold. Occasionally inflows of unusually warm tropical waters along the coast of Peru have also killed organisms that are more accustomed to cooler or moderate temperatures.

Other mortalities have been caused by lack of oxygen or presence of noxious gases. This is especially the case in lakes and bays that are fairly deep and somewhat isolated. If circulation of water is poor, then oxygen deficient bottom layers of water can build up. The bottom sediments become rich in hydrogen sulfide. Organisms suddenly entering or overcome by oxygen-deficient or $H_2S$-enriched waters will be suffocated or poisoned.

Severe storms also are responsible for catastrophic kills. Birds, fish, and invertebrates can be killed in great numbers by storms. During hurricanes and other severe storms bottom sediment can be stirred up to a considerable depth and can easily bury animals. During one Gulf Coast hurricane huge numbers of oysters were killed and in some places buried under at least a foot of mud.

There is absolutely no question that modern day catastrophes are constantly occurring and that in many of these catastrophes enormous numbers of a wide variety of organisms are not only killed but also buried by rapidly deposited sediment. In short, fossils and fossil graveyards are being formed today. The creationists are certainly right in saying that fossil graveyards are generally evidence for some catastrophic mode of formation, but they are wrong in assuming that no catastrophes are observable today and that only the Genesis Flood could account for these deposits.

In *The Genesis Flood,* Whitcomb and Morris quoted from Brongersma-Sanders to the effect that most animals in the sea die by being captured by other animals and that others dying in other ways are usually eaten by scavengers.[8] They quoted this authority to support their contention that fossils are not formed today because processes of sediment deposition are too slow, but curiously they chose to downplay, if not ignore, the evidence for catastrophic killing cited by Brongersma-Sanders. She stated that killing of thousands of vertebrates is repeatedly occurring and that the scavengers also are decimated. She also said that chances of preservation are good in some cases as when volcanic ash falls in quiet bays or when animals are quickly embedded in a porridge-like mass of dead plankton from waterbloom under anaerobic conditions. Fossil graveyards are therefore not necessarily evidence for a global catastrophe.[9]

## Preservation of Fossils

It has been further suggested that the remarkable state of preservation of many fossils is also an indication of extremely rapid burial and therefore of the Flood. An example of such reasoning is found in a paper by Bernard E. Northrup of Baptist Bible School of Theology, on the Sisquoc diatomite fossils beds.[10] Northrup made some observations on the Sisquoc diatomite beds near Lompoc, California, and concluded that he had found evidence that supports the global-Flood theory and opposes the uniformitarian view. In the diatomite beds are fish fossils; some of these are remarkably well preserved.

> These fish are not mere carbonaceous impressions. In a number of specimens which the author opened, intestinal materials were still preserved as fine red dust which lay loosely in the body cavity. Often the delicate form of an eye was completely observable.
>
> Frequently every scale was in place, and the only distortion visible was that of dislocation in the spinal cord and the pressing of the delicate rib bones and the lower fins out of alignment as the body was compressed to a few thousandths of

an inch in thickness. In one case, a slight fault had displaced the head of a herring in two planes by one half of an inch. The distortion otherwise leaves the physical form well preserved in every way.[11]

Northrup questioned whether the fish fell to the bottom after death to be covered by a slow rain of diatoms from above. He says:

> The supposed gradual deposition of millions of carcases, intruded by other bottom feeding fishes, and their painfully slow burial by the postulated $1/1500$ to $1/2$ inch per year deposition rate simply is not possible. The body structures of these fossils were preserved without any indication of deterioration and putrefaction.[12]

Moreover, other fossils are said to show clearly that the rate of deposition was extremely rapid. Some fish have been violently dismembered so that fins and scales have been found in layers above and below the skeleton. Many fish show signs of dying in agony. Their bodies are twisted and backs are arched. Now to explain all these phenomena, Northrup argued for rapid burial and presented a scenario in which the Flood catastrophe was responsible. He plainly felt that uniformitarian geology, which he assumed believed in extremely slow sedimentation and gradual deposition and burial of fish could not account for these facts.

The writing of Northrup is just one example of the general tendency in the creationist literature to misunderstand or downplay the character of modern-day fossilization processes. While it is admitted by some creationists that fossilization can occur today, it is stressed that the conditions favorable for fossilization are rare and difficult to fulfill, that fossils being formed today are few and far between, and certainly that modern fossilization processes are totally inadequate to account for the vast amounts of fossil material in the rocks. Moreover, modern fossilization is often represented (as in Northrup's paper) as occurring only very slowly with burial of animals one at a time.

Several things need to be noted about the creationist arguments. In the first place it should be observed that fossils in the geologic record are not quite so abundant as creationists seem to imply. It is, of course, true, that many strata are just packed with fossils and in some cases virtually the entire formation may be composed of fossil fragments. Such is particularly the case with many marine limestone beds. However, by no means are all strata like this. The majority of strata are either devoid of observable fossils or contain relatively few of them. This is particularly the case for sedimentary rocks of obviously terrestrial derivation, which is to be expected inasmuch as conditions favorable to fossilization are not as good on land as they are in the sea.

In the second place we agree that modern fossilization is relatively rare in the sense that the overwhelming majority of individual animals that die are not preserved whatsoever. Even their hard parts eventually disintegrate and are totally destroyed. But one must keep in mind that billions upon billions of individuals die. Even if only a very minute percentage of the multitudes of an individual species stand a chance of survival as a fossil, a large number of fossils will survive. Furthermore, if this process is continuing over long periods of time, it is certainly possible to find a sedimentary pile that will contain a substantial number of fossilized individuals.

Finally, even though the conditions favorable to fossilization are rarely met, they do exist and are capable indeed of producing fossils. The preservation and fossilization of modern organisms is an aspect of geology that has not received as much attention as it should have, but more recently a number of investigators have been studying the manner in which modern day organisms die, are buried, and preserved. Perhaps the outstanding proponent of what has come to be known as "actuopaleontology" is Wilhelm Schäfer, who spent his entire scientific life carefully observing the death habits of organisms in the North Sea. The results of his life's work have fortunately been translated into English in an extremely valuable work entitled *Ecology and Paleoecology of Marine Environments*.[13] It is important to refer to this work so that the reader may gain a better understanding of fossilization today. Examples will be selected from Schäfer's observations on fish, echinoderms, and whales.

Schäfer maintained that entire fish skeletons will be preserved only if the dead fish carcass never floats to the surface.[14] If the fish carcass does float after death, then the gradual decomposition and bloating of the body with gases under the influence of bacteria will tend to disaggregate the skeleton so that individual skeletal parts will fall to the sea floor and the remains will be scattered by currents across the floor.[15] However, relatively high salt contents and anaerobic conditions, which are especially prevalent in rather deep water, tend to inhibit the growth of bacteria that aid in the decomposition of the fish.[16] Under such conditions the carcass may never float to the surface after death inasmuch as not enough decomposition gas is produced. The carcass remains on the sea floor and the skeleton may be retained entire in such cases, especially if the bottom is quiescent and free of scavengers.[17] Such conditions may be met in deep enclosed basins, which become stagnant at the bottom.[18] Schäfer indicated that such conditions generally do not occur in at least the southern North Sea because it is too shallow, and thus the bottom remains agitated so that whole skeletons are not preserved.[19] However, he maintained that organic-rich muds produced by periodic waterblooms are capable of preserving whole fish skeletons very nicely elsewhere. Incidentally, he noted that waterblooms are the only cause of mass mortality in the North Sea because volcanic activity and floods are lacking.[20] The waterblooms either poison or suffocate huge masses of fish. In areas other than the North Sea such waterblooms serve as perfect resting places for dead fish.

Upwelling, nutrient-rich water in these areas permits explosive phytoplankton blooms which may turn into red tides and cause widespread deaths among nekton and plankton. The effect is all the more devastating since the bloom itself attracts large swarms of fishes and other marine animals. Large amounts of organic matter accumulate on the sea floor as a consequence and may well cause depletion of oxygen on the sea floor and formation of sapropel muds. Nutrient-rich, ascending water allowing explosive phytoplankton bloom is not restricted to coastal waters but occurs also in the open ocean. Consequently, one may expect organic-rich muds to form in areas of periodic upwelling in the open ocean, independently from the existence of enclosed euxinic basins. Areas that extend over many hundreds of nautical miles may receive more organic material than can be oxidized even by the generally abundant oxygen supply of the deep sea floor. The sediment becomes a rotting gyttja-mud whose surface lies only occasionally within a region of oxidation and which is well suited as a repository of undisturbed fish skeletons together with soft parts. The low rate of sedimentation of inorganic material in these depths combined with a high rate of introduction of organic material, leads . . . to the preservation in the sediment of the very organic material which also causes the oxygen depletion.[21]

Schäfer also noted that "fossil fish with well-preserved skeletons are found with remnants of their soft parts, and that the enveloping sediments bear all the characteristics of a former sapropel."[22] Preservation of whole fish skeletons in the Sisquoc diatomite beds is precisely what one would expect with an explosive bloom of diatoms.

Now the data that Schäfer outlined are totally different from what Northrup suggested is the case. We can almost completely agree with Northrup that "the supposed gradual deposition of millions of carcasses, intruded by other bottom feeding fishes, and their painfully slow burial by the postulated $1/1500$ to $1/2$ inch per year deposition rate simply is not possible." He is correct; it isn't possible. But that is not what modern geology says about fish fossilization. It doesn't suppose the "gradual deposition of millions of carcasses," certainly not in every instance. We have just seen from Schäfer's studies that millions of fish can be killed and deposited in one brief catastrophic episode, not at all gradually. Not only that, modern geology does not suppose that deposition of carcasses always occurred in places that are "intruded by other bottom feeding fishes." We have just seen that in waterblooms and in other catastrophic mass kills, bottom feeding fish and other scavengers are going to be killed, too, so that scavengers are completely eliminated. Nothing is left to eat the dead fish that are lying on the sea floor. Not only that, modern geology does not say that sediment deposition rates are everywhere and at all times between "$1/1500$ and $1/2$ inch per year." That may be a worldwide average when considered over a long period of time, but it certainly does not rule out the possibility of local catastrophic sedimentation now here and now there. Again we have just seen that rapid sedimentation does occur with the development of thick organic muds produced by settling of phytoplankton blooms. In other places locally rapid sedimentation occurs during storms, as we will see in Schäfer's discussion of preservation of invertebrates. Northrup's argument against "painfully slow burial" is certainly a good one, but by absolutely no stretch of the imagination does that argue cogently for the existence of a worldwide catastrophic Flood. Other explanations are equally valid.

Schäfer also dealt at great length with the death, burial, and preservation of a variety of invertebrates in the North Sea. We will here consider briefly just the ophiuroids or brittle-stars, which are slender-armed starfishlike creatures. Ophiuroids prefer areas of quiet water and very light sedimentation and thus heavy sedimentation generated during a strong storm can lead to their disappearance.[23] If during a storm the bottom sediment is agitated so that as little as 5 cm thickness of sediment covers the brittle-stars they will perish.[24] They are unable to wriggle out of this depth of sediment. Some species found buried in mud, that is, those with long, flexible arms, have their arms tightly coiled in death position. This is precisely the manner in which many fossil brittle-stars are found. Shorter-armed species often keep their arms extended in death.[25] To be sure, many brittle-stars that die by being buried in mud will be released into the water as the bottom sediment is later agitated and the body will be fragmented into smaller skeletal parts. However, because brittle-stars are gregarious, large numbers can be permanently preserved under favorable conditions when the bottom sediment is not agitated to a sufficient depth to release the dead animals into the water.[26] Schäfer also pointed out that other echinoderms like starfish and echinoids can be preserved in large numbers by similar burial in storm-generated sediment.

Schäfer also discussed in considerable detail the death, decomposition, and burial of whales, dolphins, and seals. In general these animals decompose and float on the surface owing to the gases in the body cavity and individual skeletal parts are released and gradually scattered over the sea floor.[27] However, many entire animals are beached and eventually completely covered over by the drifting beach sands.[28] The mummified bodies are in this way preserved nearly entire. Likewise we can well expect that any animals that entered a region of plankton-rich water would likely be poisoned or suffocated and their skeletons preserved entire in the organic-rich muds. Schäfer's book includes a number of photographs of small whales whose bodies are becoming completely entombed in blowing beach sand. Thus there are certainly numerous instances occurring today where even whole skeletons of animals can be preserved without being destroyed by scavengers or wave or current action. Admittedly such occurrences are not the norm, but they do occur repeatedly, and given the fact that billions of animals are continually dying should easily account for many complete skeletons encountered in the fossil record. The occurrence of whole skeletons certainly does not require a global catastrophe but only rapid burial, which as we have seen does occur today. Moreover, it is particularly instructive that whole fossil skeletons are found in rocks that are indicative of the same kinds of environments in which we would expect whole skeletons to be preserved today.

## Polystrate Trees

Creationists have also pointed to the existence of fossil trees standing upright through several feet of strata as indicative of an extremely rapid rate of burial. Morris, Rupke, and Coffin have discussed such fossil trees at considerable length, and they have called attention to several localities around the world where this phenomenon has occurred.[29] Of particular interest is a locality at Joggins, Nova Scotia, at the upper end of the Bay of Fundy. Here there are numerous fossil trees that seem to have root systems embedded in underlying soil. Hence most geologists have generally regarded the trees as having grown in place and then later been buried in sediments. Virtually all geologists, however, have recognized that at this locality there must have been extremely rapid sedimentation in order to preserve the trees before complete disintegration. Creationist Rupke has even listed many of the geologists who have advocated extremely rapid burial of the trees.[30] Yet this has hardly made catastrophists out of them. Even Charles Lyell visited Joggins on his travels to North America in the nineteenth century and did not return to England as a catastrophist.

Rupke has also taken issue with the idea that these trees grew in place. He has argued cogently from the field evidence that in reality the trees were transported into place[31] and has suggested the possibility that the Flood catastrophe did this. Following his lead, other creationists have also argued that these fossil trees were rafted into place, many in an upright position, rather than having grown in place in accordance with the traditional uniformitarian view.

Even if Rupke is right concerning the transportation origin of the trees, modern geology is in no danger. Plant paleoecologist Krasilov seems to agree with Rupke's view of transport and rapid sedimentation.[32] The point simply is that large plants can be rafted and deposited by means other than Noah's Flood. Krasilov provided many examples of modern-day rafted trees, especially in flooded rivers of tropical rain forests.[33] Whole trees, often floating upright, may be swept along by flooding rivers. In some cases they take root downstream. In other cases large areas of tropical rain forests can be swept bare and buried under highly fluid mudflows. The so-called polystrate trees are again evidence for rapid burial conditions, but they certainly do not require Noah's Flood for their formation.

## Evidences of Slow Deposition

Creationists have rightly called attention to numerous evidences in the rock record of rapid or catastrophic burial. They are perhaps performing a service in so doing because there probably has been a tendency in modern geology to overlook the "catastrophic" aspects of geologic history. Geologists should be more aware of the catastrophic aspects of nature and the role that they play in geology.[34] Creationists, as we have seen, like to maintain that only a global Flood can account for these evidences of catastrophe. They have a number of reasons for doing so apart from the fact that most of them think the Bible requires them to believe in an absolutely global Flood. Among these reasons are: (1) that they think rapid sedimentation is incompatible with modern uniformitarian geology, and (2) that they think a global Flood is consistent with the principle of simplicity, i.e., it is simpler to postulate the existence of one great catastrophe rather than a whole series of smaller catastrophes.[35]

We have just been pointing out that catastrophes of a small, temporary scale are hardly inconsistent with uniformitarianism since such catastrophes occur all the time. They are normal to the course of nature. Therefore we may dismiss the first reason. With regard to the second reason, we must remember that the principle of simplicity doesn't mean that nature is simple. It just means that we ought to propose and test simple hypotheses before proposing complicated ones. It does not mean that simple hypotheses are always the right ones, and it certainly does not mean that we adopt a simple hypothesis when there is a great deal of evidence against it. We must deal with such considerations in proposing the global-Flood hypothesis. While there seems to be evidence that suggests extremely rapid sedimentation and accumulation of the Earth's sedimentary rock record in one year, there are also numerous evidences against such a suggestion. In addition to those sedimentary rocks that suggest very rapid deposition, there are also sedimentary rocks that suggest slow deposition. We now turn our attention to some of these.

Creationists have, of course, been aware of the problems posed for their theory by rocks that supposedly require a very slow rate of deposition, and therefore imply that the Earth is very ancient. Whitcomb and Morris made an honest and valiant effort to face up to many of these problems in *The Genesis Flood*.[36] They have not succeeded, however, as two examples will show.

## Coral Reefs

Whitcomb and Morris recognized the problem that coral reefs pose for flood catastrophism because coral reefs generally are regarded as structures that are built up rather slowly. Geologists have found numerous examples of what they consider to be ancient fossil reefs in the sedimentary rock record. These reefs are not always coral reefs, but they are basically similar in structure to the coral reefs of today. Inasmuch as reefs are formed at slow rates today we would expect that fossil reefs would be formed likewise. Slow growth rates would be incompatible with reef formation during a brief part of the Flood year. Whitcomb and Morris claimed that the rate of growth of coral reefs is great enough that modern, currently existing reefs could have been built up in the few thousand years since the Flood,[37] and they also claimed that fossil reefs may simply be eroded, redeposited reefs that existed in the warm antediluvian seas. The erosion and redeposition supposedly occurred during the Flood. Other creationist geologists, e.g., Nevins, have attempted to demonstrate that the famous El Capitan reef of Permian age in west Texas is not really a true reef at all.[38]

The contention that fossil reefs are really antediluvian reefs that were eroded and redeposited during the Flood is totally unsupportable. To begin with we must realize that there are vast numbers of fossil reef structures throughout the sedimentary rock record. We need consider only one example of these structures.[39] In the Silurian rocks of Wisconsin, Illinois, and Indiana, in particular, there are many fossil reef structures. Some of the structures are small, that is, ten feet high and a few feet in diameter. Some of them are almost one thousand feet in thickness and several miles in diameter.[40] Can one possibly conceive of a structure this large as being a redeposited antediluvian reef? Could even the most spectacular flood be capable of transporting a reef that large? Smaller reefs might be dislodged and transported during a torrential flood, but hardly a single object several miles in diameter. Even more unbelievable is the fact that the reefs lie stratigraphically above other carbonate rocks, which lie on top of the three hundred foot thick St. Peter Sandstone, which in turn lies on top of hundreds of feet of other clastic sedimentary rocks. Do we not stretch the limits of credulity by supposing that the Flood kept an object several miles in diameter in suspension while hundreds of feet of much finer-grained lower density sediment was deposited underneath it? Turbulent waters will tend to deposit larger objects while keeping smaller objects in suspension. This is a basic principle of hydraulics. But this theory supposes that the Flood did the reverse of what moving water generally does. What is also striking is that the St. Peter Sandstone is composed entirely of well-rounded sand-sized quartz grains. It would be very unusual for a flood to be so turbulent that it could suspend a huge reef while at the same time depositing pure quartz sand. Flood geologists are constantly referring to the intense mixing activity of the Flood, so it is hard to see why the quartz-rich sediment does not have an admixture of other minerals in it. Also, one wonders where this pure quartz sand came from in such a brief period of time. The only realistic interpretation of the evidence is to say that the reef structures grew in place on an ancient sea floor.

Another reason to be highly suspicious of the redeposition theory is that none of the reefs are upside-down. Surely with turbulent transportation of huge reef blocks, some of them would be dumped in an inverted position. The reefs grew in place on a floor of already deposited carbonate sediment. Thus, if the reefs formed during the Flood year they had to grow very rapidly (especially so to reach a height of one thousand feet). Hundreds of feet of sediment (presumably formed during the Flood) were also deposited on top of the reefs. Thus we are asking these reefs to grow to tremendous sizes in much less than a year; modern reefs do not grow rapidly, but are formed at the rate of only a few centimeters per year under the best of conditions. Reefs are also sensitive to environmental factors; they grow in lighty agitated, warm water.[41] In turbulent conditions such as hurricanes, reefs tend to be destroyed. The Flood, presumably a turbulent, stormy event is hardly likely to have provided the ideal setting for rapid growth of reefs. More likely, existing reefs would have been destroyed by the Flood, and reef growth would have been impossible. The reefs would have required several thousands of years to grow, and therefore their presence in the rock record is devastating to the idea that the Flood produced the sedimentary rocks. This suggests that the Earth is much older than creationists generally admit.[42]

## Evaporite Deposits

Creationists have also recognized that bedded evaporite deposits pose a threat to the catastrophist scheme.[43] Evaporite deposits are typically composed of minerals like halite, gypsum, and anhydrite. According to the generally accepted uniformitarian scheme, bedded or layered evaporite deposits (excluding from consideration such structures as salt domes) are the result of gradual and repeated evaporation of desert lakes or more particularly arms of the sea that are periodically cut off from the ocean and then refilled with ocean water. This theory implies slow rates of deposition and would be inconsistent with the catastrophist view.

Nevins commented on some of the difficulties of current theories of the origin of evaporites in terms of uniformitarian principles as have Whitcomb and Morris.[44] Without question such difficulties do exist. But the fact that there are difficulties on the uniformitarian view hardly proves that the Flood can account for evaporites. Nevins made no suggestions as to how we can account for evaporites in terms of the Flood. The suggestions of Whitcomb and Morris are totally unsatisfying. They suggested that evaporites were created during creation week and then redistributed during the Flood.[45] Such a suggestion is not credible, however, since a highly turbulent flood would be likely to dissolve the most soluble evaporite salts like halite and sylvite ($NaCl$ and $KCl$ respectively). Other less soluble minerals would certainly become intimately admixed with clastic sediments, but evaporites are generally free from clastic material. Also, if evaporites are being eroded by the Flood, chunks, boulders, pebbles, and cobbles of the material would be carried off by the waters. Why then do we not find cobbles or boulders of evaporites in conglomerates or other clastic sedimentary deposits above *and* below evaporite deposits?

Other hypotheses proposed included "unusual conditions of vaporization and separation of precipitates . . . caused by the locally high temperatures"[46] accompanying volcanic upheavals. In other words Whitcomb and Morris here proposed an extremely high evaporation rate on a local scale during the Flood year. This is certainly an ingenious hypothesis. There is one major thing wrong with it, and that is, that many evaporite deposits are located nowhere near any volcanic centers. As an example, we may consider the great evaporite deposits of Silurian age in Michigan, Ontario, Indiana, Ohio, Pennyslvania, West Virginia, and western New York. There are virtually no volcanic rocks whatsoever in these areas. The evaporites are interbedded with clastic and carbonate sedimentary rocks. The proposed source of heat for the high rate of evaporation of flood water simply was not there.

Let me propose one additional idea not mentioned by Whitcomb and Morris. Perhaps when the flood waters receded evaporite deposits were formed; presumably the evaporation of the flood waters would leave behind a precipitate of salts. But this does not work either because evaporites are not found on the surface but buried beneath great thicknesses of clastic sediments. Once dried up, the Flood cannot deposit more mud and sand.

Evaporites simply cannot be accounted for by a rapid, one-year process. The great thicknesses involved suggest slow deposition over considerable periods of time. Evaporite deposits suggest that the Earth is much older than creationists believe.

## The Evidence of Sedimentary Environments

If, as we are told repeatedly by creationists the entire world was covered by surging flood waters for nearly a year by the Noachian Deluge, then we have every right to expect that the kinds of sedimentary rocks that presumably were deposited by that flood should bear the characteristic marks of flood-type deposits. We ought to be able to look at the kinds of flood deposits that are produced at the present time and gain some insight as to what kinds of sedimentary materials are characteristically formed. When we look at the sedimentary rock record we find some deposits that bear evidence of having been formed by moving water and could have been formed in flood waters, but by no means are all rocks like that.

There are in the sedimentary rock record numerous examples of deposits that could not have formed in surging flood waters at all; in fact, these deposits bear all the marks of having formed in several different kinds of environments that are in existence on the Earth's surface today, environments that could not exist at a time when the whole world was covered by flood waters. The evidences in the rocks are of environments that are totally incompatible with the global-Flood hypothesis. The environments are those in which the formation of the sediments also would have required considerable amounts of time in order to develop, certainly far more time than is allowed for by the Flood theory. As examples, we will deal with the kinds of sedimentary deposits that were evidently formed in lacustrine (lake), glacial, and desert environments. It is evident that lacustrine deposits could not form during the Flood if the waters covered the entire Earth, and it is similarly the case with desert and glacial deposits. It is not possible to conceive of large quiescent lakes slowly depositing their muds while the whole world is submerged under surging flood waters. It is not possible to conceive of great ice sheets scouring rocks and moving sediment if the whole world is submerged under surging flood waters. It is not possible to conceive of a large desert with great sand dunes while the whole world is submerged under surging flood waters.

## Lacustrine Deposits

We look first at fossil lake deposits. Sedimentation in lakes is characteristically very slow, and massive or thinly laminated beds of very fine-grained material build up in the deeper parts of the lake below the base of the waves. These deposits are characteristically surrounded by river deposits inasmuch as lakes are fed and drained by rivers. Therefore we ought to look in the sedimentary rock record for laterally persistent thinly laminated or massive, fine-grained sedimentary rocks that eventually grade laterally into coarser-grained, cross-bedded river deposits. There are many examples of these kinds of deposits in the rock record. There are, for example, Lakes Uinta and Gosiute of Eocene age in Wyoming, Colorado, and Utah. The famous Green River oil shales make up a great portion of these deposits, which are up to two thousand feet thick. The Popo Agie Formation of Wyoming is Triassic in age and was developed from a lake which covered the western half of Wyoming. The deposits are hundreds of feet thick. Another example is the Lockatong Formation of New Jersey, also of Triassic age. These shales are tens of feet in thickness and are characteristic lake deposits.

These lake deposits can be distinguished from similar fine-grained marine sediments by a number of criteria.[47] The regional enclosure by river sediments suggests that we are not looking at a lagoon or quiet arm of the sea. The Lockatong Formation of New Jersey, for example, grades laterally into and is overlain by coarser cross-bedded sands and shales of the Brunswick Formation. These rocks are river (fluvial) sediments. The presence of continental organisms also sets lake deposits apart from marine deposits. Fresh-water fish and mollusks may be present. Amphibians may be found. Dinosaur tracks have been found. We might ask the question why dinosaurs were walking around if the whole world was under water. Characteristic marine fauna like bryozoans, brachiopods, cephalopods, trilobites, and echinoderms will be lacking. Certain kinds of algae will be restricted to terrestrial environments. We might expect very well preserved tree leaves to be fossilized.

Lakes also differ from seawater in chemical composition. Seawater is essentially constant in chemistry, whereas lakes show considerable variability from one lake to another depending on a variety of factors. Because of the constant chemistry of seawater only certain evaporite minerals would be expected to form during evaporation cycles in marine sediments. Likewise only certain authigenic[48] minerals would form from marine waters. Because lakes can be much more saline than seawater, minerals can be precipitated that would not be precipitated from seawater. Marine precipitate minerals include mainly halite, gypsum, calcite, and dolomite. Lakes, however, may precipitate borate minerals and unusual carbonates like trona. Minerals like analcime may also be formed; so, too, may rare hydrocarbons. Thus the presence of certain minerals in thinly laminated, fine-grained sediments, like trona or borates would be indicative of a lacustrine environment, especially if associated with strictly nonmarine fossil assemblages.

The presence of mudcracks or chips is suggestive of periods of drying and would be expected in some lakes. The sulfur isotope content of organic materials, including hydrocarbons, is generally constant in marine environments, but quite variable in lacustrine environments.

Thus lake deposits can be distinguished from marine deposits by a combination of paleontological, mineralogical, geochemical, and regional stratigraphic criteria. They can be distinguished from other terrestrial environments by a combination of physical characteristics such as bedding, sedimentary structures, grain size, sorting, and paleocurrent patterns.

Many ancient lakes, examples of which were given above, have been found using these criteria. In order to form some of the deposits, millions of years may have been required; to form two thousand feet of lake sediment with an extremely slow rate of sediment accumulation takes a lot of time.

Whitcomb and Morris again attempted to explain at least one famous ancient lake deposit, namely, the Green River Formation.[49] They suggested that during the waning stages of the Flood a vast sedimentary basin was formed by gradual uplift of the surrounding lands. Shallow turbidity currents carried soft sediment and organic slime into the basin to yield the laminated sediments. Such an explanation, however, does not explain why only terrestrial fossil remains are formed in the beds. One would think that, given the global character of the Flood, abundant marine life would also have been swept into this basinal area. It would also be somewhat difficult to account for the evaporite and authigenic minerals in the formation. These minerals would form from drying up saline lakes. One could argue that the Flood waters were also saline and that as they were diminishing from the Earth's surface these minerals were precipitated in the turbidite sediments. If this is so, however, why do we not find such minerals in all later flood deposits inasmuch as in something as well mixed as the Flood, the salinity should be relatively the same throughout? Nor is it likely that the algal reefs would form under conditions postulated by Whitcomb and Morris. The field evidence is consistent with the Green River Formation having been formed by gradual sedimentation in huge lakes; this demands large amounts of time.

Such an explanation also could not possibly work for something like the Lockatong Formation in New Jersey, for the rocks of the Lockatong are covered over by a considerable thickness of much later unconsolidated sediments, which would suggest that the Flood was still active in the vicinity long after the Lockatong had been deposited. Not only that, but the Lockatong is now situated close to the Atlantic Ocean and we might wonder why no marine fossils would have been washed into this formation.

## Glacial Deposits

Other deposits which render the Flood hypothesis untenable are those of glacial origin. There are evidences of glacial deposits from various localities and in rocks of various ages.[50] One of the best known glaciations prior to the last great ice age is the glaciation of Late Paleozoic age in India, southern Africa, Australia, and southern South America. It takes a lot of time to form glaciers and have them flow and transport sediments over great distances. It took a long time to move India to its present position from a near polar region. Glaciers of great magnitude certainly would not form in India's present location. Furthermore, glaciers do not form under water.

Again, creationists see a danger to their hypothesis from this quarter. *The Genesis Flood* attempted to dispel the notion that there really had been a Permian glaciation.[51] Whitcomb and Morris rightly did not think it too likely that glaciation would develop near the equator, and so they attempted to explain the striations and unsorted gravel deposits as evidence of catastrophic volcanic or turbidity phenomena. They felt that this fit much better with the presence of such warm weather indicators as coal. Let us now examine the field evidence.

Hamilton and Krinsley[52] reported on some of the evidence from South Africa and southern Australia. They described numerous localities where highly polished and striated bedrock of various rock types and ages is overlain by poorly sorted Permian conglomerates. That the striations and conglomerates are of glacial origin is evident from the fact that the striations or deep grooves are not just on bedrock but specifically on smoothed, rounded outcrops characterized by gentle, smooth slopes up current from the outcrop. Such outcrops are typically developed by the flow of glacial ice over bedrock; they do not develop with turbidites or mudflows or other similar erosive agents. The surfaces of these outcrops, termed roches moutonnées, not only are polished and grooved and striated as is the usual case with glaciated surfaces, they also show friction cracks (chatter marks) indicative of the flow of ice. Chatter marks are straight to crescent-shaped cracks a few inches in length that are transverse to the flow of ice. The bottom of the crack is relatively smooth on one side and generally gradually deepens in the direction of ice flow.

The conglomerates themselves bear all the characteristics of modern glacial tills and thus are called tillites. They contain unsorted sediment, polished and striated pebbles and cobbles, and much rock flour. X-ray studies have indicated that there are virtually no clay minerals present and that the very fine-grained material consists of fragments of minerals that ordinarily weather very easily. These mineralogical characteristics are typical of glacially derived rock flour.

Associated with the striated pavements and tillites are thinly laminated, glacial lake deposits. These overlie or are interlayered with the tillites and are in some places varved. These laminated deposits commonly contain dropstones, that is, polished and striated pebbles and cobbles that have been deposited from rafts of ice floating out into lakes formed at the margins of melting glaciers.

It has also been shown by electron microscopy that the surface textures of quartz grains from the various sediments are typical of modern-day quartz grain textures found in glacial deposits. Surface textures of the grains can be diagnostic of sedimentary environments.[53]

The field evidence when all put together points convincingly towards glacial origin. Thus, once more we find abundant evidence in nature of materials that required much more time to form than that which is allotted to us by the one-year Flood. First we need to deposit the underlying sediments, then consolidate them, bring them to a near polar region where glaciation can proceed, develop glaciers, have them transport sediments great distances, retreat and disappear, and then have new sediment deposited on top of the glacial materials while the southern hemisphere continents drift away from the pole toward the warmer climate of the more temperate regions of the globe where we now find this evidence.

## Desert Environments

A final example of an environment that requires time to develop and is incompatible with the Flood hypothesis is the eolian desert environment. Eolian deserts are, of course, characterized by great sand dunes that are composed predominantly of quartz sand. The grains are well rounded and generally have a frosted surface texture. Fine-grained clay and mica flakes are generally absent. The dunes characteristically show very large-scale cross-bedding. The angles of cross-bedding may be as great as 34°. It takes time, of course, to erode bedrock to a sandy condition and to blow the material into dunes. One cannot develop a large desert or dunal area in a short time. A global Flood that has submerged the entire world will not temporarily drain away to expose a large tract of land on which a desert will suddenly develop for a few days.

In the Colorado Plateau there are numerous formations of Pennsylvanian to Jurassic age which show all the signs of having been ancient coastal dune to desert dune deposits. These formations are thick sandstone layers with large-scale cross beds. There are vertebrate tracks and fossil dinosaurs in some of these units. Where did these animals come from if the Flood was busy destroying them? These ancient desert sandstones give eloquent testimony to the fact that the Flood was not covering the Colorado Plateau when the rocks we see there were being deposited.

The sedimentary rock record is replete with rocks that formed in glacial, lake, desert, reef, evaporite, and other environments that are utterly impossible to reconcile with the Flood hypothesis. These deposits all formed in environments that take considerable time to develop. They all point to the fact that the Earth is far more than just a few thousand years old as creationists would have us believe.

# —7—
# RADIOMETRIC
# DATING

IT HAS BEEN SHOWN that the sedimentary rock sequences that cover most of the surface of the Earth cannot be explained in terms of a single catastrophic flood that acted only a few thousand years ago for a period of about one year. There are far too many features in the sedimentary rocks that are incompatible with this idea. Many sedimentary rocks bear evidence of extremely slow deposition; other rocks bear evidence of having been deposited in environments totally different from a flood environment. On the one hand such evidences disprove the validity of Flood geology, but on the other hand they also suggest that the Earth has had a long, complicated history. A close look at the sedimentary rocks indicates that the Earth has experienced several successive episodes of sedimentary deposition, burial and hardening of the rocks, uplift, erosion, subsidence, renewed sedimentation, burial and hardening, further uplift, and so on, through several cycles. It would appear that these processes have taken a long time, much longer than a few thousand years if those sediments were deposited and deformed in a manner similar to what is happening today.

The problem is that even though the sedimentary rocks suggest a high antiquity for the Earth, it is not possible from the physical characteristics of the rocks to make accurate determinations of just how long ago those rock layers might have been formed. Estimates can be made, but these are based on assumptions. A more reliable means of determining the ages of rocks and the Earth itself is needed and radiometric dating provides just such a means.

One of the most productive areas in all of geological research is that of radiometric dating. It is now possible for geologists to determine the absolute ages of many kinds of rocks and of certain geological events. No longer does the geologist need to content himself with saying that a rock is

Ordovician in age, thus applying only a relative age term to the rock. With the advent of radiometric dating he may also be able to say how many millions of years ago the rock formed. He can now tell when the Ordovician period occurred. Without question the results of radiometric dating methods have proved extremely disturbing to creationists, because over and over again ages of millions to billions of years have been obtained! This evidence would clearly indicate that the Earth is extremely old. Such a conclusion is, of course, totally unacceptable to those who believe the Earth is very young. Therefore, valiant attempts have been made by a number of creationists to discredit the radiometric dating methods.

There are a large variety of dating methods. In this chapter only the most common radiometric dating methods are considered, namely those based on the radioactive decay of the chemical elements rubidium, potassium, uranium, and thorium. Radiometric dating is based on the fact that certain atoms of some chemical elements spontaneously "decay" or change into atoms of entirely different chemical elements. The atom that decays spontaneously, that is, undergoes radioactive decay, is termed the parent. The atom into which the parent is transformed is termed the daughter. Parent atoms can decay into daughter atoms by means of a number of processes.

## Beta Decay

One common radioactive decay process is that of beta decay. During beta decay the parent atom emits a beta particle ($\beta$) from its nucleus and thus is changed into an atom of the daughter element. A beta particle is essentially an electron,[1] and since a neutron[2] is essentially equivalent to a proton[3] and an electron, the result of beta decay can be written as if a neutron decayed to a proton and an electron

$$n \rightarrow p + e \text{ or } n \rightarrow p + \beta \tag{1}$$

where n stands for the neutron, p the proton, and e the electron. The result of this process is that during beta decay the number of neutrons in the radioactive atom is reduced by one, the number of protons is increased by one, and an electron or beta particle is emitted (Figure 1). It is the increase in the number of protons that changes the atom of the parent element into an atom of the daughter element because each chemical element is defined on the basis of the number of protons in the atomic nucleus.

The most important geological example of beta decay is that of rubidium 87 ($^{87}Rb$) into strontium 87 ($^{87}Sr$). A rubidium 87 atom contains 37 protons and 50 neutrons in its nucleus. The 37 protons define the atom as a rubidium atom. A strontium 87 atom contains 38 protons and 49 neutrons in its nucleus. The 38 protons define such an atom as a strontium atom. Rubidium 87 decays by beta decay into strontium 87. The overall effect of the beta decay is as if one of the 50 neutrons of $^{87}Rb$ decays into a proton and an electron. Thus only 49 neutrons remain in the nucleus but another proton is added to the 37 already present thus giving 38 and making the atom a strontium atom. An electron is emitted.

## Alpha Decay

A second very common type of radioactive decay is alpha decay. In alpha decay, an alpha particle ($\alpha$) is ejected from the atomic nucleus (Figure 1). An alpha particle consists of two protons and two neutrons. It is basically the nucleus of a helium atom. Thus, helium gas is typically generated as a by-product of alpha decay. An example of alpha decay is that of uranium 238 ($^{238}$U) into thorium 234 ($^{234}$Th). A uranium 238 atom contains 92 protons and 146 neutrons. The 92 protons define the atom as a uranium atom. A thorium 234 atom contains 90 protons and 144 neutrons. During alpha decay the uranium 238 atom ejects an alpha particle, that is, 2 protons and 2 neutrons. Thus the number of protons is reduced from 92 to 90, making a thorium atom, and the number of neutrons is reduced from 146 to 144. Now thorium 234 is itself radioactive, as is its daughter product. A whole series of alpha and beta decays is required to transform $^{238}$U into its ultimate stable, nonradioactive daughter element, lead 206 ($^{206}$Pb).

## Electron Capture

A third important process is that of electron capture. In this process an atom spontaneously incorporates into its nucleus one of the electrons that is orbiting the nucleus in the innermost shell of electrons (Figure 1). Again since an electron does not exist as such in the nucleus, the net effect is the gain of a neutron and the loss of a proton. The result is as if the electron had reacted with one of the protons in the nucleus to make a neutron, or the reverse of equation (1). As an example, consider the decay of potassium 40

## Figure 1

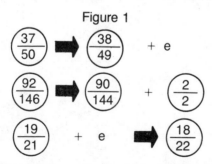

Schematic illustration of various radioactive decay processes. Circles represent atomic nuclei with numbers of protons (top) and numbers of neutrons (bottom) present in nucleus. At top, beta decay is illustrated by $^{87}$Rb nucleus decaying into $^{87}$Sr nucleus with release of beta particle (e). In middle, alpha decay is illustrated by $^{238}$U nucleus decaying into $^{234}$Th nucleus with release of alpha particle. At bottom, electron capture is illustrated by $^{40}$K nucleus capturing an electron (e) and thereby decaying into $^{40}$Ar nucleus.

($^{40}$K) into argon 40 ($^{40}$Ar). Potassium 40 contains 19 protons, which makes it potassium, and 21 neutrons. Argon 40 contains 18 protons, which makes it argon, and 22 neutrons. In this decay the potassium 40 atom "captures" an orbiting electron and incorporates it into the nucleus. In effect, a proton reacts with that electron to give an extra neutron. Thus the number of protons is reduced from 19 (K) to 18 (Ar), and the number of neutrons is increased from 21 to 22.

## The Rate of Decay

Exactly when a given radioactive atom will spontaneously decay into its daughter atom cannot be predicted. The decay of individual atoms is a purely random process. But the rate of decay for a very large number of radioactive atoms can be determined. This rate of decay is different for each particular kind of radioactive atom and is generally measurable experimentally. The rate of decay is expressible mathematically as the decay constant[4] or as the more familiar half life.[5] The half life is the period of time in which one half of a large sample of isotopes[6] of a radioactive element disintegrates to some daughter product. The meaning of the half life is shown in Figure 2, which illustrates the decay of $^{238}$U with a half life of 4.5 billion years. If a sample of pure $^{238}$U consists of 10 million atoms, then at the end of 4.5 billion years half of those atoms would have decayed so that only 5 million atoms would be $^{238}$U. The other 5 million atoms would consist of the various daughter elements in the $^{238}$U decay chain. At the end of 9 billion years half of the remaining 5 million atoms of $^{238}$U would be left so that we would have 2.5 million atoms remaining. At the

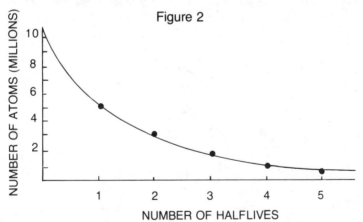

Decay curve for radioactive atoms. A sample of 10 million $^{238}$U atoms would spontaneously decay into various daughter elements so that at the end of one half-life of $^{238}$U, namely 4.5 billion years, only 5 million $^{238}$U atoms would remain in the sample. At the end of 2 half-lives, or 9 billion years, only half of the 5 million, or 2.5 million atoms, would remain in the sample.

end of 13.5 billion years we would have 1.25 million atoms of $^{238}U$ left. Thus as time progresses the ratio of parent atoms to daughter atoms in a sample gradually decreases as more and more daughter atoms are produced. The ratio of parent atoms to daughter atoms is thus a relatively simple function of time, or the age of a material.

If the radioactive decay of an element in a mineral is used to determine the age of that mineral we must be reasonably certain that the decay constant or halflife for the radioactive element is really a constant. So far no evidence has turned up to indicate that the decay constant does vary in isotopes of interest to dating geological samples.

Increased pressure and temperature seem to have no effect whatever on decay constants. The decay constant for geologically important radioactive elements remains the same when those elements are placed in different kinds of compounds. There is some evidence that electrical fields may have a very slight influence on the decay rate of iron 57, but this isotope is not of any importance geologically. The decay constants for some geologically unimportant atoms have been found to vary slightly from one compound to another. While it is possible that there are factors that may influence significantly the decay constants of the radioactive elements, nothing is known of these as yet. It has been suggested by creationists that heightened cosmic ray incidence should speed up decay rates of radioactive elements, but even if this were true radiometric dating methods would generally be unaffected because cosmic rays do not penetrate very far into the ground. Most samples collected for dating have been taken from fresh roadcuts that were originally several feet below the surface where they would not be affected by cosmic radiation. Thus available evidence indicates that decay constants are indeed constant and have been so throughout Earth history.

## Gain or Loss of Elements

Radiometric dating is thus based on measurement of ratios or amounts of parent and daughter elements in minerals or rocks where these ratios are functions of age. But certain other things must be known before we can apply radiometric methods legitimately. First of all, if a mineral or rock is to yield a correct age, a geologist must ordinarily be certain that during the history of that mineral or rock none of the parent or daughter isotope has been added to it or escaped from it. If a mineral is one million years old but some of the daughter atoms have escaped from the mineral during those years, the mineral will appear younger than it actually is. The same will be true if parent isotope atoms have been incorporated into the mineral since it formed. On the other hand if parent atoms have escaped from the mineral or daughter atoms have been added to the mineral during its history, the age will appear to be greater than the actual one million years.

One cannot always be positive that a mineral has acted as a closed system during its history, that is, has neither gained nor lost atoms of the radioactive element or its daughter product, but the possibility of error from this source can be minimized. In collecting material for radiometric analysis geologists are careful to collect samples that are as free from weathering as possible. During weathering, elements unquestionably migrate away from minerals. Geologists also avoid collecting specimens near or in fault zones or other highly fractured zones. Fracturing opens up the possibility of influx of water, which in turn allows migration of elements into or out of minerals and rocks. In other words geologists try to select specimens for dating from geological situations in which the probability of element migration and contamination would be at a minimum.

## Determining the Original Amount of Daughter Element

In properly applying radiometric methods to minerals and rocks it is also necessary to know how much of the daughter element may have been present in the mineral at the time of its formation. When the amount of a daughter element in a mineral is measured in terms of a ratio to the amount of parent element we will obtain the true age only if we know the amount of daughter element actually produced by decay of the parent in that mineral. Thus the geologist needs to know how much of a daughter element was already incorporated into the mineral when it was formed. The reader may well wonder how it is possible to know this, but the problem is not really so serious as it may seem. It is usually possible to make an estimate. For example, a mineral that is datable by the potassium-argon method usually can be considered to contain little if any argon at the time of formation since argon is an inert gas element and is not at all easily bound chemically to the structures of minerals. Exceptions have been found, but usually argon is not present in a mineral when it forms. The argon generally develops in the mineral by radioactive decay of potassium.

A mineral such as zircon that is datable by the uranium-lead method probably contained some $^{206}Pb$, the ultimate daughter product of $^{238}U$, when it was formed. It is usually possible to determine how much $^{206}Pb$ was present in the following way. When a zircon crystal forms it also very likely incorporates some $^{204}Pb$ into its structure. No $^{204}Pb$ at all is produced in the zircon by any type of radioactive decay, for it is not a radiogenic isotope. Therefore if no Pb is lost or gained by the zircon during weathering the amount of $^{204}Pb$ will remain constant through time. The amount of $^{206}Pb$ in the zircon at the time of formation can be determined by determining the ratio of $^{206}Pb/^{204}Pb$ in a closely associated mineral that is the same age, perhaps a feldspar or galena in the same or nearby rock. When a granite or other igneous rock crystallizes, the chances are excellent that the rock will contain both zircon and feldspar. Both will incorporate $^{206}Pb$ and $^{204}Pb$ into their structures at the time they crystallize in the rock. The ratio of $^{206}Pb/^{204}Pb$ should be identical in both minerals when they form. There is no compelling evidence to indicate that one mineral preferentially incorporates either $^{206}Pb$ or $^{204}Pb$ compared to the other mineral. So the ratio in the zircon when it formed should be the same as in the feldspar that crystallized at essentially the same time. Zircon also incorporates uranium into its structure and in time the uranium decays to $^{206}$Pb so that the $^{206}$Pb/$^{204}$Pb ratio in zircon increases as time goes on. Feldspar structures, however, do not readily incorporate uranium atoms. As a result, there is virtually no further addition of $^{206}$Pb to feldspar through radiogenic processes and the $^{206}$Pb/$^{204}$Pb ratio stays the same as it was when the mineral first formed. Therefore the $^{206}$Pb/$^{204}$Pb ratio in a feldspar from the same igneous rock as a zircon will tell us the probable initial $^{206}$Pb/$^{204}$Pb ratio of the zircon.

Geologists have also found legitimate methods for estimating or determining the original amount of $^{87}$Sr in a sample to be dated by the rubidium-strontium method. This is done by determining the ratio of $^{87}$Sr/$^{86}$Sr initially present in the sample. We will look at these methods in more detail when we specifically discuss the rubidium-strontium dating method.

## The Potassium-Argon Method

We now consider each of the three major radiometric dating methods and discuss the criticisms of each of these methods that have been made by various creationists. We first consider the potassium-argon (K-Ar) method. Natural potassium-bearing minerals, for example, the very common feldspar and mica minerals, contain a quantity of an isotope, potassium 40 ($^{40}$K), whose nucleus contains 19 protons and 21 neutrons. $^{40}$K spontaneously disintegrates in accordance with the laws of radioactive decay, but it is unique in that it decays into two different daughter elements. The majority of $^{40}$K atoms decay to atoms of calcium 40 ($^{40}$Ca) by emission of a beta particle. The other $^{40}$K atoms in a sample decay spontaneously to atoms of $^{40}$Ar by capturing an electron from the innermost shell of electrons orbiting about the nucleus. This process, as we have seen, is termed electron capture. Geochronologists generally are not interested in utilizing the decay of $^{40}$K to $^{40}$Ca because $^{40}$Ca is an extremely common isotope and there would be great difficulty in distinguishing between ordinary $^{40}$Ca and radiogenically produced $^{40}$Ca. The amount of common $^{40}$Ca in a mineral would greatly exceed the amount of radiogenic $^{40}$Ca. This would lead to very large errors in ages determined by this method. Hence interest focuses on the decay of $^{40}$K to $^{40}$Ar. In order to utilize this decay for purposes of dating rocks and minerals it is necessary to determine the decay constant for this reaction. To be sure, there are some experimental difficulties in determining this decay constant[7], but the value for the decay constant of $0.585 \times 10^{-10}$/year is reasonably accurate and widely accepted[8]. One criticism of the K-Ar method made by a number of creationists[9] is that the decay constant is uncertain and that a more exact determination of the decay constant is needed. Without doubt it is true that a more exact determination is needed, but this fact is of absolutely no value to creationists. The need for a slightly more exact decay constant does not in the least discredit the K-Ar method. It has been pointed out by geochronologists[10] that a 5% error in the decay constant for a rock one billion years old will result in only a 3.9% error in the age determination. This would be an error of 39 million years. That sounds like a lot, but there is not a staggering difference between something 1000 million years old and something 1039 million years old or something 961 million years old. A small error in determination of the decay constant by no stretch of the imagination makes rocks only a few thousand years old. Dalrymple and Lanphere[11] have estimated that the actual error in the decay constant is only about 3%.

Creationist D. O. Acrey[12] made the point that argon can be lost from minerals by diffusion, thus rendering inaccurate ages. This is true, but in geochronological studies we try to avoid the collection of samples from which there has likely been diffusion of atoms out of or into the sample. This is especially a problem with K-Ar dating, because argon is an inert element and can readily be lost from a crystal structure that is thermally disturbed. The result of argon loss, however, is that a mineral will give an anomalously young age. If all the argon produced by radioactive decay of $^{40}K$ contained within a mineral were retained, then the true age would be obtained and that age would be *greater* than if argon had leaked out. If creationists wish to argue that minerals dated by K-Ar are useless because of diffusion, then they must accept the fact that the minerals are actually much older than the already very high ages they yield! The fact that radiogenic argon can leak out of a mineral certainly does nothing to help an argument in favor of a recent creation.

Creationist Slusher[13] has said that the Earth's atmosphere contains far too much argon to have been derived by radioactive decay of potassium even if the Earth were really 4.5 billion years old. From this, Slusher argues that the Earth must have been created with a large amount of initial argon 40. Slusher also maintained that the results of geochronologists are "highly questionable," because they assume that errors due to the presence of initial $^{40}Ar$ are small. He does not see how this assumption can be made if so much atmospheric argon was once underground and presumably available to contaminate all sorts of samples. Slusher's thinking is unfounded, however. One can assume that there is a great quantity of argon down in the crust and even argon in magmas, but a rock that is crystallizing from the magma is generally likely to contain very little Ar at first for the simple reason that argon as an inert element will generally be rejected from the crystal structure of the growing minerals. There are known exceptions, but this is generally to be expected. This argument does not make the method questionable.

But then Slusher goes on to say that since argon diffuses readily and since the pressure is greater at depth within the Earth than it is near the surface, therefore argon would migrate toward the surface. As a result there should be an "abnormally large amount" of argon in the surface where rock samples for dating are found. These samples should have a lot of excess argon, thus making them appear older than they really are. While it is no doubt true that argon will tend to be degassed from the interior of the Earth, it is very likely that diffusing argon will migrate predominantly through fracture systems much more so than by diffusion through rocks. Nor is such argon likely to enter into mineral structures. If indeed there were any such argon it would be adsorbed on grain boundaries where it likely would be removed during sample preparation. There is little reason to expect significant argon contamination within mineral structures because of continuing migration of argon from depth.

Another criticism by creationists concerns the possibility of contamination by atmospheric argon. Approximately 1% of the Earth's atmosphere is composed of argon, and of that, most is $^{40}$Ar. Thus, when lava is erupted onto the Earth's surface, some argon could be absorbed into the liquid from the atmosphere. Upon solidification of the lava this atmospheric argon may be trapped in the volcanic rock. Thus the rock has some $^{40}$Ar in it that was not produced by radioactive decay of $^{40}$K within the lava. As a result the age of some volcanic rocks might appear to be anomalously old. Geochronologists are well aware of this problem and so a method has been devised to correct for atmospheric argon contamination. The atmosphere also contains $^{36}$Ar as well as $^{40}$Ar whereas crustal rocks contain virtually no $^{36}$Ar. In the atmosphere today the ratio of $^{40}$Ar/$^{36}$Ar is 295.5. The amount of $^{40}$Ar contamination in a sample can thus be determined by measuring the $^{36}$Ar content in the sample and multiplying by 295.5. The amount of $^{40}$Ar is then subtracted from the total $^{40}$Ar. It is, of course, possible that contamination may arise during crushing of samples for analysis in the laboratory or that tiny amounts of atmospheric argon may be trapped in the sample preparation and analytical equipment. Thus corrections are routinely made during analysis to eliminate the possible effects of atmospheric argon contamination.

Robert L. Whitelaw, a leading creationist, in two major articles,[14] claims to have found a major flaw in the K-Ar method with regard to this atmospheric correction factor. He says that the K-Ar method has been "constructed on a brilliant deduction based on a colossal oversight!"[15] This "colossal oversight" is that geologists assume that the "ratio of Ar-36 to Ar-40 in the atmosphere *has remained exactly the same as it was the day the rock was formed*. One could scarcely find a more glaring example of the uniformitarian faith!!"[16] Whitelaw goes on to argue that $^{36}$Ar is produced by cosmic rays in the upper atmosphere and therefore the $^{40}$Ar/$^{36}$Ar ratio has decreased through time down to its present 295.5 value. This means, he says, that an "old" specimen that was contaminated with atmospheric argon would have a very high $^{40}$Ar/$^{36}$Ar ratio. But since geologists would apply the present-day correction which is much too low, we would greatly underestimate the amount of atmospheric $^{40}$Ar contamination. Therefore too much of the $^{40}$Ar in a mineral or rock would be attributed to radioactive decay of $^{40}$K and we would assign much too old an age to the rock. Not only that, if creation were only a few thousand years ago, the present $^{36}$Ar level in the atmosphere could be built up from zero by cosmic ray bombardment. Thus a rock formed at creation only a few thousand years ago and trapping atmospheric argon contamination would contain only $^{40}$Ar and no $^{36}$Ar. This rock could thus appear to be extremely old when it really was only a few thousand years old. Thus Whitelaw thinks he has found the Achilles heel of the K-Ar method. He concludes his article,

> This then is the timeclock without hands—without even a face—upon which evolutionary faith now depends to prop up its desperate belief in a world that never began, a creation that never occurred, and a creator who never created and no longer exists!
>
> And the record of Scripture was never so sure![17]

The basic flaw in Whitelaw's argument is that specimens that are collected for analysis have generally not been in contact with the atmosphere until the present day. If one is going to sample a granite for K-Ar dating, one does not sample a chunk that is lying right on the surface in contact with air. One wants to avoid as much as possible the problem of contamination, not meet it head on. Geologists sample fresh, unweathered material that is not exposed to air and that is as free of fractures as possible. This minimizes the possibility of contamination. It is unlikely that atmospheric argon will diffuse into an outcrop and into mineral grains that are a couple of feet below the surface. So it does not matter what the $^{40}$Ar/$^{36}$Ar ratio in the air was at the time of the rock's formation. The rocks sampled generally were not formed in the presence of air (some volcanic rocks excepted) and even those that are rarely absorb much argon.

Another way of checking on this matter is by sampling rocks from the moon, so that we need not worry about the problem of atmospheric contamination. The moon has virtually no atmosphere, and the chances of contamination are virtually nil. Any $^{40}$Ar in a sample is likely to be derived by radioactive decay of potassium. It is therefore significant that K-Ar ages of lunar basalts from the mare regions are 3 to 4 billion years and in general agreement with dates yielded by other methods. In no way does this data support the young Earth view, but it does support the ancient Earth and solar system theory.

The K-Ar method has further been criticized in that the initial concentration of potassium and argon in a sample can be known only by guesswork. This simply is not true with regard to potassium. If a specimen is fresh and free from effects of weathering and groundwater, there is no particular reason to expect that its potassium content is any different from the time when it was formed excepting for the slight loss of potassium due to radioactive decay. There is, however, some guesswork involved with the initial argon content. Because of argon's inertness it generally makes sense to assume that virtually no argon is incorporated into a crystal structure that is crystallizing from, say, a magma. There are, however, some exceptions to this. For example, some volcanic lava flows of the last few years have been found to contain some argon at the time they were erupted. As a result, the measured age of the lava flows may turn out to be much greater than their true age, which is essentially zero. Another creationist, Sidney Clementson,[18] has seized on this fact in order to discredit the whole of radiometric dating. He has noted that some Hawaiian volcanics give very large ages when they are really only a few years old. This is true, but it does not invalidate the radiometric dating in general or even K-Ar dating in particular. In the first place, it should be noted that there have also been numerous historic lava flows from places like Japan, Sicily, Hawaii, Iceland, and elsewhere that have contained essentially no excess $^{40}$Ar when they were formed. So their measured age would be the same as their true age, namely zero.[19] Second, there is a good reason why some lavas contain excess $^{40}$Ar. Submarine lavas tend to retain any excess Ar because of the pressure of the overlying ocean water. The effect is greater at greater depths because of greater pressure. That is, a basalt lava erupted deep onto the sea floor is more likely to retain its dissolved $^{40}$Ar and thus give an anomalously high age compared to a lava erupted near the surface. It has also been found that the amount of excess argon increases from the core to the rims of the individual "pillows" of submarine lavas.[20] Thus it is known that volcanic rocks may solidify from magmas that already contain some dissolved excess $^{40}$Ar, but the resulting error in the measured age of the lava flow can be minimized by selecting subaerial rather than submarine basalts for analysis. If a submarine flow must be dated, then error can be minimized by sampling the centers of the lava "pillows" from which most of the initial Ar will have escaped.

None of the criticisms leveled by creationists against the K-Ar dating method have any real merit. Although there are elements of truth in these criticisms, they are not sufficient to discredit the method because other factors have been overlooked.

## The Rubidium-Strontium Method

The method of rubidium-strontium dating has likewise been assailed by creationists. Here again, however, the criticisms are invalid and lend no support to the idea of a young Earth.

For many years the only kind of rubidium-strontium dating was that done on individual minerals from igneous and metamorphic rocks. Because of their similar electrical charge and size, rubidium (Rb) ions substitute for potassium (K) ions in the structures of common potassium-bearing minerals like biotite, muscovite, and feldspar so that these minerals were commonly used for dating purposes. These minerals may also contain strontium (Sr) at the time of formation. When the mineral forms, it should not only incorporate the non-radiogenic isotope $^{86}$Sr but also some of the radiogenic isotope $^{87}$Sr that is incorporated into the mineral at the time of formation. The problem is how to distinguish between $^{87}Sr$ that was incorporated into the mineral when it was formed and the $^{87}Sr$ that formed in the mineral since its formation by radioactive decay of $^{87}Rb$. It is only the latter $^{87}Sr$ that will give us the age of the mineral. The problem is that we don't know how much $^{87}Sr$ was incorporated into a mineral when it was first formed and therefore we don't know the so-called initial strontium ratio $(^{87}Sr/^{86}Sr)_0$. Slusher is thus in a limited sense right when he suggests that "there is no really valid way of determining what the initial amounts of $^{87}Sr$"[21] were. What the geochronologist must do then is to make a reasonable estimate as to what the initial $^{87}Sr/^{86}Sr$ ratio was in a mineral when that mineral was first formed. Slusher, however, charges that "these values can be adjusted so that any age desired is obtainable."[22] No doubt these values can be adjusted, but this does not mean that they are. What geologists do is to select a reasonable possibility for the initial Sr ratio by using ratios that are measured in materials like seawater, river water, and basalts, which contain relatively little Rb. The $^{87}Sr/^{86}Sr$ ratios in these materials are all on the order of 0.700-0.710. Values in this range are generally used. Also it should be kept in mind that geochemical studies indicate that minerals do not preferentially incorporate either $^{87}Sr$ or $^{86}Sr$ so the ratios of these isotopes should be essentially the same in the minerals as in the solutions or magmas from which they form. When such ratios of 0.700 to 0.710 are used, we obtain ages of millions to hundreds of millions of years old and in some cases more than a billion years old.

These numbers certainly suggest that the Earth is far more than a few thousand years old. But the initial strontium ratio was not selected in order to give us the huge ages. Ratios were selected that are already commonly found in Rb-deficient materials. The initial $^{87}Sr/^{86}Sr$ ratio would have to be far higher than 0.7 (on the order of 0.9) to give ages of only a few thousand years. There is absolutely nothing to indicate that such ratios occur in minerals when they form. They certainly haven't been found in minerals known to have formed only recently.

Of course, it is always better to know what the initial ratio really was rather than simply to make an intelligent guess, so the Rb-Sr mineral dating technique is rarely used now and has given way to a superior technique, the whole-rock isochron method. This technique is discussed in detail shortly.

Slusher also charged that in Rb-Sr dating the ease of diffusion of Sr is completely ignored.[23] This charge is completely unfounded. Even if it were true, would it help the young-Earth theory? When severely heated or exposed to groundwater, a mineral containing Sr may well lose some of that Sr. The Sr may migrate out of the structure by diffusion and be permanently lost. It has been shown that weathering and heating cause this loss of Sr.[24] What then is the result? If a mineral that has lost Sr is dated, a young age is obtained. There is less radiogenic Sr in the mineral than there should be since some has leaked out. So the mineral looks too young. So when, for example, S. R. Hart[25] reports an age of 54 million years for strongly heated biotite from Colorado, the biotite is really much older, because Sr has diffused out of the biotite during heating. Diffusion of Sr does nothing to aid the young-Earth cause. Once again, geologists generally try to avoid collecting samples that are badly weathered or exposed to groundwater or heavily fractured or faulted. All these situations would tend to be favorable to diffusion of Sr, and we like to minimize such effects in order to get the most accurate age possible.

It was mentioned previously that dating individual minerals is less desirable than dating whole rocks by the Rb-Sr method. The whole-rock method is superior in that the geologists can actually determine mathematically what the initial amount of $^{87}Sr$ was in a rock when it was originally formed in terms of the ratio $^{87}Sr/^{86}Sr$. The whole-rock method also is sensitive to the possibility of Sr diffusion. That is, from the results, one can generally determine whether or not diffusion has taken place. The whole-rock method has been applied to a variety of rock types but is most reliable for the dating of igneous rocks, that is, those that have crystallized from magma.

Imagine that a hot magma exists somewhere within the Earth's crust. The magma is composed of a great variety of atoms. Most of these atoms are of common elements like potassium, sodium, calcium, iron, magnesium, aluminum, silicon, oxygen, hydrogen, and titanium, but there will also be trace amounts of other elements like scandium, barium, uranium, nickel, rubidium, and strontium. Of all the strontium atoms, several isotopes will be present. Of these strontium isotopes, we are especially interested in $^{87}Sr$ and $^{86}Sr$. $^{87}Sr$ differs from $^{86}Sr$ only in having an extra neutron in its nucleus. This makes $^{87}Sr$ a slightly heavier atom than $^{86}Sr$. In spite of the slightly greater mass of $^{87}Sr$ atoms, we can predict that the ratio $^{87}Sr/^{86}Sr$ throughout the magma will be essentially uniform, that is, constant. There is no available evidence to indicate that $^{87}Sr$ atoms preferentially migrate to one portion of a body of magma. Although it is not known what this initial ratio $^{87}Sr/^{86}Sr$ was at the outset of an investigation, the ratio can eventually be determined. It does not matter that we do not know how much $^{87}Sr$ is present at the time of crystallization, and it doesn't matter that this $^{87}Sr$ is not derived by later decay of $^{87}Rb$. This ratio $^{87}Sr/^{86}Sr$ is termed the initial strontium ratio and is expressed mathematically as $(^{87}Sr/^{86}Sr)_0$.

Suppose that the magma with a uniform initial $^{87}Sr/^{86}Sr$ ratio begins to crystallize. Several different kinds of minerals will begin to form, each of which has a different internal atomic crystal structure. If the magma is a granitic magma, then the major minerals to form will be feldspar and quartz with possibly substantial amounts of hornblende or mica minerals like biotite or muscovite. Suppose that the magma crystallizes to a biotite-bearing granite. The crystal structure of quartz is such that it is virtually pure silicon dioxide ($SiO_2$). Atoms of elements that are of interest to geochronology like Rb and Sr will be excluded from the quartz structure because they have the wrong electrical charge and are too big to substitute for the major atoms in that structure. Some Rb and Sr, however, will be incorporated into such minerals as biotite and feldspar. Traces of Rb and Sr will probably substitute for K in the biotite structure. Rb will generally substitute for K in the feldspar structure and Sr will generally substitute for Ca since the charges and sizes of these atoms are similar.

Once the granite has crystallized, the ratio $^{87}Sr/^{86}Sr$ will be essentially constant throughout the body of rock because virtually no $^{87}Rb$ has yet decayed to produce new $^{87}Sr$. However, at the time of formation some samples of the granite will be relatively enriched in Rb and others will be relatively enriched in Sr. For example, samples of granite that have higher percentages of biotite and K feldspar will have higher ratios of Rb/Sr than samples of the granite that have higher contents of quartz and plagioclase feldspar and lesser amounts of biotite and K feldspar. This is so because the Rb of the granite will be concentrated in the K-rich minerals like biotite and K feldspar, and the Sr will be concentrated in Ca-bearing minerals like plagioclase. Thus the ratio of Rb/Sr and therefore $^{87}Rb/^{86}Sr$ will vary quite a bit from one specimen of the granite to another. If then we were to sample several chunks of granite just after it had crystallized, and if we analyzed the ratios $^{87}Sr/^{86}Sr$ and $^{87}Rb/^{86}Sr$ in those samples and plotted the data on a graph we would obtain a diagram like that portrayed in Figure 3. None of the above is wild guessing. It is based on the observed behavior of strontium and rubidium isotopes in mineral structures. The line on the diagram

## Figure 3

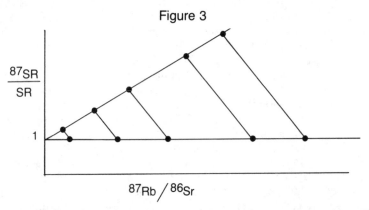

Isochron diagram. Horizontal line shows orientation of an isochron at time of crystallization of a magma. At that time all minerals crystallizing will have virtually identical $^{87}Sr/^{86}Sr$ ratios (I = initial ratio) but will have different Rb/Sr ratios. As time progresses after crystallization, $^{87}Rb$ in individual minerals decays into $^{87}Sr$ thus lowering the $^{87}Rb/^{86}Sr$ ratios and raising the $^{87}Sr/^{86}Sr$ ratio for each mineral. Hence each data point through time follows a path with negative slope. Thus at some time long after crystallization the data points will have migrated to the positions on the isochron with the positive slope. The greater the slope of the isochron, the older the age of the rock.

in Figure 3 is called an isochron and the slope of the line is a function of the age of the rock. For a rock of zero age, that is, one that has just formed, the slope of the isochron will be zero. It will therefore be a horizontal line.

How will the diagram appear for a granite that has aged somewhat? How does the position of the isochron vary as the granite gets older? As the granite becomes older some of the rubidium 87 atoms spontaneously decay by beta particle emission into strontium 87 atoms in accordance with the radioactive decay law. This means that, with time, the ratio of $^{87}Rb/^{86}Sr$ of any sample of granite will gradually decrease. The more time that elapses, the more the ratio decreases because $^{87}Rb$ is being lost from the sample. At the same time the $^{87}Sr/^{86}Sr$ ratio of the sample increases because $^{87}Sr$ is being added by decay of $^{87}Rb$. Consequently a data point on the isochron diagram shifts its position through time as shown in Figure 3. The older the sample becomes, the farther along the arrow the data point is shifted.

All the points will shift along paths with the same slope as indicated in Figure 3. In a given amount of time, points with the highest Rb/Sr ratios will shift the most because they have higher Rb contents and thus a greater amount of Rb will be converted into $^{87}Sr$ by decay. As a result the isochron line will pivot around the point of $(^{87}Sr/^{86}Sr)_0$ through time. The slope of the isochron will become steeper the older the granite is. This change in slope of the isochron through time is illustrated in Figure 3.

Mathematically the isochron may be expressed by the equation

$$\frac{^{87}Sr}{^{86}Sr} = \frac{^{87}Rb}{^{86}Sr} \times \left[ e^{\lambda t} - 1 \right] + \frac{^{87}Sr}{^{86}Sr_0} \quad (2)$$

Equation (2) has the form of the equation of a straight line: $y = mx + b$. Thus $(^{87}Sr/^{86}Sr)_0$ is the y-intercept and $(e^{\lambda t} - 1)$ is the slope of the isochron on a plot of $^{87}Sr/^{86}Sr$ vs. $^{87}Rb/^{86}Sr$.

To obtain an isochron it is necessary to collect several large samples of granite with variable mineral contents to insure a fairly wide range of Rb/Sr ratios. The $^{87}Sr/^{86}Sr$ and $^{87}Rb/^{86}Sr$ ratios now present are measured analytically and plotted on the diagram. These points generally fall on a straight line whose slope gives the age of the rock. The isochron diagram also yields the initial $^{87}Sr/^{86}Sr$ ratio of the magma from the intercept on the y-axis. If samples had been seriously affected by diffusion of Sr out of the rock then the data points would fall considerably off the isochron and to the right.

According to Slusher,[26] Melvin Cook has objected that the isochron line has nothing to do with age, but is simply a result of natural isotope variations in the rock. Slusher pointed out that Cook says that one can obtain similar straight lines using other isotope ratios where none are radiogenically related. For example, if one plots $^{54}Fe/^{86}Sr$ vs. $^{58}Fe/^{86}Sr$ one can also obtain a straight line that has nothing to do with age.

This argument, however, is misleading because the relationship of $^{54}$Fe to $^{58}$Fe is not at all like that of $^{87}$Sr to $^{87}$Rb. When one plots $^{54}$Fe/$^{86}$Sr vs. $^{58}$Fe/$^{86}$Sr one naturally obtains a straight line, for one sees only the effect of a constant ratio of $^{54}$Fe to $^{58}$Fe, which is completely independent of the $^{86}$Sr content in a suite of rocks from a given rock body. Table I on page 109 lists some purely hypothetical values of $^{54}$Fe, $^{58}$Fe, and $^{86}$Sr contents in a suite of rocks. One would have every reason to expect that the $^{54}$Fe/$^{58}$Fe ratio would be essentially constant in a suite of rocks from a given rock body. One may also legitimately expect the $^{86}$Sr content to vary independently of the Fe isotope contents because Sr and Fe will be preferentially incorporated into different minerals whose abundance may vary from one rock to another. If the hypothetical data in Table I are plotted on a diagram in terms of $^{54}$Fe/$^{86}$Sr vs. $^{58}$Fe/$^{86}$Sr as in Figure 4 a straight line resembling an isochron is indeed obtained. But, as Cook points out, the line has nothing to do with age. However, to infer, as he does, that a plot of $^{87}$Sr/$^{86}$Sr vs. $^{87}$Rb/$^{86}$Sr is also simply a matter of natural isotope variation is completely incorrect. The straight line on such a plot *is* a function of age, for the $^{87}$Sr/$^{87}$Rb ratio *cannot* be a constant as is $^{54}$Fe/$^{58}$Fe. The ratio *must* continuously vary in all rocks as a function of time because of the decay of $^{87}$Rb into $^{87}$Sr. Moreover, Rb and Sr are preferentially incorporated into different minerals. Also, the $^{86}$Sr content is not independent of the other isotope contents. To be sure, the form of the line is the same, but its meaning is totally different. The slope of a line on a plot of $^{87}$Sr/$^{86}$Sr vs. $^{87}$Rb/$^{86}$Sr must be related to age.

Slusher[27] has further criticized the whole rock-isochron method by say-

## Figure 4

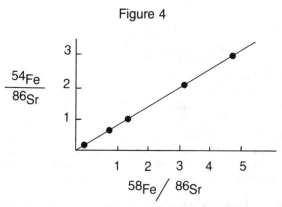

A psuedo-isochron obtained by plotting hypothetical data (Table I) of $^{54}$Fe/$^{86}$Sr vs. $^{58}$Fe/$^{86}$Sr. The straight line is obtained because of the constant ratio of $^{54}$Fe/$^{58}$Fe in rocks and will not change through time. Fe content is independent of Sr content. The isochron diagram is fundamentally different, however, because $^{87}$Sr and $^{87}$Rb must continuously change in rocks owing to radioactive decay, and thus the isochron will change position through time.

ing that there is too much nonradiogenic strontium that needs to be subtracted in order to obtain an accurate age. But Slusher shows with this comment that he does not understand the method, for as we have seen, the method nicely takes care of the problem of nonradiogenic strontium. In no way does this nonradiogenic strontium invalidate the method.

Slusher is also worried about strontium diffusion and contamination, but again, these present no serious problem for the isochron method. To begin with we avoid collecting samples that may be affected by diffusion. Second, if diffusion or contamination has occurred, the points on the isochron diagram should be scattered so as not to yield a straight line. Or perhaps, especially if diffusion has occurred, the isochron may have a lower slope than it would if no diffusion had occurred. All this means is that the rock is older than it appears to be from the isochron. This is small comfort to those who think the Earth is only a few thousand years old.

---

### Table I

Some hypothetical values of $^{54}Fe$, $^{58}Fe$, and $^{86}Sr$ that might be found in an imaginary suite of rocks. (These "values" are plotted in Figure 4.)

| $^{86}Sr$ | $^{54}Fe$ | $^{54}Fe$ $^{86}Sr$ | $^{58}Fe$ | $^{58}Fe$ $^{86}Sr$ |
|-----------|-----------|---------------------|-----------|---------------------|
| 60 | 30 | 0.5 | 45 | 0.75 |
| 20 | 60 | 3.0 | 90 | 4.5 |
| 100 | 10 | 0.1 | 15 | 0.15 |
| 30 | 30 | 1.0 | 45 | 1.5 |
| 10 | 20 | 2.0 | 30 | 3.0 |

These "values" have been selected to give a constant $^{54}Fe/^{58}Fe$ ratio from one sample to another which is consistent with what might be expected in nature. $^{86}Sr$ content is completely unrelated to Fe content. When data are plotted as in Figure 4 as $^{54}Fe/^{86}Sr$ vs. $^{58}/^{86}Sr$ a straight line superficially resembling an isochron is obtained.

---

The suggestion has been made by Cook[28] that the Rb-Sr method be abandoned because of uncertainties over the decay constant of $^{87}Rb$. To be sure there are considerable variations in the values obtained for the decay constant by different investigators. Not only that, but some of the better determinations of the decay constant yield values that when applied to dating do not yield ages that agree with those obtained by the U-Pb methods. Some geochronologists have used a decay constant for $^{87}Rb$ that was adjusted so that agreement would be obtained with U-Pb ages. The suggestion to abandon the entire method, however, is premature. The different determinations of the decay constant vary only by a few percent, and in any case, no matter what decay constant is used, the ages of minerals would still be exceedingly great.

More importantly, two very recent studies[29] utilizing completely different methods, have provided perhaps the most reliable determinations yet of the decay constant of $^{87}Rb$. Not only were the two experimental determinations done by two independent methods, but the values obtained were in excellent agreement, yielding halflives of $4.89 \times 10^{10}$ yr. and $4.88 \times 10^{10}$ yr., respectively. These two values also have the benefit of yielding ages that are concordant with those obtained by other methods without doing any adjusting of the constant to obtain such agreement. With the two new determinations of the decay constant, Rb-Sr radiometric methods are more reliable than ever.

## Uranium-Thorium-Lead Methods

We turn finally to a consideration of the U-Th-Pb methods of radiometric dating. These methods, involving the radioactive decay of uranium and thorium into lead, are generally used in conjunction with one another. There are several radiometric methods based on the decay of uranium and thorium, and a number of these methods are no longer used. Today the main methods are based on the decay of the isotope uranium 238 into lead 206, the decay of uranium 235 into lead 207, the decay of thorium 232 into lead 208, and the ratio of radiogenic lead 207/lead 206. Only these four methods are treated here.

The elements uranium and thorium are typically found in great abundance in the mineral uraninite, a uranium dioxide ($UO_2$). Many dates from uranium ore bodies and from pegmatites have been obtained from radiometric studies of uraninite. For the more routine dating of igneous rocks, especially granites, and of metamorphic rocks, however, the mineral zircon is analyzed most often. Other relatively common minerals such as apatite, sphene, and monazite are also used for dating purposes. Zircon is a zirconium silicate ($ZrSiO_4$) mineral that is almost invariably present in small quantities in granite and similar igneous rocks and in many metamorphic rocks. During crystallization of zircon from magma small quantities of uranium isotopes and thorium isotopes may be incorporated into the structure of the zircon because uranium and thorium ions have the same electrical charge as zirconium ions (+4) and they are also similar in size to zirconium ions. As a result uranium and thorium ions may substitute readily for zirconium ions in the zircon structure. Moreover, some lead ions may also be incorporated into zircon structure, and these, too, are likely to substitute for zirconium, but less readily than will uranium and thorium.

As time goes on, the radioactive uranium and thorium atoms in the zircon crystals will spontaneously disintegrate and ultimately be converted into lead atoms. As a result, the amount of lead will gradually increase in the zircon and the amounts of uranium and thorium will decrease provided

110

that no disturbances result in the gain or loss of uranium, thorium or lead by diffusion.

Dating of igneous and metamorphic rocks by analysis of zircon is a routine procedure and typically yields ages of rocks several hundred millions or even billions of years. Therefore this method also has been assailed by creationists as being completely unreliable and fraught with all sorts of unreasonable assumptions. We shall examine just a few of these criticisms. Slusher, once again, has summarized a number of these.[30] It has been argued, for example, that gains and losses of uranium from the Earth's surface affect the validity of these dating methods.

> U is being carried into the oceans from the rocks at a rate variously estimated from 10,000 to 5,000,000 tons per year. Also, meteors, meteorites, and micro-meteorites are bringing U and Th into the atmosphere and onto the surface of the earth. Further, U and Th are brought to the surface by volcanic action. These changes will affect the correctness of the measurements of U and Th, thus producing error in the equations for the time calculations.[31]

It may be quite true that uranium is being accreted onto the surface of the Earth all the time by means of meteorite bombardment as well as by volcanic action. What, however, does this have to do with the dating of an individual mineral or a rock body that contains a radioactive mineral, unless that added uranium somehow or other gets into the minerals we are using for dating? Where does most of this uranium go? Of course, most of it will end up in the oceans inasmuch as they cover about 70% of the Earth's surface area. The meteoritic or volcanic uranium which falls onto land, is largely going to be incorporated into surface soil. In the soil it will easily be oxidized, become soluble, and be carried away by groundwater or running water. The chances of the uranium ever percolating into rock are relatively slight. Even assuming that some of the uranium and thorium could get into rocks beneath the mantle of surface soil, it would merely adhere to grain boundaries as a thin film of oxidized material. The likelihood of its penetrating into already crystallized minerals like zircon is very small. Sampling procedures avoid rocks that have coatings of oxidized uranium material, and, furthermore, precautions are taken to remove any possible oxidized and weathered material from samples even if it cannot be seen. Every precaution is taken to remove all possible contaminants so that when analyses are made, they are made on cleaned and purified zircon which is not very likely to have incorporated contaminating uranium from outside. The uranium and thorium in a zircon is almost certainly going to be original material dating from the time of crystallization unless contamination can be proved. So it doesn't really matter that new uranium is being added to the Earth's surface by meteorites and volcanoes. This does not affect dating procedures.

But suppose, for the sake of argument, that the creationists were right and that the addition of uranium and thorium to the Earth's surface by volcanic action and meteorite infall somehow or other invalidated the ages obtained from rocks. What would be the result? Well, if some of the uranium and thorium in zircons in a granite had not really been present in that zircon at the time of its crystallization, but had actually migrated into the zircon by virtue of contamination subsequent to its time of crystallization, then the measured uranium to lead ratio is greater than what it actually should be. If we subtract the uranium that was present in the zircon by contamination then the uranium/lead ratio that resulted only from radiometric decay would be considerably lower. All this means is that the true age of the zircons is even greater than what it was thought to be. The effect of contaminating a uranium-bearing mineral by adding uranium to it is simply to lower the apparent age. If thousands of measured zircons and uraninites have been yielding ages of hundreds of millions or even billions of years, just think what their real ages are if a lot of the uranium in them was added to them after they formed! Arguing that influx of uranium from outer space and from volcanoes could contaminate radioactive minerals does absolutely nothing to help creationists in their quest for a young Earth.

But then it was also argued that a lot of uranium is being carried into the oceans each year, presumably because of weathering of surficial rocks and release of contained uranium. Without question, it is true that uranium is entering the oceans, and rocks at the surface are weathered and in the weathering process uranium in minerals can become oxidized and in its oxidized form it is soluble and can readily be transported away in running water. This can introduce significant errors into radiometric dating if the geochronologist selects samples that are weathered or fractured or that have been subjected to the continuing action of groundwater. Many geo-chronologists have indeed recognized that some of their samples have been subjected to loss of uranium and as a result yielded unreliable ages. But by no means can it be said that all uranium-bearing minerals yield unreliable ages just because some do. Furthermore, loss of uranium can generally be detected in a suite of zircons by graphical means.[32]

A second criticism of the U-Th-Pb methods stems from the fact that different ages are frequently obtained from the same mineral by means of the four different methods. Such different ages are said to be discordant. For example, a zircon from the Boulder Creek batholith[33] in Colorado yielded the following results: the age obtained from the $^{238}U-^{206}Pb$ method was 1402 million years. The age obtained from the $^{235}U-^{207}Pb$ method was 1522 million years. The $^{232}Th-^{208}Pb$ method gives an age of 1283 million years, and the $^{207}Pb-^{206}Pb$ method gives an age of 1688 million years. So four distinct, discordant ages are obtained by the four methods. The question arises as to exactly when did the zircon in that batholith crystallize. The zircon in this particular example is no rare exception either. In fact it is very common to obtain discordant ages from zircons from an igneous rock when the four different methods are used. Also, these discordant ages usually follow a well-defined pattern in that the age obtained by the $^{207}$Pb$-^{206}$Pb method is higher than the $^{235}$U$-^{207}$Pb age, which in turn is higher than the $^{238}$U$-^{206}$Pb age, which in turn is higher than the $^{232}$Th$-^{208}$Pb age. Geochronologists generally agree that the $^{207}$Pb$-^{206}$Pb age is the closest to giving the original age of crystallization. The reason for discordant ages is lead leakage from the mineral after it has crystallized, thus making some ages appear younger than they really are. It is expected that if lead leaks out of a mineral the ratio $^{207}$Pb/$^{206}$Pb will be identical to that retained in the mineral, so that an age based on the $^{207}$Pb/$^{206}$Pb ratio is not likely to be affected too strongly by lead loss. Moreover, geochronologists have developed a method whereby they can determine the age of crystallization and also the time at which lead loss may have occurred by analyzing not just one zircon sample, but a whole suite of zircons from a group of rocks from the same igneous rock body.

Melvin Cook has argued quite extensively in *Prehistory and Earth Models*[34] that these discordant ages are one reason why U-Th-Pb dating methods are no good. The argument is that if the methods were really reliable then we should expect that the ages from all four methods would agree. Since they do not agree, the methods obviously are invalid. Cook proposed an alternative explanation for the abundances of various lead isotopes in uranium-bearing minerals that would be perfectly consistent with discordant apparent ages and also, supposedly, yield true mineral ages that are virtually zero, indicating that the minerals were formed only very recently.

Cook argues that much of the $^{207}$Pb and $^{208}$Pb isotopes in uranium-lead-bearing minerals were not produced by radioactive decay of $^{235}$U and $^{232}$Th but by neutron bombardment. He proposed that the $^{208}$Pb atoms in uranium minerals were formed mainly by neutron bombardment of $^{207}$Pb atoms already in the mineral, not by decay of $^{232}$Th. In addition he argued that a large proportion of the $^{207}$Pb atoms in the mineral were formed by neutron bombardment of $^{206}$Pb atoms, not by decay of $^{235}$U. The neutrons are alleged to be generated by bombardment of various elements in the vicinity of the uranium-lead mineral by alpha particles being emitted by radioactively decaying uranium. If this is the case then clearly we cannot obtain an accurate age of the mineral for much of the lead was not derived radiogenically. Cook selected two examples of uranium deposits to show how his neutron bombardment theory could explain the observed distribution of lead isotopes and yet yield essentially zero ages for the deposits. He selected data from a table given by geochronologist Henry Faul[35] for the Shinkolobwe uranium deposit in Katanga and for the Martin Lake deposit in Canada. The ratio of radiogenic $^{206}$Pb/$^{207}$Pb of ore from the Shinkolobwe deposit is 16.5. Such an isotopic ratio, if the lead were truly radiogenic, yields an age for the deposit of about 600 million years. The $^{206}$Pb/$^{207}$Pb ratio for the Martin Lake deposit is about 9.9, a value that yields an age of 1650 million years. In general the higher the value of $^{206}$Pb/$^{207}$Pb, the younger is the material containing the lead isotopes.

These ages are much too high to suit Cook and so he devised a means for changing the lead ratios to provide ages that would be effectively zero. The ratio of lead isotopes for extremely recent uranium materials is on the order of 21.5-21.7, and thus Cook adjusts the lead 206/lead 207 ratios much closer to that value by arguing that some of the lead in these two deposits was not radiogenic at all but formed by neutron bombardment.

Cook noted that these two deposits had virtually no thorium present, certainly not enough to account for, but that they did have $^{208}Pb$. Hence he argued that the lead 208 could not have been generated by the radioactive decay of thorium in the deposit. Where did the lead 208 come from? Was it already present as a component of common lead at the time when the deposit was formed? No, said Cook because there is no lead 204 in the deposits either, and there is always some lead 204 present in common lead, that is, in the lead that may be incorporated into minerals at the time when a uranium deposit is first formed. Instead, suggested Cook, the lead 208 was formed by neutron radiation of the lead 207 atoms and likewise a lot of the lead 207 was formed by bombardment of lead 206. On this basis Cook calculated what the $^{206}Pb/^{207}Pb$ ratio would be if he considered only that amount of those isotopes which had formed by radioactive decay and ignored the neutron-produced lead. Cook's calculations showed that the readjusted $^{206}Pb/^{207}Pb$ ratio would be 21.1 for the Shinkolobwe deposit and 20.7 for Martin Lake. These ratios are much closer to those expected in extremely recent deposits, and thus do not indicate any great antiquity for the uranium deposits he is discussing. Cook assumed that one could make similar arguments for the recency of any other uranium deposit.

Cook's tortuous argument is intriguing but full of flaws. For example, in the original paper in which the data on lead isotopes for the Shinkolobwe deposit were presented,[36] and from which Faul obtained his data, A. O. Nier, a pioneer of geochronology, made it quite plain that the lead 208, small amount though it was, was indeed attributable to common lead. A very small amount of lead 208 was incorporated into the deposit at the time of its formation. Creationist Cook said there was no lead 204 in the deposit and therefore the lead 208 could not be common lead, but that is not what Nier said. Nier said that the amount of lead 204 was so small that it was not worth the effort to make a detailed measurement. His specific words are "where the abundance of $Pb^{204}$ was very low no attempt was made to measure the amount of it as the determination would be of no particular value."[37] The reason is that "in common lead, $Pb^{208}$ is more than twice as abundant as any of the other isotopes."[38] If the amount of $^{208}Pb$ in common lead was very small, then the amount of $^{207}Pb$ and $^{206}Pb$ present as common lead would have been considerably smaller, and no substantial difference would have been made in age determinations by subtracting that little bit from the amount of total lead. It is unnecessary to come up with some unusual source of $^{208}Pb$ such as proposed by Cook.

There are several other flaws in Cook's argument. Cook calculated that the corrected ratio of $^{206}$Pb and $^{207}$Pb would be 21.1 for the Shinkolobwe deposit. "The corrected age would then be practically zero because the ratio $^{206}$Pb/$^{207}$Pb for modern radiogenic lead is 21.5, which agrees with this value well within the uncertainties involved."[39] If it is assumed that Cook's calculations are perfectly valid and the ratio of 21.1 for the lead isotopes is compared with a table of lead ratio vs. age,[40] one will find that the lead could still be nearly 100 million years of age. His Martin Lake example would even be a little older in spite of the recalculations.

Another problem for Cook is that even after his calculations there is still a very sizeable amount of $^{206}$Pb and $^{207}$Pb in the uranium ore that was derived by means of radioactive decay of various isotopes of uranium. The data indicate that the Pb/U ratio is nearly 0.1, which means that nearly ten percent of the uranium had decayed inasmuch as no common lead to speak of was present. Certainly the substantial amount of $^{206}$Pb would still yield very large ages on the basis of the $^{238}$U$-^{206}$Pb method. If Cook wishes to explain the $^{206}$Pb as a result of catastrophic fissioning of uranium under the influence of bombardment by various particles he will need to predict exactly what other isotope abundances ought to be present in the ore and then demonstrate the existence of those abundances. As an example of this point, we can certainly challenge Cook to explain why we do not find substantial amounts of $^{205}$Pb in many uranium deposits. If other lead isotopes can be produced by neutron bombardment, then why cannot substantial amounts of $^{205}$Pb be produced by bombardment of $^{204}$Pb? To be sure, we should not expect this to happen in the Shinkolobwe deposit inasmuch as no $^{204}$Pb to amount to much was there to begin with, but in many other uranium deposits there is a substantial amount of $^{204}$Pb. Would we not expect a lot of it to be converted into $^{205}$Pb by neutron bombardment? $^{205}$Pb is a radioactive isotope but it has a long half-life on the order of tens of millions of years and so there should be plenty of it detected. If Cook is to verify his neutron bombardment mechanism we should expect him to show us substantial amounts of $^{205}$Pb in other uranium deposits where we find a fair amount of $^{204}$Pb.

In conclusion, it is highly unlikely that the neutron-generating mechanism will work in rocks considering that the appropriate target atomic nuclei are not always present, and moreover, the high energy neutrons that are presumably being emitted in all likelihood would not be absorbed by the lead in the deposit itself. If geochronologists suspected that some of their isotopes could be generated by neutron bombardment, they would investigate the possibilities.

Numerous other efforts have been made by creationists to discredit radiometric dating. We have dealt with some of the most frequent criticisms and concluded that they are typically based on misunderstanding of the geological environment in which radioactive elements and their daughters occur. No geochronologists will ever take seriously such arguments. It is hoped that Christian lay people will not take them seriously either, for they are poor arguments. The young-Earth theory certainly cannot be supported by attempting to discredit radiometric methods. These methods are continually improving and consistently yielding extremely high ages. Calculations based on the distribution of radioactive elements and their daughters in the Earth, the Moon, and in meteorites clearly imply that these objects were formed about 4.5 to 4.7 billion years ago. Independent astronomical evidence also suggests a similar age for the formation of the solar system.

# —8—
# THE EARTH'S
# MAGNETIC FIELD

SOME CREATIONISTS HAVE BEEN impressed with a paper by Thomas Barnes, professor of physics at the University of Texas at El Paso.[1] It is the contention of Dr. Barnes that evidence from studies of the magnetic field of the Earth argues strongly for the recent creation of our planet. The Earth is, says Barnes, only a few thousand years old, and the physics of terrestrial magnetism seems to demand that conclusion.

In order to evaluate Dr. Barnes' argument, one needs to consider briefly the nature of the terrestrial magnetic field. The magnetic field of the Earth is very complex. It consists of several components. The main component of the Earth's field is known as the dipole component. In other words, most of the Earth's field can be explained as if the Earth were a gigantic magnet with two poles somewhat like a typical bar magnet. The field of a dipolar magnet is symmetrical (Figure 5). There are, however, local deviations from the symmetry of a perfect dipole field. These deviations are caused by smaller nondipole contributions to the Earth's magnetic field. For example, a large iron ore body located very near to the Earth's surface causes a local deviation from the Earth's dipolar field. Larger sources of permanently magnetized material in the crust and mantle would produce larger deviations from the dipole field. In addition, minor externally controlled factors also influence terrestrial magnetism. An example of this would be the influence of the Sun's magnetic activity. It is the main, or dipole, component of the geomagnetic field that is of particular interest to the argument developed by Barnes. The dipole field of a magnetic sphere can be characterized by a number of properties. One of these properties is the *dipole moment*, which is a function of the intensity of the magnetic field and the volume of the spherical magnet.[2] Thus the magnitude of the dipole moment is dependent on changes in the value of the intensity of the dipole component of the Earth's magnetic field.

## Figure 5

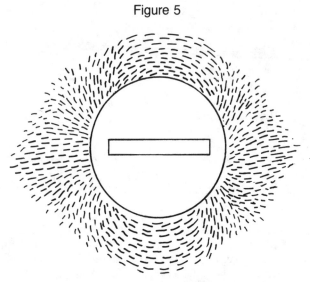

Schematic illustration of Earth's dipolar magnetic field.

In recent years it has been possible to make direct measurements of the intensity of the Earth's magnetic field and therefore to calculate the strength of the magnetic dipole moment. Several values have been recorded at various times since 1835 to the present. The values of the dipole moment, measured in units of gauss•$cm^3$, are tabulated in Table II and plotted in Figure 6. The data clearly indicate that the dipole moment has been steadily decreasing since 1835. Now Barnes has argued that the rate at which the dipole moment has been decreasing indicates that only a few thousand years ago the dipole moment would have had an astronomically high value. For example, only 20,000 years ago the value of the dipole moment would have been almost 4000 times greater than at present. Barnes thus concludes that the Earth was created only a few thousand years ago with a very strong magnetic field caused by electrical currents in the Earth's core. He further argues that these electrical currents have been gradually dissipating through time and that the electrical energy of the core is gradually being converted into heat energy. As the electrical currents in the core thus dissipate, the magnetic field diminishes in strength inasmuch as magnetic fields are produced by electrical currents. The dipole field should therefore eventually decay to zero strength on this point of view.

## Table II

Measured Strength of Earth's Magnetic Dipole Moment
(Units of gauss•cm$^3$ × 10$^{25}$)
Data are plotted in Figure 6

| Year | Dipole Moment |
|---|---|
| 1835 | 8.558 |
| 1845 | 8.488 |
| 1880 | 8.363 |
| 1885 | 8.347 |
| 1905 | 8.291 |
| 1915 | 8.225 |
| 1925 | 8.149 |
| 1935 | 8.088 |
| 1945 | 8.066 |
| 1955 | 8.035 |
| 1960 | 8.053 |
| 1965 | 8.013 |

The problem with Barnes' argument is that the Earth's magnetic field probably is not generated by gradually dissipating electrical currents but by some sort of self-sustaining dynamo mechanism and therefore the dipole moment does not necessarily have to decrease continuously but indeed can

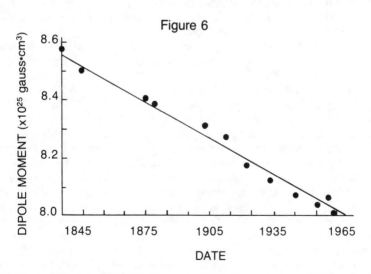

Figure 6

Measured values of strength of Earth's magnetic dipole moment from 1835 to present.

fluctuate considerably over a long period of time. Geophysicists today explain the terrestrial magnetic field in terms of the dynamo theory. The Earth's core is believed to behave somewhat like a gigantic dynamo. Such a dynamo, according to geophysicists, would naturally lead to considerable variation, that is, periodic increases and decreases, in the strength of the magnetic dipole moment. Moreover, occasional reversals in magnetic polarity would also be expected whereby the north and south geomagnetic poles would interchange positions. The dynamo theory is exceedingly complex and fraught with difficulties; the details of the dynamo process are not known. It is not clearly understood what kinds of fluid motions and electrical phenomena do occur in the core to cause the dynamo-like mechanism.

Barnes, however, rejects the dynamo theory and favors the decaying-electrical-current theory. He, in effect, accuses geophysicists of ignoring the decaying-electrical-current hypothesis, which he favors, and of accepting the dynamo theory because of a uniformitarian, old-Earth preconception and not because of facts. Now most geologists and geophysicists certainly do favor the idea that the Earth is old, but they favor it not because of a philosophical prejudice but because of abundant evidence from outside of geomagnetics. Thus it makes sense to look for a geomagnetic theory that fits the evidence from other fields of Earth science. And we must note that the dynamo theory fits all the facts of geomagnetism far better than does the decaying-electric-current theory.

Several direct measurements of the magnetic dipole moment have been made during the past one hundred and forty years, and the value of the moment is now decreasing; this is an observed fact. But has the dipole moment been decreasing continuously from the beginning of a recent creation as Barnes asserts? The answer is no, because geophysicists have also been able indirectly to measure the strength of the magnetic field in times prior to 1835 by utilizing carefully selected archaeological and geological specimens. In effect these specimens have the effects of past terrestrial magnetic fields frozen in.[3] The results show that the magnetic field in the past has frequently been weaker than it is now.

Many rocks contain magnetic minerals such as the iron oxides magnetite, hematite, and ilmenite. When certain types of rocks are formed they may acquire what is termed a natural remanent magnetism (NRM) owing to the partial or complete alignment of magnetic domains within magnetic minerals in the rock in response to the prevailing terrestrial magnetic field. There are several kinds of natural remanent magnetism; those of particular interest to geophysicists are termed thermoremanent magnetism (TRM), detrital or depositional remanent magnetism (DRM), and chemical remanent magnetism (CRM). Thermoremanent magnetism is especially important in lava flows that are cooling down on the surface of the Earth. Iron oxide minerals are common in many lava flows and the magnetic orientation of atoms and domains within these minerals will be strongly influenced by the Earth's magnetic field at the time of crystallization. Evidence of the

Earth's past magnetic field will be "locked in" to the rock as the minerals cool below a certain critical temperature called the Curie point.[4] These minerals will be magnetically oriented in accord with the Earth's field in much the same way that iron filings line up in the field of a bar magnet. Such minerals, then, owing to their magnetic orientation, should give us information about such properties of the terrestrial magnetic field as declination, inclination, polarity, and intensity[5] at the time when the rock was formed. The greater the intensity of the field the more likelihood of strongly developed preferred magnetic orientation.

In detrital or depositional remanent magnetism (DRM) magnetic particles are aligned in the Earth's field as they settle through a fluid medium, most likely water, during the process of sedimentation. Many sediments contain iron oxide minerals, which may have been deposited in the sediment by settling out of flowing water. Such particles may succeed in obtaining a magnetic alignment reflective of the terrestrial field at the time of sedimentation.

The process of conversion of loose sediment into a sedimentary rock is known as diagenesis. During diagenesis one magnetic mineral may be converted chemically into another magnetic mineral. Magnetite, for example, may be chemically oxidized into the mineral hematite. During the chemical reaction the new magnetic mineral may take on a magnetic orientation that reflects the Earth's magnetic field prevailing at the time of diagenesis. This magnetism is termed chemical remanent magnetism.

Thus many rocks, especially volcanic rocks and sandstones and shales, contain a fossil record of the Earth's past magnetism. In like manner many archaeological artifacts such as furnaces and clay pots also contain evidence of the Earth's past magnetic field. By obtaining precisely oriented specimens of geological and archaeological materials and examining these materials in magnetics laboratories, geophysicists have been able to obtain information about the past positions of the Earth's geomagnetic poles, about the polarity of the field, and about the intensity of the field.

These paleomagnetic studies have demonstrated that the geomagnetic poles have constantly been changing in position through time. This fact, of course, has been known for a long time inasmuch as direct measurements have been made at London, England, on the declination and inclination of magnetic dip needles since about A.D. 1600. When averaged over long periods of time the geomagnetic poles essentially coincide with the Earth's axis of rotation, although at any specific time the geomagnetic poles deviate somewhat from the rotational poles as is presently the case (Figure 7).

Not only does the geographic position of the magnetic poles shift, so, too, does the polarity of the poles. That is, the Earth's poles on several occasions have become reversed so that the present-day north magnetic pole interchanged positions with the south magnetic pole. The cause of these reversals is unknown, but it is very possible that the reversals are related to changes in strength of the magnetic dipole moment.

Figure 7

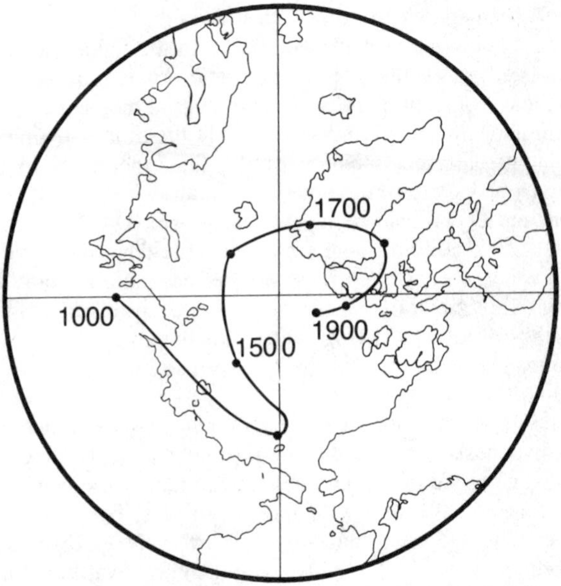

Position of Earth's north geomagnetic pole since A.D. 1000. North rotational pole is located where lines cross.

Paleomagnetic studies have also given us much information about the strength of the dipole moment. The validity of Barnes' argument for the recent creation of the Earth hinges on findings regarding the dipole moment in the past. We have already seen that paleomagnetic studies have disclosed the fact that the geomagnetic poles have reversed many times. One possible explanation for these reversals is fluctuation in strength of the dipole moment. The dipole moment might gradually decrease in strength, fall off to zero during a pole reversal, and then gradually build up in strength with the opposite polarity. The process would continue by having the dipole moment again begin to diminish down to zero through yet another reversal, then build up again, and so on. If the dipole moment in fact fluctuates in this manner, it is clear that the value of the dipole moment has at many times, especially during pole reversals, been less than it is now. Such a conclusion is in flat contradiction to Barnes' idea that the dipole moment is weaker now than it has ever been. However, it is possible that reversals are not caused by such fluctuations in the dipole moment. Nevertheless, paleomagnetic studies have produced sufficient data on the past intensity of the magnetic field, and therefore the dipole moment, to prove clearly that the Barnes' theory is incorrect. Considerable data have been collected from paleointensity measurements on geological and archaeological materials.[6]

The work of several geophysicists on archaeological intensity measurements (archaeomagnetism) indicates that the Earth's dipole moment has been diminishing in strength since about or slightly before the beginning of the Christian era. This is certainly in agreement with Barnes' argument. However, archaeological materials from the millennia before Christ yield data that indicate that the dipole moment was *increasing* in strength. In other words, the strength of the dipole moment passed through a maximum around the time of Christ or perhaps two or three centuries earlier (Figure 8). If this is the case, then Barnes' attempt to explain the origin of the magnetic field in terms of continuously decaying electrical currents in the core fails and his entire argument fails. The dipole moment has not decreased continuously from some astronomically high value. In fact it would appear that the strength of the dipole moment two to four thousand years before the time of Christ was several percent *less* than it is now.

There is also information on the strength of the ancient dipole moment from geological materials. The appropriate data are plotted in Figure 9. Again the data show that the dipole moment has not continuously de-

## Figure 8

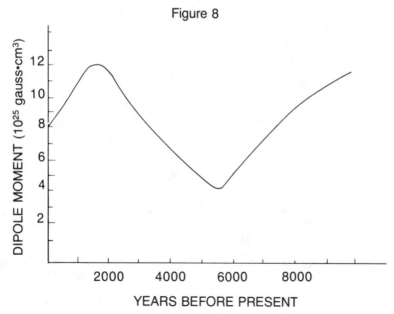

Strength of Earth's dipole moment for the past few thousand years as measured from archaeological material.

SCIENTIFIC CONSIDERATIONS

creased from some astronomically high value. Instead it appears that the value has fluctuated greatly through geological time and may even show an overall increase. The fact that creationists object to the geological time scale makes no difference here. When we make a paleomagnetic intensity determination on a rock, the chances are that we are doing so on a rock that creationists think was erupted or deposited during the Flood rather than millions of years ago. Suppose that really were the case. All the data would be showing is what we have already seen, namely, that in the few millennia before the time of Christ, the Earth's magnetic dipole moment did not have a strength that is substantially greater than now. In fact the value of the dipole moment may have been less.

Barnes' argument that the terrestrial dipole moment has diminished from an astronomically high value only a few thousand years ago is completely out of accord with the data supplied by paleomagnetic studies of rocks and archaeological artifacts. Barnes' argument for a young-Earth based on magnetic evidence is completely invalid. Terrestrial magnetism gives no support to the idea that the Earth was created recently.

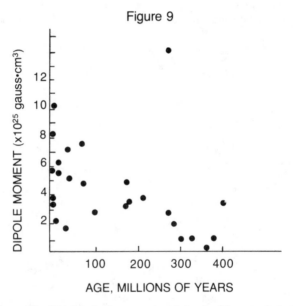

Figure 9

Values of strength of Earth's dipole moment as determined from geological materials. The data indicate that the strength of the dipole moment has commonly been much lower than it is at present.

# —9—
# GEOCHEMICAL ARGUMENTS

CREATIONISTS HAVE ALSO utilized arguments from cosmochemistry and geochemistry to suggest that the age of the Earth is only a few thousand years rather than the billions of years suggested by uniformitarian geologists.

## Meteorites and Tektites

Whitcomb and Morris have advanced the argument that the absence of meteorites and tektites in the sedimentary rock record points up the untenability of uniformitarian geology.[1] The same argument has been repeated in the curriculum materials published by the Creation Science Research Center.[2] The argument is that meteoritic material is now falling onto the Earth at a certain rate. If the Earth has been in existence for billions of years and meteoritic material has been falling onto the Earth at essentially present rates throughout that period of time, then surely meteorites should be found in rocks of all ages of the geological time scale. The fact is that tektites have not been found in any pre-Tertiary strata and real meteorites have not been found in deposits earlier than the Recent. The inference is, of course, that sedimentary rocks must have been deposited extremely rapidly and that the Earth must really be young.

A little reflection, however, on the nature of meteorites and tektites and on the nature of the sedimentary rock record will show that this result is not at all unexpected. It would actually be rather surprising if meteorites and tektites were discovered in the rock record, for their chances of survival would be relatively slim and it would be truly amazing to find one.

To begin with, the number of meteorites that have actually been found is quite small. Only a few thousand meteorites have been discovered.[3] A large percentage of these were picked up because the meteorite had actually been observed to fall to the ground. This type of discovery is referred to as a *fall*. The remainder were accidentally discovered. The great majority of this latter class of meteorites, known as *finds,* are metallic meteorites composed primarily of a nickel-iron alloy. Inasmuch as metallic iron almost never occurs naturally in the Earth's crust, owing to the fact that it oxidizes so readily, these metallic meteorites would quite naturally attract attention by their unusual appearance. They do not look like ordinary terrestrial rocks.

The great majority of meteorites are probably so-called stony meteorites, for the stony meteorites predominate among the falls. This group is composed chiefly of magnesium- and iron-rich minerals like olivine [$(Mg,Fe)_2SiO_4$] and pyroxene [$Ca(Mg,Fe)Si_2O_6$] or [$(Mg,Fe)SiO_3$]. There is relatively little metallic iron or nickel in the stones. In the Earth's crust there are some igneous rocks that are composed mostly of olivine and pyroxene, so that stony meteorites would have a more "terrestrial" appearance to them and they would be much more likely to be overlooked by the untrained observer who happened to walk past one. In addition, both olivine and pyroxene weather more rapidly than most other common rock-forming minerals, so that a stony meteorite lying on the surface of the Earth for a very long time would very likely be destroyed by chemical weathering.

This high degree of weatherability of stony meteorites is one reason it would be extremely unlikely that stony meteorites would be preserved in the Earth's layered sediments. The meteorite would likely be destroyed as an entity before it was ever incorporated into sediment. Even terrestrial pyroxene and olivine grains and pebbles of gabbro and basalt, rocks that contain much pyroxene and olivine, are uncommon in sedimentary rocks.

Iron meteorites, too, should disintegrate through time because exposure to the atmosphere will oxidize the iron. Burial in wet sediments and exposure to groundwater will further assist in oxidation of the iron and the loss of identity of the iron meteorite.

The chances of survival of a meteorite in the rock record are therefore extremely slight. Assuming, however, that some meteorites did survive and are present in the sedimentary rocks, the chances of actually discovering one are very remote. Almost half the known meteorites were observed to fall, but with fossil meteorites we must discover them accidentally. The meteorites that have been discovered by accident were discovered on the Earth's surface, a sizeable percentage of which has actually been walked on by a very large number of people. In looking for ancient rocks, however, we generally are not dealing with surface features but with sporadic outcrops and vertical cuts on highways, railroads, canyons, gullies, and valleys. Hence the actual area of rock observed by geologists is very much less than Earth's land surface area. In other words, the layers in which meteorites conceivably might be buried are largely inaccessible except for the rare edgewise view. Moreover, there are far fewer observers involved in the study of canyon walls and roadcuts, so that the chance discovery of a buried meteorite by an amateur is almost nil, whereas a large percentage of falls and finds are discovered by amateurs. The chances of finding a fossil meteorite in sedimentary rocks are remote. It is not to be expected. Therefore the argument from the absence of fossil meteorites has no validity and says nothing about the age of the Earth.

Similar comments can be made about tektites. Tektites are silica-rich glassy objects and as such would be far less susceptible to chemical weathering than any meteorite. The chances of a tektite being preserved may be somewhat better than those of a meteorite, but a tektite could easily be disintegrated through abrasion in streams or on the beach and so, too, its chances for survival are slim. The same remarks as were made regarding meteorites can be made about the chances of finding tektites.

## Nickel Content of the Crust

The antiquity of the Earth has also been questioned in terms of the nickel content of the crust assuming the present-day rate of infall of meteoritic material of "cosmic dust." Whitcomb and Morris[4] have argued that the Earth's crust shows no evidence of having accumulated meteoritic material for $4.5 \times 10^9$ years assuming present day rates of infall. Studies by Petterson on the metallic spherule content of deep sea red clays and of nearly pollution-free atmospheric dust infall suggested that approximately 14 million tons of meteoritic dust settles to Earth each year at the present time.[5] If one assumes that meteoritic material fell on the Earth at the present rate calculated by Petterson throughout all of geologic time then a layer of meteoritic dust fifty-four feet thick would blanket the Earth's surface if undisturbed.[6] One could, of course, account for this fifty-four-foot layer by mixing the meteoritic material into the crust throughout geologic time. Whitcomb and Morris say that we cannot reasonably account for this meteoritic material in terms of crustal mixing processes.

> For example, the average nickel content of meteorites is of the order of 2.5 percent, whereas nickel constitutes only about 0.008 percent of the rocks of the earth's crust. Thus, about 312 times as much nickel per unit volume occurs in meteorites as in the earth's crust. This means that the 54 ft. thickness of meteoritic dust would have to have been dispersed through a crustal thickness of at least $312 \times 54$ ft., or more than three miles, to yield the present crustal nickel component percentage, even under the impossible assumption that there was no nickel in the crust to begin with![7]

Whitcomb and Morris do not seem to think it reasonable that this meteoritic nickel is dispersed through a three mile thickness of crust.

This dispersal is not quite so difficult to explain as creationists think. Consider the geochemical behavior of nickel and some terrestrial mixing processes. Since the ocean basins comprise 70 percent of the Earth's surface, most meteoritic material will be incorporated into marine sediments. If the theory of sea-floor spreading[8] is correct, and most evidence seems to suggest that it is, then through time these sediments will migrate toward the troughs or trenches, like the Peru-Chile trench or the Puerto Rico trench, that border many of the continents. At trench sites, sea floor crust with its cover of sediment is gradually dragged downward into the crust toward the mantle. The sediments are deformed and metamorphosed. Through time these metamorphosed sediments will be heated sufficiently to be partially melted. During melting processes nickel has a very strong tendency to be concentrated in the solid unmelted residues in minerals like pyroxene and olivine where it substitutes for magnesium and iron atoms. Nickel is very highly depleted in the granitic and andesitic magmas that are generated from the partly melted sediments. In other words during partial melting of buried nickeliferous marine metasediments, nickel tends to stay in the higher density solids and does not tend to be incorporated into granitic magmas that rise toward the surface (because of low density) and make up much of the upper crust.

Geologically then one would expect meteoritic nickel to become concentrated toward the base of the crust, and much of it can ultimately be taken into the mantle. Thus it is not at all difficult to envisage nickel being dispersed through a three mile thickness of crust. Most of it is probably much deeper than that!

In conclusion it should be noted that Petterson also found from studies of deep-sea sediments that the rate of meteoritic influx appear to have varied through time and seems to have been less in the past than it is now.

## Sediment Volumes

Creationist Stuart Nevins wrote a paper entitled *Evolution: the Ocean says No!*[9] in which he sought to show that the oceans and the Earth cannot possibly be billions of years old as uniformitarian geologists say. His argument is based on a study of sediment volumes in the ocean basins and the rates of erosion of sediment from land masses today. Nevins first of all determined from available literature the total volume and total mass of sediments that are presently lying on the sea floors. His conclusion is that the mass of ocean sediments is about 820 million tons.[10] He then determined the total amount of sedimentary material that is being eroded from the present-day continents each year by various agents. His data were obtained from reliable geologists and they indicate that approximately 27.5 billion tons of sediment is being added to the oceans every year by continental erosion.[11] He also determined the total volume of continental material that exists above sealevel and found a mass of 383 million billion tons. By dividing the present mass of continental material above sealevel by the present yearly rate of erosion, Nevins concluded that it would take only 14 million years to erode the present continents down to sealevel. But for him this is a strange result, for "evolutionary-uniformitarian geologists feel certain that the continents have existed for at least 1 billion years. During this supposed interval of time the present continents could have been eroded over 70 times! Yet—miracle of miracles—the continents are still here and do not appear to have been eroded even *one* time!"[12]

Nevins then looked at his problem from a slightly different angle and asked the question as to how great a thickness of sediments in the oceans would be accumulated if the continents had indeed been eroded at the present-day rate for at least a billion years, which he says is the "alleged evolutionary age of the ocean." By multiplying 27.5 billion tons per year by one billion years he concluded that 27.5 billion billion tons of sediment would be produced. Such a mass would be equivalent to a pile 97,500 feet thick covering the entire ocean floor. Of course, if Nevins had used 4.5 billion years for the age of the Earth the thickness would have turned out 4.5 times greater yet. Obviously this huge thickness of sediments is not present on the sea floor. The thickness is only about 2950 feet on average. Also, in order to generate all that sediment a thickness of some 200,000 feet of rock on the continents would have to be eroded away. The conclusion was "if we assume the present rate of erosion and exposed continental volumes to have existed over the evolutionist's supposed 1-billion-year history of the world ocean, *we would expect a staggering layer of sediment almost 100,000 feet thick to cover the sea floor today!* Since such a monumental layer does not exist, it seems that evolutionists have grossly overestimated the age of the world ocean."[13]

Nevins also asked how long it would take to form the present amount of sediments on the sea floor assuming a constant rate of erosion and he arrived at an answer of 30 million years. That certainly does not approach the actual age of the Earth, but it is nonetheless an extremely large number, much greater than a few thousand years. Of course, Nevins believes that rates of erosion were very great at the time of the Flood, so the 30 million years is reduced. "It is eminently reasonable to believe in a young ocean with an age of 10,000 years or less."[14]

But no geologist is puzzled over where the 100,000 feet of sediment is. We suspect we know where it is, but Nevins anticipated the rebuttal. He recognized that in order to have an old ocean with a relatively thin carpet of sediments, there must be some mechanism or process that removes sediments from the sea floor. Nevins recognized that geologists would appeal to at least two means for getting rid of sea floor sediments. One, he said, is by uplifting the sea floor and returning ocean sediments to the continents. And he is exactly right. The continents are covered with great volumes of former marine sedimentary rocks. However, Nevins argued, the total amount of sediments on the continents is about equal to the amount on the ocean floor, so that if we added the continental sedimentary rocks to the oceanic sediments, we would still be far short of the anticipated 100,000 feet of oceanic sediments. "This process does not solve the evolutionist's dilemma," he concluded.[15]

The fallacy in Nevins' argument, of course, is that sedimentary materials can be continuously recycled throughout geological time. We can erode all

129

the sedimentary material we want from the continents at a specified rate for as long as we want, and the sedimentary material of the continents will not be depleted nor will the sediment contents of the ocean floors continuously increase *provided* that we return oceanic sediment to the continents at the same long term average rate as erosion is occurring. A simple example may help to illustrate my point. Suppose that we have a container of 100 ping-pong balls, representing the continents with their sedimentary rocks. Further suppose that we remove one ping-pong ball from that container every second and put it into another container, representing the ocean basins, which also contains 100 balls. Let us also suppose that we have been removing ping-pong balls from the first container for one hour, that is 3600 seconds. We can call this the old container view. Along comes a young container advocate who sees ping-pong balls being removed once a second and put into the second container. He argues that this process cannot possibly have been going on for a whole hour. Rather, he says that it is eminently reasonable to suppose that the process has been going on only for a couple of minutes. His reasoning is that if all the balls in the second container had originally been obtained from the first container then there would have been 200 balls in the first container to start with and the process could have been going on only 100 seconds to achieve the present distribution at the rate of removal of one ball per second. He argues that if this process had been going on for a whole hour then we should fully expect 3600 balls to be present in the second container, clearly an enormous number of balls, which we do not see anywhere. Where, he asks, are all these balls which ought to be there if they have been transferred at the rate of one ball per second? Obviously the process can't have been going on for an hour and so the old container view is wrong. The answer is simple; the proponent of the young container theory simply overlooks the fact that every time a ball is taken from the first container and placed in the second container, a ball is likewise removed from the second container and put back in the first. With such cycling one can continue the process infinitely long. It makes absolutely no difference how many balls are in the containers. In the same way one can continue cycling sediments forever; it makes absolutely no difference how much sediment one has to deal with. The very fact that the continents are covered by great thickness of largely marine sedimentary rocks is certainly evidence of the fact that vast volumes of material that once were under water are now back on the continents. Thus for Nevins to state ". . . the total amount of sediments on the continents is about equal to the amount on the ocean floor. Adding all the sediments on the present continents to those in the modern ocean would still be far short of the anticipated 100,000 feet of ocean sediments which should exist if the ocean is a billion years old"[16] is a totally irrelevant argument. It is tantamount to saying that adding the 100 balls in container #1 to the 100 balls in container #2 still falls far short of the 3600 balls that should exist as proof that no one has been removing ping-pong balls for one hour. Continuous recycling eliminates the validity of Nevins' argument.

Nevins also noted that geologists could appeal to the destruction of oceanic sedimentary materials by means of sea-floor spreading and argued that the rate of their destruction by such a means is far less than the rate at which new sediment is being added to the oceans at the present time. This is probably true, but we need to observe that subduction of sediments is not the only means for eliminating them from the sea floor. Uplift of continental shelves is also extremely important. Moreover, it is generally regarded by geologists that the rates of erosion at present are relatively high because of the topography of the continents. The continental land masses are believed to be much more rugged and mountainous than is usually the case, and mountainous topography speeds up rates of erosion. Thus at the present time we ought fully to expect that more sediment is being added to the oceans than is being removed. Paleogeography indicates that very often in the past the opposite was the case.

# PART THREE

# PHILOSOPHICAL AND APOLOGETIC CONSIDERATIONS RELATED TO THE AGE OF THE EARTH

# —10—
# UNIFORMITARIANISM
# and CATASTROPHISM

IN PART TWO WE sought to demonstrate that the evidence of nature strongly indicates that the Earth is extremely old, and we sought to demonstrate how well-meaning creationists have completely misinterpreted that evidence in their attempt to argue that the Earth is only a few thousand years old. Yet in spite of all that has been said on scientific grounds against the creationist's young-Earth theories, creationists might still argue that the geological evidence was evaluated in terms of a faulty philosophy of science.

It might still be implied that creationists evaluate the geological evidence in terms of a true, biblical philosophy of science. Specifically, creationists might charge that I have been guilty of viewing the evidence in terms of the principle of uniformitarianism,[1] a principle they generally claim is atheistic and antibiblical at root. It might be said that by utilizing the principle of uniformitarianism I unwittingly distort the real facts of nature in my interpretations regarding the antiquity of the Earth, and it might be maintained that I could be delivered from my false interpretations of the geological record by adhering to a biblical principle, namely, that of catastrophism.

Now the principle of the uniformity of nature, or uniformitarianism, is frequently summed up in the familiar statement that the present is the key to the past. Ever since the publication of Charles Lyell's *Principles of Geology* in 1830, most geologists have approached the study of the Earth in terms of this principle, and modern geological practice is certainly uniformitarian in outlook. Creationists, however, have frequently argued that modern geologists are fundamentally in error in their reconstructions of geologic history because of their adherence to this principle. It is argued that the principle of uniformity is incapable of explaining the observed data of the rock record. It is said to be an inadequate explanatory principle. Now in this chapter I wish to show that modern creationists do not really understand the principle of uniformity as it is generally used by geologists today, and I further wish to show that, however strongly they might deny it, flood catastrophists and creationists also subscribe to the principle of uniformity as it is applied in modern geology. Creationists are really uniformitarians who have falsely interpreted the evidence of geology. The conclusion is that one cannot argue for a young Earth by insisting on the use of a philosophical principle of catastrophism as over against a philosophical principle of uniformitarianism. This dodge will not save creationists from the weight of the natural evidence for the antiquity of the Earth.

## The Creationist Challenge to Uniformitarianism

Creationists and flood geologists generally believe that the principle of uniformity is lacking in explanatory power. It is charged that it is an inadequate principle. For example, in a book review of *Franciscan and Related Rocks and their Significance in the Geology of Western California,* theologian Bernard Northrup began by stating, "Seldom has a book been written within the interpretative framework of evolutionary macrochronological geology[2] that has so effectively demonstrated the inadequacy of that framework to explain the facts found in field research."[3] In yet another paper on the Sisquoc diatomite beds near Lompoc, California, Northrup said that he is

> convinced that reality in geological time has been grossly misrepresented on the walls of the contemporary science classroom by the deceptive shadows of evolutionary uniformitarian time values. At Lompoc this distortion is remarkably evident. The fossils that were trapped in the abrupt deposition which left this unique graveyard tell a story violently contradictory to the classroom interpretation. Every fossil found supports a denial that it has been buried at a geological snail's pace.[4]

In a general discussion of sedimentation Henry Morris stated that

> the principle of uniformity turns out to be entirely inadequate right at this most important aspect of geological interpretation. Modern processes of sedimentation are in general quite incapable of accounting for the sedimentary rocks of the geologic column. This is true whether the environment of deposition is thought to be geosynclinal, deltaic, lagoonal, or some other.[5]

Nevins commented that

> the many contradictions encountered make the Principle of Uniformity unacceptable to the historical geologist. The principle which has long been considered the basis for historical geology has been shown to be inadequate.[6]

Steinhauer maintained regarding two aspects of uniformitarianism that "one is at variance with observation; the other, though correlating with many observations, leads to logical and philosophical contradictions."[7] And finally Whitcomb and Morris repeatedly stressed the inadequacy of uniformitarianism. Regarding continental ice sheets, "the principle of uniformity is once again woefully inadequate to account for them."[8] Regarding the formation of coal, "the fundamental axiom of uniformity, that the present is the key to the past, completely fails to account for the phenomena."[9] Thus we see that, according to creationists, the phenomena of sedimentation, fossilization, volcanism, tectonism, glaciation, and the like, cannot be accounted for in terms of the principle of uniformity.

It has also been charged that uniformitarian thinking is unbiblical. Uniformitarianism is thought to be a false unchristian philosophy. So, for example, Whitcomb and Morris have appealed to 2 Peter 3:3–10. In this passage Peter warns that, in the last days, there would be scoffers who would say, "Where is this 'coming' he promised? Ever since our fathers died, everything goes on as it has since the beginning of creation." Peter then goes on to remind his readers of the flood judgment and of the coming final judgment. With regard to this passage Whitcomb and Morris said:

> Here again the Flood is used as a type and warning of the great coming worldwide destruction and judgment when the 'day of man' is over and the 'day of the Lord' comes. But the prophet is envisioning a time when, because of an apparent long delay, the 'promise of his coming' is no longer treated seriously. It is to become the object of crude scoffing and intellectual ridicule. It will be obvious to 'thinking men' in such a day that a great supernatural intervention of God in the world, as promised by Christ is scientifically out of the question. That would be a miracle, and miracles contradict natural law.
>
> And how do we know that miracles and divine intervention contradict natural law? Why, of course, because our experience shows and our philosophy postulates that 'all things continue as they were from the beginning of the creation'! This is what we call our 'principle of uniformity' which asserts that all things even from the earliest beginnings can be explained essentially in terms of present processes and rates. Even the Creation itself is basically no different from present conditions, since these processes are believed to have been operating since even the *'beginning* of the creation.' There is no room for any miracle or divine intervention in our cosmology; therefore, the concept of a future coming of Christ in worldwide judgment and purgation is merely naïve.[10]

Thus, at least in the view of Whitcomb and Morris, the principle of uniformity is an unbiblical principle.

The solution, according to creationists, is to accept the principle of catastrophe and to reinterpret the data of geology in terms of it. Now for catastrophists the principle of catastrophe involves the idea of global catastrophe, with emphasis being placed on one major catastrophe, namely the Noachian Flood[11] which supposedly inundated the entire Earth for about a year. During this period there was catastrophic sedimentation, volcanic activity, and mountain building. The catastrophic philosophy is believed to offer at least as good if not a superior explanatory principle for accounting for such phenomena as fossil graveyards, sediments, the mode of fossilization, polystrate trees, mountains, volcanoes, and the like. Thus Burdick, for example, said:

Many of the vexing problems of stratigraphy would be solved if we simply took the evidence we see at face value instead of attempting to fit it into the concept of uniformitarianism made popular by Sir Charles Lyell. Lack of space forbids a discussion of all the simplifications resulting from a return to catastrophism.[12]

Rupke argued that the polystrate fossils "constitute strong arguments in favor of cataclysmal deposition, and generally, support catastrophism as a scientific principle to interpret the earth's history."[13] From the remainder of his paper it is evident that his cataclysm is the Flood. And constantly we read statements like "The Flood seems to be a reasonable explanation for the deposition of widespread chert blankets"[14] and

it is highly consonant with the whole character of the catastrophic action attending deposition of the Deluge sediments to infer that the processes of compaction, cementation, drying, etc. leading to final lithification could have been accomplished quite rapidly.[15]

Many catastrophists would also maintain that the principle of catastrophe, unlike the principle of uniformity, is a biblical principle.[16] It is maintained that the Bible teaches a purely miraculous creation that took only 144 hours, a Fall of Adam with catastrophic implications, a catastrophic worldwide Flood. Thus Christian geologists in particular are urged to give up the principle of uniformity and adopt the principle of catastrophe.

Clearly, if we adopted a principle in terms of which rates of geological processes would have been vastly speeded up in the past (principle of catastrophe) and abandoned a principle which views past geological processes as having proceeded very slowly and peacefully, somewhat like they do today (principle of uniformity), we would have no problem regarding the age of the Earth. If we adopted the principle of catastrophe, it is suggested, a fair reading of the physical evidence would lead to the conclusion that the Earth is only a few thousand years old, whereas if we insist on reading the evidence in terms of the false principle of uniformity, we will end up with an age of the Earth that is much too high.

## Creationism's Understanding of Uniformitarianism

However, before we conclude that a switch in principles from uniformity to catastrophe would really lead us to the idea that the Earth is young, let us examine precisely what it is about the principle of uniformity that creationism finds so objectionable. What exactly does the typical catastrophist understand by the principle of uniformity?

In his discussion of uniformity Steinhauer suggested that it is possible for the

assumption of uniformity to be overextended and overextrapolated, leading to a simplistic or even grossly inaccurate view of the universe. This is indeed the case when scientists propose that those process rates and conditions presently observable have always operated in the same way or with the same intensity.[17]

He asked us to consider this assumption that process rates and material conditions are uniform and invariant when viewed on a global scale. He argued that process rates depend on material conditions so that as the latter vary so must the former. Thus process rates cannot be uniform inasmuch as material conditions have varied. Steinhauer used human population growth as an example to show that the rates of global phenomena do change. This assumption of a uniformity of process rates is a "titanic extrapolation, a blind leap of faith that contradicts what is observable in the universe. A few scientists have recently become aware of this leap and abandoned it."[18] In another paper Steinhauer stated that

> evidence comes from every quarter that the history of Earth's crust is one of trauma and cataclysm. Geologists have assembled a great volume of facts supporting global catastrophism. This is in spite of the domination of their science by the uniformitarian axiom of a peaceful Earth history.[19]

Elsewhere he said "some kinds of sediment are *not* being formed today, which contradicts an axiom of uniformitarianism."[20]

Nevins has also discussed uniformity at great length. He charged that "the possibility of catastrophic events during this evolutionary development is rejected. Characteristic of this limited thinking is the reliance on the Principle of Uniformity as a basic assumption."[21] He said that "the Principle of Uniformity sternly rejects any catastrophic event like the Flood."[22] Nevins then went on to discuss at great length an aspect of uniformitarianism that has recently been termed *substantive uniformitarianism*.[23] Basically substantive uniformitarianism is the idea that the processes and process rates of the present may be extrapolated indefinitely into the past and that geologic phenomena may be sufficiently accounted for in terms of a uniformity through time of processes and process rates. Such process rates are very slow and not cataclysmic since modern day rates are presumably rather slow in general. In opposition to substantive uniformitarianism, Nevins said that the fossil record indicates "rapid changes of environments rather than . . . slow and uniform change."[24] Also,

> evidence of continental glaciation shows that a colder climate existed at one time. There is abundant geologic evidence of former catastrophic events. Rock formations show current structures which indicate that transcontinental flood conditions once prevailed. Critics of substantive uniformitarianism have found fossil graveyards, trees buried by massive lava flows, frozen mammoths in Arctic regions, and many other exceptions to a strict adherence to the substantive uniformitarian view. The great mass of evidence indicating catastrophe has been largely ignored by geologists.
>
> Actually, the assumption that process rates must be uniform is without scientific backing. There is no scientific law which requires a natural event always to proceed at constant rate. A scientific law only describes an event under a fixed set of conditions and as conditions vary so does the rate. Conditions, not scientific law, determine the rate of a process.[25]

Finally, Nevins said that "the substantive uniformitarianism of Hutton and Lyell was an *a priori assumption* formed not upon evidence but upon a preconceived opinion of how nature must ideally operate if we are to study it by inductive means."[26] And

> the principle of simplicity and consideration of the evidence of the fossil record logically establishes a catastrophe similar to Noah's Flood recorded in Genesis. This hypothesis, however, must be carefully tested only from evidence contained in the rocks. By no means should the old argument of Lyell (substantive uniformitarianism) be used to deny the reality of the Flood.[27]

In his paper on the Sisquoc diatomite beds, Northrup gave us an inkling of his understanding of uniformitarianism when he discussed fossilization:

> It is deposition of fossils in the normal bedding plane of the diatomite that first suggested that these fishes and birds had simply fallen to the bottom after death, to be slowly covered by the slow "rain" or "snow" of diatom structures from the waters above. There are several factors, however, that make this simple uniformitarian explanation impossible.
>
> First, the perfect condition of the bodies of the fossilized fish repudiates slow deposition. . . . The supposed gradual deposition of millions of carcases, untouched by other bottom feeding fishes, and their painfully slow burial by the postulated $^1/_{1500}$ to ½ inch per year deposition rate simply is not possible. . . . Secondly, there are fossils found which show that the rate of deposition was extremely rapid. Some are clearly deposited by a violent action which has torn scales and even removed fins from the body.[28]

For Whitcomb and Morris, the idea of uniformity was essentially that

> geomorphic processes which can be observed in action at present, such as erosion, sedimentation, glaciation, volcanism, diastrophism, etc.—all operating in essentially the same fashion as at present—can be invoked to explain the origin and formation of all the earth's geologic deposits. The doctrine of uniformity thus is supposed to render unnecessary any resource to catastrophism, except on a minor scale.[29]

Further on they said, "Historical geology purports to explain all of the earth's geologic formations in terms of the essentially uniform operation of processes of nature that are now occurring and can be studied at the present time,"[30] and

> Thus it is now believed that the present day geomorphic processes (including erosion, deposition, volcanism, diastrophism, etc.), acting essentially in the same manner and at the same rates as at present, can suffice to account for all the earth's physiographic features when properly studied and correlated.[31]

Finally they said "It is processes such as these which the uniformity concept asserts can explain the earth's stratified and massive rock formations. Our basic objection to this contention, however, is that the character and rates of activity of the processes cannot have been the same in the past as in the present."[32]

It is quite clear from these representative selections from the writings of modern catastrophist-creationists that uniformitarianism is generally understood as meaning substantive uniformitarianism—not only the idea of uniformity of processes through time but also uniformity of intensity or rates of processes through time. The processes and rates are basically those presently observable. Because of their virtual identification of uniformity with substantive uniformitarianism catastrophists seem to think that uniformitarians postulate very slow process rates and a very peaceful Earth history in which there are virtually no catastrophes, inasmuch as modern processes of, say, mountain building and sedimentation are extremely slow and supposedly anything but catastrophic. Indeed catastrophists almost seem to think that uniformitarians reject a priori the very possibility of great catastrophes. And they seem to think that uniformitarianism means that there must be forming in the world somewhere today an example of every kind of rock found in the geological record since the present is the key to the past and present process rates were the same in the past. They seem to think, therefore, that since chert[33] is supposedly not forming in the world today,[34] uniformitarianism is somehow contradicted. They seem to think that very rapid, violent processes are inconsistent with uniformitarianism. They seem to think that evidence for catastrophe is inconsistent with uniformitarianism.

## Modern Geology Rejects Substantive Uniformitarianism

Substantive uniformitarianism has been repeatedly attacked by creationists, who seem to think that is the principle to which modern geologists (whether Christian or atheistic) subscribe. Often the inference is made that, since substantive uniformitarianism is incorrect, Flood catastrophism is correct, as if we had to choose between these two alternatives. It is of course true that substantive uniformitarianism is an incorrect principle. It is not in accord with the facts of nature, and there are many geologic phenomena that cannot be accounted for in terms of uniformity of rates through geologic time. So, for example, the earlier part of solar system history and of Earth history was a time of far more intense meteorite bombardment than at present. Volcanic activity on the Moon certainly was far more intense early in its history. Such activity on the Moon is virtually extinct now. Core formation in the Earth has no doubt virtually ceased. Such a process may have been extremely rapid during the earliest stages of Earth history. Continental drift may not have occurred at all during early Earth history, whereas it does occur now. Glaciation rates have certainly varied enormously through time. Extinction of fauna and flora proceeded at a spectacular rate at the end of the Cretaceous period. Thus catastrophists like Nevins are quite right when they charge that the viewpoint of substantive uniformitarianism is an imposition on nature as to how it should behave. At least this is so to the extent that substantive uniformitarianism becomes an a priori principle that we impose on nature before actually looking at the evidence contained in the rocks.

The fact of the matter, however, is that Flood catastrophists have been spending considerable effort in beating a dead horse because it is highly questionable whether any significant number of geologists has held to anything like substantive uniformitarianism for a long time.[35] The modern geological community just does not think in terms of substantive uniformitarianism. When a geologist goes out to look at rocks, he does not go out with a preconceived notion that present processes must always have operated at the same intensity throughout history. Nor does he go out with a preconceived notion that a great catastrophe (or several of them) cannot have happened. If geologists do not subscribe to Flood geology, it is because they are persuaded that the evidence from the rocks argues against it, not because they approach geology with a preconceived idea as to what rates of processes must have been like in the past. Geologists hardly feel that sedimentation and burial of fossils must always and everywhere have been excruciatingly slow, peaceful, and nonviolent. Geologists hardly feel that just because a particular rock is not in the process of being formed today this poses a serious threat to the uniformity of nature. Furthermore, geologists do not rule out the possibility of great catastrophes.[36]

Steinhauer noted that a few scientists have seen the weakness of substantive uniformitarianism and have given it up. This is an understatement of tremendous proportions. The geologic community gave up substantive uniformitarianism long ago. One might even question whether the geologic community as a whole ever did enthusiastically adhere to substantive uniformitarianism. The brand of uniformity of which catastrophists accuse geologists is not generally held by them. Catastrophists are attacking a straw man.

**Methodological Uniformitarianism**

If the geological community has abandoned substantive uniformitarianism, however, are we not then driven into the camp of the catastrophists as they would seem to infer? By no means. Modern geologists are still very much uniformitarians. They generally adhere to what has been termed methodological uniformitarianism.[37] Briefly stated, this is simply the idea that the laws of nature are invariant in time and space[38] and that Earth processes of the past behave in accord with those laws just as they do now. Catastrophists have been far more reticent about attacking this aspect of uniformitarianism than substantive uniformitarianism and with good reason, for to attack this principle is to begin undermining the very foundation of science itself. In fact, Morris has said that "true uniformity has to do with the inviolability of natural *law* (e.g., the laws of thermodynamics), and not to the uniformity of process *rates*."[39] Elsewhere Morris spoke of methodological uniformitarianism as the true uniformitarianism.[40] Steinhauer had some reservations about methodological uniformitarianism to the extent that it might exclude divine intervention into the world, but recognized that there must be some kind of uniformity of the regularity of nature and the laws that God has implanted into the structure of the universe.[41]

The Christian geologist who adheres to the principle of methodological uniformitarianism in his scientific work must not, of course, make it a complete philosophy of life. To adhere to methodological uniformitarianism for geological study does not mean that one must reject the possibility of miracles. I certainly do believe that God has performed miracles in which He suspended His laws, yet I still accept the idea of uniformity of law in the universe since God first created the initial stuff of the universe. God is very economical with miracles, however, and miracles in Scripture are closely tied in with the history of redemption; they have little if any bearing on geological history. The catastrophists have not proved from the Bible the contention that Creation, the Fall, and the Flood were shot through and through with all kinds of miracles in which God dispensed with the laws of nature as definitely as is the case with, say, the floating axehead and the Virgin Birth and Resurrection of Jesus Christ. When I look at rocks, I have no reason to believe from the Bible that what I am looking at is the result of a whole series of miracles.[42] In order for geology to be a science we must operate with methodological uniformitarianism, but this does not compel us to reject God or the miraculous.

If we are to look at the Earth's past scientifically, we must interpret the formation of rocks and landforms in terms of processes that are either known to us now or are somehow conceivable in terms of the laws of nature. Processes analogous to those of the present may be consistent with such laws. The rates of those processes must be consistent with the laws of nature although not necessarily constant throughout time and not necessarily even slow. This is all we ask of methodological uniformitarianism. The processes and rates and material conditions are inferred from the evidence of the rock record. None of this implies an a priori rejection of catastrophes on a global scale. If there have been such catastrophes, all we ask is that those catastrophes be interpretable in terms of the laws of mechanics, dynamics, optics, meteorology, chemistry, electricity, and so on. Methodological uniformitarianism cannot reject a priori the Flood geology theory without looking at rocks. After all, flooding is a process that occurs in nature in accordance with laws. It is clear from their writings that catastrophists generally try to interpret the Flood in terms of natural laws even though the Flood was sent as a divine judgment.[43] There is relatively little attempt to treat the Flood as a pure miracle in which natural law was suspended.

## Modern Flood Catastrophists are Uniformitarians

Although they are not aware of it, modern Flood catastrophists are really proceeding on the same principle as do modern uniformitarian geologists.

We both accept the idea that rocks should be explicable in terms of processes that behave in accord with the laws of nature. It is clear that catastrophists are talking in terms of a modern-day observable process, a flood, and that this Flood behaves in accordance with natural laws. The only difference is one of scale. But they expect their Flood to do things that floods do. And so we find statements such as the following by Nevins in reference to certain layers of rock rich in fossil clams:

> How was this clam layer formed? The best explanation seems to be that the clams were *washed* into their present location and buried alive. If the clams had died prior to the burial, the shells would have been open rather than tightly closed. The clams must have been transported because they could not have lived amassed in the layer in which they are found. Turbulent and flowing water seems to be the only mechanism which could rapidly transport and deposit heavy objects like clams. Some catastrophe like the Flood seems to be a most reasonable explanation.[44]

In spite of the appeal to the Flood catastrophe, this is uniformitarian thinking if ever there were such. The appeal is not to the unknown and the unknowable, but the appeal is from the geological evidence to experience with modern-day processes, i.e., washing, the way clams die, turbulent transportation in water, and so on. Nevins' appeal is to knowable and known processes with which we have experience in the modern world, processes that he expected to have behaved in the past as they behave today because they obey the laws of nature.

Also notice what Nevins said in regard to graded bedding and turbidites:

> It is noteworthy that the Flood would have generated turbidity currents as well as conditions very similar to turbidity currents. The waters of the Flood would have stirred up a heavy and viscous load of sediment. When the turbidity of the waters decreased, very rapid deposition would have occurred over vast areas. Minor oscillations in current would have introduced new sediment which could have been deposited on previous beds producing the characteristic repeating graded beds.[45]

Notice how frequently "would have" is used. Again Nevins said "would have" with some degree of confidence because in uniformitarian fashion he is appealing not to some unknowable miraculous occurrence but to his experience with present-day observable phenomena and processes. Nevins' Flood acts the way we would expect flooding waters to behave. It produces the kinds of phenomena we would expect a great flood to produce.

Or take this statement from Whitcomb and Morris regarding the formation of evaporites from brines:

> Perhaps it is not too presumptuous to suggest that these unusual brines may have been generated during the volcanic upheavals accompanying the Deluge and that unusual conditions of vaporization and separation of precipitates may likewise have been caused by the locally high temperatures accompanying these same upheavals.[46]

Again it is clear that we have no appeal to miracle, but uniformitarian construction of a hypothesis appealing to knowable processes which operate in accord with natural laws. When we speak of high temperatures generated by volcanic activity, and of vaporization of water and precipitation of chemicals caused by those high temperatures, we are arguing on the basis of our experience of present processes, and in so doing we are doing what any modern uniformitarian geologist does.

This is not to say that Flood geologists are consistent uniformitarians, for they are not, but they are uniformitarians nonetheless. They are not always consistent in making reasonable inferences from the geological data in terms of natural processes and laws. We usually find them making their most reasonable inferences when the data seem to support their Flood hypothesis. Then they become quite consistent uniformitarians. But we find them making their most outrageous inferences when the data flatly contradict their Flood hypothesis. Even then their false reasonings are cast in terms of natural laws and they argue in terms of what "would have" happened. Thus when it is not so convenient, Flood catastrophists become less consistent, but even then they cannot escape being uniformitarians.

Some further examples should help to illustrate that this is so. As we saw earlier, Northrup argued that dismembered fossil fishes implied turbulent water action and rapid burial. Very well preserved fishes also implied rapid burial. He thought all this was against uniformitarianism, but it is not. It is very good uniformitarian thinking in spite of the fact that he attributes this violence and rapidity of deposition to the Flood. It is uniformitarian because he argued from evidence to what would likely happen in the world today. Very turbulent water action and rapid burial probably would dismember some fish and preserve them from predation of scavengers. Flood catastrophists are often consistent uniformitarians when dealing with stratigraphy, but the consistency of their uniformitarianism diminishes when we move into other aspects of geology. For example, as we noted in chapter 8, Barnes maintained that the Earth's magnetic moment has steadily and exponentially decreased from an astronomically high value at creation only a few thousand years ago to its current value. He wanted to show that the Earth is very young. Of course, one could counter that the evidence from radiocarbon dating alone shows that the Earth has been in existence much more than just a few thousand years, thus bringing into question the whole idea of recent creation. But, reasoning in uniformitarian fashion, Barnes argued that increased values of the magnetic moment in the past would increase the shielding effect of the Earth from cosmic rays. Since cosmic rays would be deflected away from the Earth's atmosphere, there would be less carbon 14 production in the upper atmosphere. This in turn would completely upset radiocarbon dating. Other Flood catastrophists such as Whitelaw have expressed similar ideas. They have criticized the validity of radiocarbon dates because of what the Earth's magnetic field would do to cosmic ray production during the Flood. Now Barnes,

Whitelaw, and the other catastrophists have not done a particularly good job of interpreting the scientific evidence in this matter. Their inferences and conclusions are wrong because they have neglected abundant archaeological and geological evidence from the field of paleomagnetics as we saw in chapter 8, which clearly indicates that the Earth's magnetic moment has not decreased exponentially from the beginning but has fluctuated greatly throughout time. Yet in spite of their distortion of and ignoring of much evidence regarding the Earth's magnetism the catastrophists have unavoidably reasoned from the evidence which they did choose to consider in a uniformitarian manner. They constantly stress, as do modern geologists, the causal interrelationships between the magnetic field, cosmic rays, and carbon 14. Barnes, Whitelaw, and the others spoke in terms of such causal interrelationships not only at present but in the past as well. In other words they accepted the idea that the same laws of magnetics that are in existence now were in existence in the past and that cosmic rays and radiocarbon production responded in accordance with those laws. This kind of thinking clearly makes uniformitarians out of the catastrophists. They are arguing in the same way as modern geologists do except that they ignore the evidence that contradicts their most fundamental world hypothesis.

## Why the Big Difference in Opinion?

One might think that if modern geologists do not, as some perhaps did years ago, insist that rates of processes be slow so that no global catastrophes are needed, and if we have no a priori principial objection to the possibility of a global catastrophe, and if creationist catastrophists and modern geologists are both arguing essentially from methodological uniformitarian premises, then there would not be such a great rift between the two groups. Why do creationists and most Christian geologists interpret the history of the Earth so very differently? I must conclude that the creationist, flood catastrophists are, for some reason, unwilling to read the totality of the available geological evidence. They are unwilling to abandon their young-Earth, global-Flood hypothesis even when the evidence, properly interpreted, shows it to be untenable. They have ignored or distorted a vast body of evidence which is contrary to their preconceived notion of what Earth history must have been like. They have focused only on what is favorable to their own theory. They claim continually to argue from the evidence, from the facts of nature, but they have repeatedly ignored what is inconvenient for them. It is true that many phenomena of the sedimentary rock record might be interpretable in terms of a great Flood. But many of the phenomena to which they appeal, such as fossil graveyards and graded bedding, are easily explicable in terms of much smaller scale processes than global catastrophic floods. More importantly, Flood catastrophists have ignored abundant evidence of glacial deposits, lake deposits, desert deposits, delta deposits, shore deposits, reef deposits, and evaporite deposits in the rock record. The presence of all of these as we saw in chapter 6 argues completely against a global Flood having deposited almost the totality of the sedimentary rock pile. Furthermore, catastrophists have ignored the evidence from heat flow from cooling magmas, metamorphism, and the kinetics of mineral formation.[47] They have tried to make the evidence from radiometric dating say something opposite from what it does say as we pointed out in chapter 7. Although a fraction of the geological evidence might suggest a global Flood when considered in isolation from other evidence, the overwhelming totality of evidence argues mightily against it.[48] Yet a firm commitment to the infallibility and inerrancy of Scripture does not require a Christian to believe the theories of Creation and the Flood to which creationists so doggedly hold. The data of the Bible certainly do not demand that we hold to these views. Christians need to relax and stop being afraid that somehow or other some scientific evidence will disprove the Bible. We should not be afraid of the evidence that God has put into His world.

The only recourse that Flood catastrophists have to save their theory is to appeal to a pure miracle and thus eliminate entirely the possibility of historical geology. Even catastrophists seem unwilling to go that far.

In conclusion, recent creationists have charged those who hold to the idea that the Earth may be on the order of 4.5 billion years in age with adhering to a false principle that leads them to misinterpret the geological evidence. This false principle is supposedly the principle of uniformitarianism. By uniformitarianism, young-Earth creationists understand a principle that almost a priori rejects the very possibility of global catastrophes and maintains that Earth processes have always proceeded at very slow, peaceful, constant rates throughout geological time. Because of adherence to this principle of slowness of rates, geologists have supposedly vastly overestimated the amount of time that it has taken the Earth to form.

Creationists, however, claim to hold to a principle of catastrophism that says that rates of geological processes in the past, particularly at the time of the Flood, were speeded up incredibly compared with what they are now, so that much less time than millions of years was required to form the Earth.

The problem is that creationists have completely misunderstood the nature of the uniformitarianism used by modern geologists. We do not reject a priori catastrophes nor do we automatically assume that geological process rates have always been "excruciatingly slow." We infer rates of processes from the record of the rocks. Where rocks contain features like polystrate trees we are ready to infer that sedimentary deposition was extremely rapid in that place when the deposition occurred. But when rocks contain features like lake deposits, we infer that sedimentation was very likely extremely slow. Both creationists and modern geologists infer process rates from the rock record. The creationists, however, have looked only at those rocks that were probably formed relatively rapidly. Geologists have looked at all the rocks. The evidence of the rocks suggests strongly that it took several billions of years for the Earth to form, and no amount of arguing about uniformitarianism as over against catastrophism, for that is a false dichotomy, can alter the fact.

# —11—
# CREATIONISM, EVANGELISM, and APOLOGETICS

IN PART TWO WE have examined several scientific arguments that are said by creationists to indicate that the Earth is only a few thousand years old at most. Since most creationists think Scripture teaches that the Earth is young, they enthusiastically believe and advance such arguments. However, it has been shown that these scientific arguments for a young Earth are not valid, and they do not establish a young age for the Earth at all. These so-called scientific evidences are based on incomplete information, wishful thinking, ignorance of real geological situations, selective use of data to support the favored hypothesis, and faulty reasoning. The fact of the matter is that the scientific evidence considered as a whole, and as we have it now, compellingly argues for the great antiquity of the Earth.

It is entirely possible that in the future some new discoveries may be made that will lead the scientific community to abandon belief in the great age of the Earth. There have certainly been great revolutions in scientific thought in the past, and we must expect more of them in the future. Possibly some factor will turn up that will cause us to look at the evidence in wholly new ways that we had not ever dreamed possible. I am inclined to doubt that evidence overturning the idea of the antiquity of the Earth will be found, but there is always that possibility. In any case, in our present situation with the abundant evidence that we have before us there is nothing that would remotely lead us to conclude that the Earth is anything other than extremely old. The totality of the evidence just does not point to the Earth being only a few thousand years old, no matter how ardently creationists might wish that it did. No amount of juggling can change the overwhelming weight of the evidence.

Where then does this conclusion lead Christians? Specifically, what does the scientific evidence mean with reference to the truth of the Christian religion? With reference to the truth of the Bible? Is the Genesis account really reliable after all? Does the Bible contain only myths about creation rather than accurate information about it? Or are there perhaps other ways of understanding Genesis when it speaks of creation? Does the Bible contain mistakes about the nature of the world in which we live?

## Is Faith Damaged by an Ancient Earth?

Many Christian people have been, are, and will continue to be very greatly disturbed by the conclusion that the Earth is extremely old. They simply cannot bring themselves to accept the idea that the Earth and the universe are billions of years old. They cannot understand why God should have taken so long to make the world. Indeed they might well feel that if the antiquity of the Earth is accepted then somehow or other God's power and sovereignty are limited. They would feel that we scientists had badly misinterpreted the evidence and would hope that something would turn up to convince us that the Earth is young. And there is always the impression that scientists are somehow engaged in a conspiracy to doctor the evidence. I have been asked, "Why do you want the Earth to be that old?" as if I had some preference in selecting an age I thought the Earth ought to be. It is shattering for many Christians to face the idea that the Earth really is old because they have for so long been persuaded that the Bible emphatically, unequivocally teaches that the Earth is very young. To establish conclusively the antiquity of the Earth, as I have been attempting to do, would in their minds suggest that the Bible might really be wrong about creation and therefore not reliable any more. This is a consequence that large numbers of Christian people simply cannot face. Their faith would be damaged, and so because of an unnecessary connection between the antiquity of the Earth and the possibility of error in the Bible, they steadfastly resist the conclusion that the Earth is old.

With such Christian people I have the utmost sympathy. I can appreciate the struggles and anguish such a person must go through, for I have gone through some of those struggles myself. I do, however, want to persuade fearful Christian brethren that they should not fear the idea of the antiquity of the Earth. They should not be afraid that the overwhelming available evidence that the Earth is billions of years old is somehow damaging to Christianity. The available evidence from science in no way undermines the Bible or our Christian faith.

On the other hand, what is much more likely to undermine Christian faith is the dogmatic and persistent effort of creationists to present their theory before the public, Christian and non-Christian, as in accord with Scripture and nature, especially when the evidence to the contrary has been presented again and again by competent Christian scientists.[1] It is sad that so much Christian energy has to be wasted in proposing and refuting the false theory of catastrophic Flood geology. But Christians need to know the truth and to be warned of error. Creationist articles constantly make sweeping statements to the effect that Christianity is now on surer ground because of the discoveries and theories that creationists have concocted. The article by Whitelaw[2] is an extreme case in point. "Proving" the Bible or Christianity with a spurious scientific hypothesis, can only be injurious to the cause of Christ. We do not defend truth by arguing error in its behalf. The Bible is God's Word and is neither more nor less certain because some scientific theory seems to confirm or deny it. The Bible is true, it is infallible, it is without error no matter what our theories of geology may be.

I do not want to put a muzzle on any Christian. We ought to have freedom of responsible expression in Christian circles. We ought to explore new ideas and new ways of looking at things. Christians ought to be creative and ought to have the right to put forward some new thoughts in a tentative manner. At the same time we have a responsibility not to mislead our reading public. We have the responsibility to learn as much as possible about what we are saying before we publish. It may be that overzealous Christian scholars have stepped out on a limb and made pronouncements that were not properly grounded in fact.

I find it puzzling that the spurious arguments of creationism are repeated over and over again in so many books, articles, and periodicals. Creationists need to learn how to receive criticism when they are told that they have spoken on a matter about which they know relatively little. When they are criticized they ought to listen to the criticism and profit from it and correct their mistakes or be silent in the future. The creationist movement seems unwilling to receive criticism in a gracious manner and profit from criticisms of its arguments by competent Christian scientists. The same arguments are put before the Christian public in book after book, in article after article. Christian people are still being misled. The creationists can make a real contribution by doing scientific work in fields that really are problematic. The work by Gentry on pleochroic halos[3] is indeed problematic for current theories of radiometric dating and decay constants of radioactive nuclides. But creationists should concentrate their energies in trying to solve such problems with the help of modern research rather than continuing to propagate the same fallacious arguments.

Many people, even Christians, attach too much authority to scientific theories. The faith of many Christian people could be hindered when they ultimately realize that the teachings of the creationists are simply not in accord with the facts. But imagine the trauma of accepting the possibility of an old Earth in these days. Christians believe that the Bible is God's Word and is free of error, and many of them have been thoroughly indoctrinated to believe also that creation occurred in six twenty-four-hour days, that the entire globe was completely submerged for an entire year by the Flood, that uniformitarian geology is based on a godless philosophy, that Flood geology offers a superior explanation of the facts of nature, and that "genuine science" supports the creationist-catastrophist view of the Bible.

Imagine the trauma and shock of finally realizing that Flood geology, which has been endorsed so enthusiastically by well-meaning Christian leaders, is nothing more than a fantasy. A Christian could easily become disillusioned in circles where Flood geology has been regarded as an article of faith or as *the* biblical view of nature.

Furthermore, creationism and Flood geology have put a serious roadblock in the way of unbelieving scientists. Although Christ has the power to save unbelievers in spite of our foolishness and poor presentations of the gospel, Christians should do all they can to avoid creating unnecessary stumbling blocks to the reception of the gospel. Some people who might otherwise be open to the gospel could be completely turned off by Flood geology. If acceptance of Christianity means accepting Flood geology, some might not want to become Christians. No non-Christian geologist is ever going to accept Flood geology or the young-Earth theory these days; the flaws and weaknesses are obvious to any practicing geologist.

Christians must not try to prove the Bible from science. We need not twist or misinterpret the facts in order to get agreement between the Bible and science. Christians must realize that the Scriptures do not require us to believe in six twenty-four-hour days of creation.[4] There is legitimate internal biblical evidence to indicate that the days of creation may have been indefinite periods of time.[5] Moreover, the genealogies of Genesis 5 and 11 need not be taken in a rigidly literal fashion.[6] Christians also need to realize that accepting the universality of the Flood hardly requires one to adopt Flood geology as the only possible explanation. Moreover, it is not entirely clear that the Bible is talking about a geographically universal flood.[7] Why then are some Christians so rigidly dogmatic about matters on which the Bible itself is not dogmatic? There is considerable room for legitimate variation of interpretation of the Creation and the Flood. Christians should not paint themselves into a corner by being more rigid than the Bible.

Just suppose for the sake of argument that the Bible and the scientific evidence do not seem to agree at every point anyway. Does it really advance the Christian cause by forcing the facts of nature to fit into a preconceived theory of the Earth as is done by the creationist movement? No, it harms our cause. Christ has called us to truth and honesty. We are to tell the truth in love, but we are not telling the truth if we insist that the facts of nature indicate that the Earth is very young and that the Earth was totally covered and renovated in one year by the Flood as described by Flood geologists. I am *not* accusing creationists of lying or deliberate distortion. No doubt they have honorable intentions, but if they continue to espouse their theories when other Christian brethren have repeatedly called attention to the falsity of their theories, they must be challenged to stop. It is a far better procedure to follow the evidence of nature wherever it may lead, even if it seems, at first, to run counter to our interpretations of Scripture. Let me indicate why this procedure is better, and in so doing point out why the antiquity of the Earth does not at all undermine Christian faith.

## The Unity of Revelation

We are dealing with God's world and with God-created facts. The world is not a brute, wholly uninterpreted entity with which we may do as we please, but it is a God-interpreted world. We must make our interpretation of the world after the pattern of God's interpretation. We must handle the data reverently and worshipfully, yet we should not be afraid of where the facts may lead. God made those facts, and they fit into His comprehensive plan for the world. God has brought the world into its current state of existence, and thus the facts of geology and all other facts owe their existence to His sovereign counsel. When a geologist finds a rock composed of 30% quartz, 40% alkali feldspar, 20% plagioclase, and 10% biotite, the rock is that way because God willed it to be so, not because the geologist made it up or because of fate or ultimate chance. The fact about that rock's composition is every bit as much a fact as any fact that can be found in the Bible. It is as true as any fact in the Bible. It is just as much a fact as the fact that Christ died for our sins. To be sure, it is a much less important fact. One's life will not be significantly different for either being aware of it or not being aware of it, but it is nonetheless still just as much a fact. It is a very different kind of fact from the facts we find in the Bible. The facts of the Bible are expressed verbally; those in nature are not. The facts of the Bible primarily tell us what we are to believe concerning God and what duty He requires of us. The facts of the Bible are ethically normative for our lives; the facts of nature are not. The Bible generally tells us what we ought to do; nature generally does not. Thus in the Bible and in nature we are dealing with different kinds of revelation of God, with different kinds of facts, but we are dealing in both cases with facts of divine origination.

We see much the same thing on the human level, for mankind has been made in God's image. People can express themselves both verbally and creatively. For example, the monumental Ninth Symphony of Gustav Mahler is very expressive of the personality of its creator. In listening to the music again and again we gain insight into the nature of Mahler himself. We sense something of the kind of person he was. We begin to know what he was like. When, for example, we listen to the poignant introspection, the exquisite, almost unbearable nostalgia of the Finale of the Ninth Symphony, we sense something of the tragic inner life of Mahler, of his inner turmoil, of the struggle of his entire life to find meaning in existence, particularly as he faces imminent death. This symphony is a genuine revelation of the character, of the being, of Gustav Mahler, every bit as much as the letters he wrote and the words he spoke. While the music is revelatory of its composer, it does not express his will in a directly recognizable way. If Mahler's wife, Alma, wanted to know what he expected of her or what she should really think of him, she would not learn this so much from his music as from his verbal expressions and commands. His verbalizing would be normative for her, but not his music, even though both the verbalizing and the music were equally genuine expressions of the character of the composer. In a similar way if we want to know what God wants us to do we listen to His words in the Bible, but in the study of nature the redeemed Christian also learns to appreciate the character of God as Psalm 19 and Romans 1 make plain. Creation reveals God's character and expresses His nature, although not in the same direct way that the Bible does.

The facts of the Bible and the facts of nature, therefore, do not disagree but form one comprehensive, unified expression of the character and will of our Creator and Redeemer. Nature and Scripture form a unity, for God is one. Although man, because of his sinful nature, reveals himself in inconsistent and contradictory ways, God *cannot* do so. But the fact that God's words and works are a perfect unity does not by any means indicate that we can always see how they agree or fit together.

We must of necessity engage in the interpretation of both nature and Scripture in order that we might see how the facts fit together, in order that we might see the interrelationships of those facts. In the matter of interpretation God has no problem, because for Him the universe, His word and works, is wholly transparent. Inasmuch as He is creator of the world and author of Scripture, He comprehensively sees and knows all the facts of His universe at a glance. His "interpretation" of the facts coincides with the facts. God sees the interrelationships of the facts as He sees the facts themselves, for He has created in accordance with His plan. All is light to Him; no facts are new. No facts are discovered by Him. No facts are unknown to Him. No facts are unintelligible to Him. The case, however, is much different for us, for we are creatures. Our interpretations of the facts do not coincide with our knowledge of the facts, but must be constructed by reasoning processes from the facts. For us the facts precede the understanding of interrelationships. We collect the facts and then think about their meaning. As creatures, too, we do not have immediate access to all the facts. Our knowledge of the facts is incomplete. Then, too, we are sinners and sin mars our interpretations of God's truth. As sinners, our intellects have been harmed, and we resist to some degree dealing in a responsible way with God's works and words. Our interpretations do not always wholeheartedly accept the facts God has given us. At times we distort their meaning. Sometimes we do this unconsciously. The fact that we must interpret the unified world in which God has placed us means that we do not always see that unity. We do not always understand how everything fits together because of our creatureliness and our sinfulness. Hence it may on occasion appear to us that the Bible and nature do not agree, but the disagreement is not between the Bible and nature, rather between our understanding of the Bible and our understanding of nature. It is our interpretation of the God-given data that leads us into discrepancy, conflict, and disagreement. And so, as Christians, we should not be too dismayed if such conflicts seem to appear between nature and the Bible. They are not real conflicts between nature and the Bible, but only conflicts between natural science and theological exegesis.

Let us see further why we should not be too upset over such discrepancies. We recognize that the Bible is a unity, too. We believe that the Bible has one redemptive story to tell from Genesis to Revelation. The Bible story begins in the garden of God and it ends there. We affirm that all parts of the Bible agree and are in perfect harmony with one another, but we do not always see this harmony fully. There is much in the Bible that from our limited perspective does not seem to fit together too well. There are many examples of apparent discrepancies that we cannot fully reconcile. There are, for example, parallel accounts of the same event in the different gospels. We cannot fully reconcile the differences in detail between the accounts. Matthew refers an Old Testament quotation to Jeremiah the prophet when in fact the majority of the quote comes from Zechariah. Here is a statement that has puzzled theologians. Even the understanding of all the relevant information will not provide a fully satisfying explanation.

One could mention many other apparent contradictions in the Bible as well as many paradoxes such as the divine-human nature of Christ. These data of Scripture present us with difficulties for our scientific theology. All the facts of the Bible do not fit neatly together in our human understanding. Faithful as we may be in interpreting the data of the Bible regarding the personality of our Lord, we still cannot fully grasp how a person can be God and man with the characteristics of each at the same time. How can Jesus know everything and know things only partially at one and the same time? No one knows. But we believe it in spite of the tensions this causes for us because the Bible tells us that Jesus was God and that He was man. Just because of these discrepancies or tensions or apparent contradictions in the Bible, Christians do not reject the facts or reject the Scripture. We certainly ought not to start charging the Bible with mistakes at those points where there appear to be differences, as, for example, in the various Resurrection narratives. The increasing tendency on the part of evangelical Christians to suspect that the Bible might be in error in some of its narratives is to be viewed with alarm. By its very nature as a revelation of God, the Bible cannot be erroneous any more than God Himself can be erroneous. As Christians we must accept the biblical statements, properly interpreted, as correct, as genuine facts, and accept any resulting tensions. As a result, our theology, which has the character of a science built on the data of Scripture,[8] God's verbal revelation, has some loose ends in it. In God's mind there are no loose ends, no tensions, but in our theology there are. Theology cannot be an air-tight, closed system. We must learn to live with loose ends in our theology.

At the same time, we should not thereby become careless in our theologizing and satisfied with an increasing number of dangling facts. As interpreters of the Word of God we should continue to endeavor to explore and explicate the underlying unity of the Bible and we should do our best to resolve conflicts and tensions. Where there are differing accounts of the same event, we should continue to do our best to harmonize the two accounts without forcing facts to fit theories. Where there are seemingly contradictory doctrines, we ought to continue to do our best to develop improved formulations of doctrines that are increasingly faithful to biblical facts and biblical principles and motives. Theologians should not necessarily be content with the formulation of the doctrine of predestination that was worked out after the Reformation, excellent though that formulation may have been. They should seek, if possible, to develop the doctrine further, bringing it into ever greater conformity with the Word of God. They should continue to explore ways in which the tension between that doctrine and the doctrine of human responsibility might be relieved to some degree. Although as creatures engaged in creaturely interpretation of God's world we will forever be faced with some tensions and loose ends in our theological interpretive endeavors, we should do our best to eliminate them, not artificially, but by becoming more faithful to the truths God has given us.

The same kind of tensions exist in our understanding of nature. Very frequently there are loose ends in natural science because of our limited understanding of the facts of nature. One very prominent illustration of such a tension comes from nineteenth-century science. Geologists were generally of the opinion that the facts gleaned from the rocks suggested that the world was several hundred million years old. On the other hand the evidence of physics in the eyes of Lord Kelvin[9] suggested that the world was less than a hundred million years old. Here were two bodies of facts drawn from different parts of nature which when interpreted by competent scientists indicated two mutually exclusive ideas regarding the age of the Earth. Now either the world is more than a hundred million years old or it is not. Consequently, there were loose ends, tensions, in scientific thinking of the nineteenth century. The facts were leading to seemingly different conclusions. Now what happened within the scientific community during the nineteenth century? There was tremendous controversy, especially between geologists and physicists. Each group was convinced the other was badly misinterpreting the evidence at hand. Yet at the same time there remained a deep persuasion that nature was a unity and that nature was only giving one answer regarding the age of the Earth. Attempts were made to work out a plausible "harmonization" of the discrepancies between the facts of physics and the facts of geology. Geologists have always been a little bit intimidated by the mathematical sophistication of physics, and so perhaps they were not so sure of themselves as the physicists were. Hence geologists made a real effort to reexamine the data of the Earth to see if it was possible to come up with a legitimate age that would fit the facts and be satisfying to the physicists. Toward the end of his life Kelvin was suggesting that the Earth was probably not much more than 20 million years old; hence, physicists were greatly pleased when the outstanding geologist, Clarence King, proposed on geological grounds an age of 24 million years for the Earth. Presumably a harmonization was achieved.

We must note what did not happen. Geologists did not abandon facts of nature, nor did physicists. No one accused nature of contradicting itself. No one accused nature of being in error, as an increasing number of modern evangelical theologians are doing with the Bible. They admitted the tension and tried to resolve it, fully persuaded of the unity of nature. Now it turns out that the geologists were right and the physicists wrong, not because either of them had badly misinterpreted evidence or distorted facts. The fact of the matter is that the phenomenon of radioactivity was discovered. A new piece of the puzzle was discovered. A whole new set of facts of nature was discovered that had to be taken into account. Radioactivity provided a source of heat that was wholly unknown to Kelvin and therefore which he could not have taken into account in his calculations on the age of the Earth. The old "harmonization" was abandoned, and the scientific tension was eventually resolved in this case because of the discovery of new facts with attendant new and improved interpretations of those facts.

As a geologist, I have developed a detailed regional map of an area in which I thought I had a good understanding of the basic relationships of the rocks. I thought I knew how they behaved and I was usually able to predict what kind of rock I would find at the top of the next hill. But once in a while I would find an outcrop that did not fit into my larger, generally valid picture of the geology. The outcrop just did not make sense to me. Although I did not know what it was doing there, there was a set of facts (in the form of the rock outcrop) that was supposed to be there. The outcrop is a part of the unity of nature. It made perfect sense in terms of the whole geological picture of the area I was working. I could not see how it fit in, but I certainly cannot deny the existence or factuality of the outcrop, but neither can I completely overthrow all the other work I did. I cannot reject the large regional picture simply because I have been unable to figure how one fact fit into it. I accept all the facts, but with a certain unresolved tension, with a loose end. I simply confess that there is an outcrop I do not know what to do with and hope that in time I or another geologist will be able to figure out what it's doing there and how it fits in with all the other outcrops.

There are always loose ends, discrepancies, contradictions in natural science, too, owing to the fact that scientists are human, our understanding of nature is limited, and we don't always have access to all the facts that are pertinent to the situation. Nevertheless even though I may not have all the facts or may not have apprehended all the facts I still proceed to develop my natural science or my theology on the basis of the facts that I do have. I should be very much surprised if we ever had a theology that had no loose ends, and I should be very surprised if we ever had a natural science that had no loose ends. We ought to be able to clear up some of those loose ends as time goes on and our knowledge improves and new discoveries are made, but there are always going to be loose ends because we are human.

In the same way I should be very much surprised if we had a unified knowledge of both the Bible and the world that had no loose ends. Why should theology and natural science ever be expected to agree fully when each by itself has plenty of loose ends? The problems and apparent contradictions do not exist between nature and the Bible, but between our understandings of these two very different revelations of God. Therefore, we should not panic over discrepancies between science and theology any more than we panic over discrepancies in theological exegesis or discrepancies in scientific study of rocks. It simply should not be a matter of great concern to the Christian if the facts of nature do not seem to dovetail with the facts of Genesis 6–9 regarding the Flood. In reality the facts do dovetail perfectly, but we may have a hard time seeing how they do. The fact that there appears to be disagreement between the Bible and nature should not cause us to reject Genesis 6–9 or deny the reality of the Flood. Nor should this situation cause us to reject nature or attempt to falsify the evidence to make it come into conformity with what we think is in Genesis. We should be content to let both bodies of revelation speak for themselves and listen as carefully as we can. If there is apparent disagreement or tension between theological science and natural science, so be it. We ought to try to resolve the tensions, but not be upset if we cannot. We know that in the mind of God all the facts regarding the Flood agree and dovetail into a neat system with no loose ends. We must therefore be cautious in using science as an apologetic device. We should not fall into the trap of thinking that somehow Scripture is more reliable or trustworthy if it is at every point backed up by scientific evidence, nor should we somehow suspect that Scripture may be untrustworthy if science does not back it up at every point.

Perhaps we might be justified in getting upset over areas of apparent disagreement between the Bible and the realities of nature and history if indeed the Bible was at nearly every point at odds with the rest of reality. The fact of the matter, however, is that for the most part the areas of apparent disagreement between the Bible and nature, geography, archaeology, and history are rather minor. With only occasional areas of tension between the Bible and other realms of reality why should we be any more distressed than in geology or physics where internal agreement of data is remarkably good and there are only occasional problematical areas?

Much too often those of us who have been involved in the discussion of the interrelationship between biblical interpretation and natural scientific investigation have been guilty of accepting or rejecting hypotheses on the basis of how well or how poorly the hypothesis fit a set of data to which it was not particularly applicable. By this I mean that we have sometimes been guilty of exegeting Scripture more on the basis of data from nature than on the data of Scripture and this is something we should not do. As one example, Henry Morris has rejected the classic day-age hypothesis of interpreting Genesis 1.[10] He has rejected that hypothesis on exegetical grounds. That is a perfectly legitimate procedure whether one agrees with his exegesis or not. But he has also rejected the validity of the day-age hypothesis as a biblical view on the grounds that the order of events suggested by geological investigation does not correspond with the order of events listed in Genesis 1. Morris has listed a number of points at which he believes there is poor or contradictory correspondence between the sequence in Genesis and the sequence of geology. This comparison between the Bible and nature is not, however, a legitimate ground for rejecting the day-age hypothesis. That hypothesis is an interpretation of Scripture and should be defended or rejected solely on the grounds that Scripture affirms or denies it. It is independent of the facts of nature. The facts of nature cannot determine what the Bible says about any particular subject. Therefore simply because the order of events in nature is somewhat different from the order in Genesis 1 certainly does not prove one way or another that the days of Genesis 1 were long periods of time in which much geological activity may have taken place. That is a question that must be decided on the basis of the internal data of Scripture. If there is a discrepancy then we are in an area of tension, where our interpretation of the data may be in error, or where we simply do not have enough information to see how the two accounts, one of Scripture, the other of nature, fit together.

On the other hand, opponents of recent creationism perhaps have made the mistake of arguing that the days of Genesis 1 cannot be twenty-four-hour days. Their argument is that the facts of nature, especially those of geology, are so overwhelmingly convincing that the Earth is extremely old, that the Bible cannot possibly teach that the Earth is only a few thousand years old. We must therefore find another interpretation of the days of Genesis 1 that spares us the embarrassment of thinking that the Bible teaches a very recent creation; the days cannot be 24 hours long. I am sympathetic toward this point of view, but I believe that it is wrong. The data of nature can only make us take another hard look at the data of the Bible to see if we have interpreted them correctly the first time. Nature, however, cannot force upon us an interpretation of the Bible. The Bible must finally be interpreted in terms of its own facts even though information from other sources, for example, literature or archaeology may help us to ask proper questions of the biblical text in our interpretive task. The question of the length of the days of Genesis 1 must be decided by the text of Scripture and the analogy of Scripture. It cannot be decided by information from nature. Sometimes the second look at Scripture that is prompted by the investigation of nature may lead us to change our interpretation of Scripture, as was certainly the case in the days of the Copernican controversy. Nevertheless the new biblical interpretation in that case is one that is consistent with the data of Scripture, and not one that was forced on the Bible by the facts of nature. Tayler Lewis was quite right in his criticism[11] of many of the nineteenth-century harmonists that they often allowed their science to do their exegeting of Scripture, and that they fell into the trap of thinking that because science argued for the antiquity of the Earth therefore the restitution hypothesis or the day-age hypothesis, depending upon which hypothesis one favored, was *the* teaching of Scripture. We cannot reject the twenty-four-hour hypothesis simply because it doesn't agree with science. The length of the days is an exegetical question. There is biblical evidence to indicate that the days of Genesis 1 were long periods of indeterminate length, consistent with the day-age hypothesis, but on the other hand, the exegetical arguments for the twenty-four-hour-day hypothesis also have support in Scripture, although I personally do not favor that hypothesis.

## Apologetics

A Christian believer should not be bothered by the idea that the Earth is extremely old. He should not feel that Christianity is threatened or that the veracity of the Bible is undermined because the evidence of nature suggests the antiquity of our planet. His faith should not be weakened by adherence to such an idea. It may well be that historically the church has generally held to the view that the Earth is only a few thousands of years old, but what has traditionally been held is not necessarily what the Bible teaches. There seems to be a genuine conflict between what most in the church traditionally believed regarding the age of the Earth until the nineteenth century and what scientific evidence is suggesting. But it must be stated again that seeming contradictions or tensions between biblical understanding and our understanding of nature are neither grounds for rejection of the Bible nor grounds for undermining the historic Christian faith. We should not expect a tension-free interrelationship between science and biblical interpretation any more than we should expect a completely tension-free physics or biology or geology with no problems left to solve. The Christian must not allow unresolved discrepancies to undermine his faith in Scripture as God's Word.

In our dealing with unbelievers we may need to admit the existence of these tensions and discrepancies. As we present the gospel, particularly to scientifically-trained unbelievers, and defend Scripture as God's truth, we may well be confronted with questions about the interrelationship between the Bible and science. It may be charged that there are contradictions or tensions, or areas of disagreement, and we may find that the unbeliever cannot cross the intellectual barriers raised by these difficulties. Because of such barriers he may be unable to bring himself to believe that the Bible is really God's Word after all. He may feel that the Bible is mistaken in matters of science. Our temptation in such instances may be to sweep all the difficulties under the rug and pretend that everything is all right and that there are no contradictions or tensions. We may be tempted to twist Scripture or to twist nature to eliminate all the conflicts and thus present a false unity. This temptation must be resisted at all costs. In dealing with non-Christians we must be totally honest and above-board and freely admit that we do not have all the answers. We must admit that there are indeed some loose ends that cannot be satisfactorily explained by us or anyone else. We can certainly suggest some plausible ways of reconciling these tensions, but we must freely admit that even our best harmonizations still have difficulties. The non-Christian will respect our presentation of Christianity far more if we present the truth in love and humility and a willingness to say "I don't know the answer" when indeed we do not know the answer. The unbeliever will see through attempts to distort the Bible or nature to eliminate apparent disagreements.

I am convinced nonetheless that the tensions or disagreements between theology and geology are nowhere near as awkward and embarrassing as is usually thought to be the case. I am convinced that the antiquity of the Earth suggested by nature is not at variance with what the Bible has to say. I believe that there are exegetical grounds for maintaining that the six days of creation were long, indeterminate periods of time. This is also the view of several distinguished theologians in the last two centuries.[12] Although this interpretation comes from a perfectly valid exegesis already hinted at by Augustine and other church fathers, and although it eliminates any conflict with scientific investigation on the question of the age of the Earth, it must freely be admitted that it is an exegesis that still leaves us with some areas of tension and unsolved problems. It certainly leaves us with far fewer tensions and contradictions than does the twenty-four-hour-day view of the six days. In dealing with the unbeliever we have every legitimate right to state that the common impression that the Bible unequivocally teaches that the universe was created in six twenty-four-hour days is false. We must state, however, that this is only one possible interpretation that is faithful to the words of the text. We have every right to state that the long, figurative day interpretation is equally legitimate, and it has been supported by many of the greatest theologians in church history. We should in all fairness make plain that there are legitimate exegeses of Scripture that allow for plausible harmonizations with scientific thinking. In doing so we can still willingly admit that these harmonizations are not perfect and that they do have difficulties.

Again we need to remind our unbelieving friends that the difficulties in these harmonizations are no greater than many of the difficulties presented to us by any of the natural sciences. And besides, we can remind those to whom we witness that in the vast bulk of material in the Bible that could be corroborated by historical or archaeological methods, the amount of agreement with modern investigation is generally overwhelming. The areas of tension are relatively minor in amount when compared with the areas of compatibility. If the unbeliever refuses to admit that the Bible is God's Word simply because of a few apparent contradictions or discrepancies, we need to remind him that these discrepancies are in our understanding of the data, not in the data themselves, and that he should also abandon physics, or astronomy, or geology, until those sciences also completely rid themselves of all perplexing problems. We do, however, need to realize that in the matter of the age of the Earth there really is no contradiction between possible interpretations of the Bible and legitimate interpretations of the facts of nature. There is agreement; let us point this out.

We must not distort Scripture or the findings of nature in order to obtain a forced agreement between the two. I fear that some theologians are trying to force Scripture in the matter of the origin of man. They are trying very hard to make it say something other than what it says in order that accommodation with the theory of evolution may be obtained. We should resist this tendency. Certainly we can try new exegeses of the relevant data of the Bible, but the exegeses must be faithful to the data as they are. We need to exercise considerable caution in our handling of the Bible in areas that have bearing on scientific work. On the other hand, far too many Christians are willing to distort science in order to gain an accommodation with what they are persuaded is the only possible legitimate interpretation of Scripture. This is the case with the modern creationist movement. Creationists have generally persuaded themselves that the days of Genesis 1 must be twenty-four hours long, and that the genealogies of Genesis allow for only a few thousand years at the most. They have persuaded themselves that the story of the Flood in Genesis can be interpreted only as a flood that completely covered the entire globe and that the mountaintops all around the world were under water. They typically have not recognized other valid interpretations of Creation and the Flood. Having locked themselves into these rigid interpretations they are in disagreement with modern scientific ideas. Not willing to allow tensions to exist, they have sought for harmonization with the facts of nature or with science not by reevaluating their biblical exegeses but by wholesale distortion of science and the facts of nature. They have tried to make nature say things it is not saying. In this book we have documented that creationists have ignored data when convenient and have been very selective in the use of other data. They have misinterpreted data and scientific theories and have attempted to develop a wholly new science. Their wholly new science agrees with their biblical interpretation, and the conflict is removed; the problem is that their wholly new science has nothing to do with the real world in which we live. It has almost nothing to do with the facts of the Earth, rocks, chemical element distribution, fossils, and so on, except in the most superficial way. Their theory of a young Earth and a global-Flood catastrophe has been superimposed not only on the Bible, but on nature as well. Such an approach to the harmonization of the Bible with nature is no harmonization at all, for it harmonizes by ignoring the real world in which God has placed us, which

God himself made and controls, a real world whose factuality has been determined and given by the sovereign God of the universe.

The maintenance of modern creationism and Flood geology not only is useless apologetically with unbelieving scientists, it is harmful. Although many who have no scientific training have been swayed by creationist arguments, the unbelieving scientist will reason that a Christianity that believes in such nonsense must be a religion not worthy of his interest. Mixing the gospel with creationism could raise a barrier in the way of a person's acceptance of the gospel. Modern creationism in this sense is apologetically and evangelistically ineffective. It could even be a hindrance to the gospel.

Another possible danger is that in presenting the gospel to the lost and in defending God's truth we ourselves will seem to be false. It is time for Christian people to recognize that the defense of this modern, young-Earth, Flood-geology creationism is simply not truthful. It is simply not in accord with the facts that God has given. Creationism must be abandoned by Christians before harm is done. The persistent attempts of the creationist movement to get their points of view established in educational institutions can only bring harm to the Christian cause. Can we seriously expect non-Christian educational leaders to develop a respect for Christianity if we insist on teaching the brand of science that creationism brings with it? Will not the forcing of modern creationism on the public simply lend credence to the idea already entertained by so many intellectual leaders that Christianity, at least in its modern form, is sheer anti-intellectual obscurantism? I fear that it will.

The creationists are to be praised for their desire to provide an alternative to a thoroughgoing atheistic, materialistic, naturalistic evolutionism. But recent-Earth creationism is not the only alternative to such evolutionism. The Bible is indeed the infallible, inerrant[13] Word of God. It is absolutely true in matters of science and history as much as in matters of salvation and religion. But nature is also from God, and nature would lead us to believe that the Earth is extremely old. Scientific investigation of the world God gave us is an exciting enterprise that God would have us engage in. We do not need the flight-from-reality science of creationism. We need more of the vigorous approach to both nature and Scripture that we found in men of the nineteenth century like William Buckland, Hugh Miller, Thomas Chalmers, and John Fleming. May I plead with my brethren in Christ who are involved in the young-Earth movement to abandon the misleading writing they provide the Christian public. I urge them to study geology more thoroughly. Geology cannot be learned from a few elementary textbooks. There is far more to it than that. I also urge creationists to be less dogmatic about Scriptural texts over which there has been substantial diversity of interpretation within the historic Christian church. If they would be of service to Christ's kingdom, they should do some honest-to-goodness scientific thinking that takes facts seriously, facts that were created by the God they wish to defend and serve. We Christians need to stop expending our energies in defending a false creationism and in refuting a false creationism. Let us spend our energies on interpreting the Bible and the world that God in His mercy and grace has given us. A vigorous Christian science will be of far more service in meaningful evangelism and apologetics than the fantasies of young-Earth creationism.

# Appendix

**THE GEOLOGICAL TIME SCALE**

| Eras | Periods | Approximate Time of Beginning (millions of years) |
|------|---------|-------------------------------------------------|
| CENOZOIC | Quaternary | 2 |
| | Tertiary | 65 |
| MESOZOIC | Cretaceous | 140 |
| | Jurassic | 195 |
| | Triassic | 230 |
| PALEOZOIC | Permian | 280 |
| | Pennsylvanian | 310 |
| | Mississippian | 345 |
| | Devonian | 400 |
| | Silurian | 435 |
| | Ordovician | 500 |
| | Cambrian | 600 |
| | Precambrian | 4,650 |

# Notes

## Chapter One

[1]H. Miller, *The Testimony of the Rocks* (Boston: Gould and Lincoln, 1858), p. 428.

[2]For an excellent summary of the many ways in which Christians have looked at geology, see B. Ramm, *The Christian View of Science and Scripture* (Grand Rapids: Eerdmans, 1955), pp. 119–78.

[3]For more detailed views on some relevant exegetical questions, see D. A. Young, *Creation and the Flood* (Grand Rapids: Baker, 1977).

[4]A. J. Desmond, "The Discovery of Marine Transgression and the Explanation of Fossils in Antiquity," in *American Journal of Science* 275 (1975), pp. 692–707.

[5]Hippolytus, "Refutation of All Heresies," in *Ante-Nicene Fathers* (Grand Rapids: Eerdmans, 1951), 5:17.

[6]Herodotus, *The Histories* (Baltimore: Penguin Books, 1954), p. 106.

[7]Strabo, *Geography* I (London: Heinemann, 1931), pp. 181–83.

[8]Aristotle, *Meteorologica* (London: Heinemann, 1952), pp. 107–9.

[9]Ibid., pp. 119–21.

[10]Theophilus, "To Autolycus," in *Ante-Nicene Fathers*, 5:119.

[11]J. Africanus, "Chronography" in *Ante-Nicene Fathers*, 6:130–31.

[12]Basil, *On the Hexameron* (Washington: Catholic University of America Press, 1963), p. 14.

[13]Lactantius, "The Divine Institutes," in *Ante-Nicene Fathers*, 7:94–95.

[14]Lactantius, "The Epitome of the Divine Institutes," in *Ante-Nicene Fathers*, 7:237.

[15]Augustine, "The City of God," in *Nicene and Post-Nicene Fathers* (Grand Rapids: Eerdmans, 1956), 2:315–16.

[16]Clement, "The Miscellanies," in *Ante-Nicene Fathers*, 2:498.

[17]Ibid., p. 501.

[18]A. Kuyper, *Principles of Sacred Theology* (Grand Rapids: Eerdmans, 1965), p. 642.

[19]"The Epistle of Barnabas," in *Ante-Nicene Fathers*, 1:146.

[20]Irenaeus, "Against Heresies," in *Ante-Nicene Fathers*, 1:557.

[21]Hippolytus, "Fragments from Commentaries," in *Ante-Nicene Fathers*, 5:179.

[22]Methodius, "Fragments," in *Ante-Nicene Fathers*, 6:301.

[23]Lactantius, "Divine Institutes," p. 211.

[24]John of Damascus, "Exposition of the Orthodox Faith," in *Nicene and Post Nicene Fathers*, 9:19.

[25]Theophilus, "To Autolycus," pp. 118–20.

[26]Theophilus, "Commentary on the Hexameron," *Ante-Nicene Fathers*, 2:100–104.

[27]Clement, "The Miscellanies," pp. 332–33, 513–14.

[28]J. Africanus, "Chronography," pp. 131–38.

[29]Augustine, "The City of God," p. 233.

[30]Ibid., pp. 300–301.

[31]Hippolytus, "Fragments from Commentaries," p. 179.

[32]Origen, "De Principiis," in *Ante-Nicene Fathers*, 4:341.

[33]Basil, *On the Hexameron*, p. 34.

[34]Hilary, "On the Trinity," in *Nicene and Post-Nicene Fathers*, 9:228.

[35]Augustine, "The City of God," pp. 208–9.

[36]Ibid., p. 208.

[37]Augustine, "Confession," in *Nicene and Post-Nicene Fathers*, 1:178.

[38]Ibid., p. 207.

[39]*Ante-Nicene Fathers*, 1:301–2.

[40]M. Luther, *Lectures on Genesis* (St. Louis: Concordia, 1958).

[41]J. Calvin, *Institutes of the Christian Religion* (Grand Rapids: Eerdmans, 1957), p. 141.

[42]Quoted from E. Hitchcock, *The Religion of Geology* (Boston: Phillips, Sampson, 1851), p. 42.

## Chapter Two

[1]For an excellent and stimulating study of the history of thought on the nature of fossils see M. J. S. Rudwick, *The Meaning of Fossils* (New York: Science Publications, 1976).

[2]Aristotle, *Meteorologica* (London: Heinemann, 1952), pp. 29–35, 205–23.

[3]E. Grant, ed., *A Source Book in Medieval Science* (Cambridge: Harvard, 1974), pp. 616–20.

[4]M. Lister, "Fossil Shells in Several Places in England," in *Philosophical Transactions Royal Society of London* (1671), p. 2282.

[5]J. Ray, *Three Physico-Theological Discourses* (London: Innys, 1713). Arno Press, New York, reprinted this work in 1978.

[6]Ibid., pp. 149–56.

[7]Ibid., pp. 146–49.

[8]R. W. T. Gunther, *Further Correspondence of John Ray* (London: no publisher, 1928), letters 151, 154.

[9]Tertullian, "On the Pallium," in *Ante-Nicene Fathers* (Grand Rapids: Eerdmans, 1951), 4:6.

[10]T. Burnet, *The Sacred Theory of the Earth* (London: Centaur, 1965), p. 26.

[11]Ibid., pp. 27–30.

[12]Ibid., pp. 33–35.

[13]Ibid., pp. 53–64.

[14]Ibid., p. 67.

[15]Ibid., pp. 67–68.

[16]Ibid., pp. 68–73.

[17]Ibid., pp. 98–99.

[18]J. Woodward, *An Essay toward a Natural History of the Earth* (London: Wilkin, 1695), p. 1. Arno Press, New York, reprinted this work in 1978.

[19]Ibid., pp. 3–4.

[20]Ibid., pp. 5–7.

[21]Ibid., pp. 6, 11.

[22]Ibid., pp. 15–33.

[23]Ibid., pp. 34–44.

[24]Ibid., pp. 74–75.

[25]Ibid., pp. 75–76.

[26]Ibid., pp. 76–79.

[27]W. Whiston, *A New Theory of the Earth* (London: R. Roberts, 1696), pp. 123–26. Arno Press, New York, reprinted this work in 1978.

[28]Ibid., pp. 69–76.

[29]Ibid., pp. 79–94.

[30]Ibid., pp. 94–104, 173.

[31]Ibid., pp. 126–156.

[32]Ibid., pp. 199–205.

[33]Ibid., p. 82. Quotation from Authorized Version.

[34]Ibid., pp. 82, 84. Quotation from Authorized Version.

[35]Ibid., pp. 86–87.

[36]Ibid., pp. 89–91.

[37]R. Hooke, *Lectures and Discourses of Earthquakes and Subterraneous Eruptions* (New York: Arno Press, 1978), pp. 280–90.

[38]Ibid., p. 283.

[39]Ibid., pp. 318–19.

[40]Ibid., p. 290.
[41]Ibid., pp. 290–91.
[42]Ibid., pp. 293–94.
[43]Ibid., p. 293.
[44]Ibid., pp. 297–320.
[45]Ibid., pp. 323–44.
[46]Ibid., p. 320.
[47]N. Steno, *Prodromus Concerning a Solid Body Enclosed by Process of Nature Within a Solid* (New York: Hafner, 1968), p. 230.
[48]Ibid., pp. 223–30.
[49]Ibid., pp. 228, 232.
[50]Ibid., pp. 228–29.
[51]Ibid., pp. 262–70.
[52]Ibid., pp. 267–69.

## Chapter Three

[1]Igneous rocks are those that have solidified from very hot liquid called magma. Metamorphic rocks are crystalline rocks that have crystallized in the solid state under very high temperature and pressure.
[2]A. G. Werner, *Short Classification and Description of the Various Rocks* (New York: Hafner, 1971).
[3]G. Buffon, *The Natural History of Animals, Vegetables, and Minerals, with the Theory of the Earth in General* (London, 1976), pp. 358–73.
[4]G. Buffon, *Les Epoques de la Nature* (Paris: Editions du Museum, 1962), pp. 70–71.
[5]Ibid., pp. XC–XCI.
[6]Ibid., p. 21.
[7]J. Hutton, *Theory of the Earth* I (Edinburgh: Creech, 1795), pp. 19–20. Stechert-Hafner reprinted this work in 1972.
[8]Ibid., pp. 20–27.
[9]Ibid., pp. 33–164.
[10]Ibid., pp. 165–200.
[11]Ibid., pp. 198–200.
[12]Ibid., pp. 429–40.
[13]Ibid., pp. 320–38.
[14]Ibid., p. 200.
[15]See Playfair's defense of Hutton against Richard Kirwan's charge of atheism in J. Playfair, *Illustrations of the Huttonian Theory of the Earth* (Edinburgh: Creech, 1802), p. 120.
[16]Plutonic action refers to igneous or metamorphic activity occurring deep within Earth's crust.
[17]R. Kirwan, *Geological Essays* (New York: Arno Press, 1978).
[18]J. A. Deluc, *An Elementary Treatise on Geology* (London: no publisher, 1809).
[19]Ibid., p. 414.
[20]Playfair, *Illustrations of the Huttonian Theory of the Earth*, p. 120.
[21]Ibid., p. 121.
[22]Ibid., pp. 121–22.
[23]Ibid., pp. 125–26.
[24]Quoted in F. C. Haber, *The Age of the World: Moses to Darwin* (Baltimore: Johns Hopkins Press, 1959), p. 201.
[25]G. Cuvier, *Essay on the Theory of the Earth* (Edinburgh: Wm. Blackwood, 1817), pp. 7–23. Arno Press, New York, reprinted this work in 1978.
[26]Ibid., pp. 23, 181.
[27]Ibid., pp. 146–71.

[28]W. Buckland, *Geology and Mineralogy Considered with Reference to Natural Theology* (London: Wm. Pickering, 1837), pp. 8–9. Buckland's work is volume 6 of the Bridgewater Treatises that were designed to set forth "the power, wisdom, and goodness of God as manifested in the creation."

[29]Ibid., p. 13.

[30]Ibid., pp. 16–17.

[31]Ibid., p. 19.

[32]Ibid., pp. 23–26.

[33]A moraine is an irregular, somewhat sinuous pile of gravel that is deposited at the melting margin of a glacier.

[34]Among the most vigorous advocates of "scriptural" geology were Granville Penn who wrote *A Comparative Estimate of the Mineral and Mosaical Geologies* (1822) and George Fairholme who in 1837 brought out his *New and Conclusive Demonstration both of the Fact and Period of the Mosaic Deluge and of its Having Been the only Event of the Kind that has ever occurred upon the Earth.*

[35]The Rev. Adam Sedgwick was elected Woodwardian Professor of Geology at Cambridge in 1818 and was responsible, along with Roderick Murchison, for deciphering much of the Lower Paleozoic stratigraphy of England and Wales.

[36]Conybeare, like Sedgwick, was also an ordained minister. His fame rests largely on his coauthorship, with William Phillips, of the *Outlines of the Geology of England and Wales*. In the introduction to that work, Conybeare took occasion to discuss the matter of the antiquity of the Earth as it relates to both Scripture and geology. Conybeare was convinced that the Earth was indeed ancient, but he saw no conflict with Scripture on that account. Conybeare briefly discussed several possible harmonizations, and, although he wasn't sure which harmonization was best, was confident that reconciliation was genuinely possible.

## Chapter Four

[1]For a survey of many of the theories of harmonization see Ramm, *The Christian View of Science and Scripture*. For American attempts to integrate geology and the Bible see H. Hovenkamp, *Science and Religion in America* (Philadelphia: University of Pennsylvania Press, 1978). See especially Chapter 7. For European thought see C. C. Gillispie, *Genesis and Geology* (New York: Harper, 1959).

[2]J. H. Kurtz, *The Bible and Astronomy*, 3rd ed. (Philadelphia: Lindsay and Blakiston, 1857), pp. 131–36, 232–42.

[3]Ibid., pp. 238–39.

[4]Ibid., pp. 89–101.

[5]Ibid., pp. 103–11.

[6]Ibid., pp. 112–27.

[7]R. Bakewell, *An Introduction to Geology* (New Haven: H. Howe, 1833). This work, the second American edition based on the fourth London edition, was reprinted in 1978 by Arno Press, New York. As the American editor, Benjamin Silliman of Yale added a supplement in which he discussed at length "the consistency of geology with sacred history." This discussion includes pp. 389–466 of Bakewell's work.

[8]J. D. Dana, "Creation: Or, the Biblical Cosmogony in the Light of Modern Science." in *Bibliotheca Sacra* 42 (1880), pp. 201–24.

[9]A. Guyot, *Creation* (New York: Scribner, 1884).

[10]J. W. Dawson, *The Origin of the World according to Revelation and Science*, 7th ed. (London: Hodder and Stoughton, 1898).

[11]F. Delitzsch, *A New Commentary on Genesis* (Edinburgh: T. and T. Clark, 1899).

[12]J. P. Lange, *Commentary on the Holy Scriptures: Genesis* (Grand Rapids: Zondervan, n.d.).

[13]A. Maclaren, *Expositions of Holy Scripture: Genesis, Exodus, Leviticus and Numbers* (Grand Rapids: Eerdmans, 1932).

[14]C. Hodge, *Systematic Theology* (Grand Rapids: Eerdmans, n.d.).

[15]W. G. T. Shedd, *Dogmatic Theology*, 2nd ed. (New York: Scribner, 1889).

[16]J. Orr, *The Bible under Trial* (London: Marshall, 1907), pp. 212–15.

[17]A. H. Strong, *Systematic Theology* (Philadelphia: Griffith and Rowland, 1907).

[18]J. Miley, *Systematic Theology* (New York: Eaton and Mains, 1892).

[19]T. Lewis, *The Six Days of Creation* (Schenectady: Van Debogert, 1855), pp. 127–32, 192–212, 307–14.

[20]W. H. Green, "Primeval Chronology," in *Bibliotheca Sacra* 47 (1890), pp. 285–303.

[21]B. B. Warfield, "On the Antiquity and the Unity of the Human Race," in *Biblical and Theological Studies* (Philadelphia: Presbyterian and Reformed, 1952), pp. 138–61.

## Chapter Five

[1]C. Lyell, *Principles of Geology*, 10th ed. (London: Murray, 1867–8), 1:271–82, 291–301.

[2]J. C. Goodchild, "Some Geological Evidence regarding the Age of the Earth" in *Proceedings of the Royal Physical Society of Edinburgh* 13 (1896), pp. 259–308.

[3]C. Darwin, *The Origin of Species* (London: Murray, 1859), pp. 282–87.

[4]J. Phillips, *Life on the Earth: Its Origin and Succession* (London: Macmillan, 1860), pp. 122–37.

[5]J. Joly, "An Estimate of the Geological Age of the Earth," in *Smithsonian Reports* (1899), pp. 247–88.

[6]For an account of Kelvin's contributions to the question of the age of the Earth see J. D. Burchfield, *Lord Kelvin and the Age of the Earth* (New York: Science History Publications, 1975).

[7]Ibid., pp. 171–79.

[8]See G. Faure, *Principles of Isotope Geology* (New York: John Wiley, 1977), pp. 227–31.

[9]Ibid., pp. 107–11.

[10]See S. R. Taylor, *Lunar Science: A Post-Apollo View* (Elmsford, N.Y.: Pergamon, 1975) and N. M. Short, *Planetary Geology* (Englewood Cliffs, N.J.: Prentice-Hall, 1977).

[11]Ibid.

[12]H. O. Wiley, *Christian Theology* I (Kansas City: Beacon Hill, 1959).

[13]F. J. Hall, *Creation and Man* (New York: Longmans, Green, 1921).

[14]F. Bettex, *The Six Days of Creation in the Light of Modern Science* (Burlington, Iowa: Lutheran Literary Board, 1924).

[15]J. Pohle, *God and the Author of Nature and the Supernatural* (St. Louis: Herder, 1934).

[16]J. O. Buswell, Jr., *A Systematic Theology of the Christian Religion* I (Grand Rapids: Zondervan, 1962).

[17]B. Ramm, *The Christian View of Science and Scripture* (Grand Rapids: Eerdmans, 1955).

[18]R. C. Newman and H. J. Eckelmann, Jr., *Genesis One and the Origin of the Earth* (Downers Grove: InterVarsity, 1977).

[19]R. Maatman, *The Bible, Natural Science, and Evolution* (Grand Rapids: Reformed Fellowship, 1970).

[20]D. A. Young, *Creation and the Flood* (Grand Rapids: Baker, 1977).

[21]H. Bavinck, *Our Reasonable Faith* (Grand Rapids: Eerdmans, 1956).

[22]E. J. Young, *Studies in Genesis One* (Philadelphia: Presbyterian and Reformed, 1964).

[23]D. Kidner, *Genesis* (Downers Grove: InterVarsity, 1967).

[24]R. L. Harris, *Inspiration and Canonicity of the Bible* (Grand Rapids: Zondervan, 1957).

[25]R. L. Katter, *The History of Creation and Origin of the Species* (Minneapolis: Theotes Logos Research, 1967).

[26]A. C. Custance, *Without Form and Void* (Brockville, Canada: Custance 1970).

[27]M. G. Kline, "Because It Had Not Rained," in *Westminster Theological Journal* 20 (1958), pp. 146–57.

[28]F. Pieper, *Christian Dogmatics* (St. Louis: Concordia, 1950).

[29]J. T. Mueller, *Christian Dogmatics* (St. Louis: Concordia, 1934).

[30]H. C. Leupold, *Exposition of Genesis* (Columbus: Wartburg, 1942).

[31]H. Hoeksema, *Reformed Dogmatics* (Grand Rapids: Reformed Free Publishing Association, 1966).

[32]L. Berkhof, *Systematic Theology* (Grand Rapids: Eerdmans, 1930).

[33]V. Hepp, *Calvinism and the Philosophy of Nature* (Grand Rapids: Eerdmans, 1930).

[34]G. M. Price, *The New Geology* (Mountain View, Calif.: Pacific Press, 1923).

[35]B. Nelson, *The Deluge Story in Stone* (Minneapolis: Bethany Fellowship, 1968).

[36]H. Clark, *The New Diluvialism* (Angwin, Calif.: Science Publications, 1946).

[37]A. Rehwinkel, *The Flood* (St. Louis: Concordia, 1951).

[38]D. W. Patten, *The Biblical Flood and the Ice Epoch* (Seattle: Pacific Meridian, 1966).

[39]M. Cook, *Prehistory and Earth Models* (London: Max Parrish, 1966).

[40]R. M. Daly, *Earth's Most Challenging Mysteries* (Grand Rapids: Baker, 1972).

[41]For example, *The Twilight of Evolution, Studies in the Bible and Science, The Genesis Record, Biblical Cosmology and Modern Science, Many Infallible Proofs,* and others.

[42]Published by Baker Book House, Grand Rapids.

[43]W. E. Lammerts, ed., *Why Not Creation?* (Philadelphia: Presbyterian and Reformed, 1970).

[44]W. E. Lammerts, ed., *Scientific Studies in Special Creation* (Philadelphia: Presbyterian and Reformed, 1971).

[45]G. E. Howe, ed., *Speak to the Earth* (Philadelphia: Presbyterian and Reformed, 1975).

[46]Daly, *Earth's Most Challenging Mysteries,* pp. 185–86. Daly accuses Lyell of introducing four basic assumptions into geology that have ever since served as a foundation for geological thought. One of these assumptions is said to be that "all life has evolved from the simple to the complex, from the one-celled to man, and all rocks are in a corresponding ascending sequence." How such an evolutionary theory can be attributed to Lyell is amazing! In fact Lyell argued against such evolutionary schemes because he felt they violated his conception of uniformity in nature!

## Chapter Six

[1]See, for example, the decidedly catastrophist book by a uniformitarian geologist, D. Ager, *The Nature of the Stratigraphic Record* (New York: John Wiley, 1973). Also of interest are a number of recent papers that argue persuasively for some kind of catastrophic cause for the very extensive Cretaceous-Tertiary boundary extinction, e.g., S. Gartner and J. P. McQuirk, "Terminal Cretaceous Extinction Scenario for a Catastrophe," in *Science* 206 (1979), pp. 1272–76 and L. W. Alvarez, W. Alvarez, F. Asaro, and H. V. Michel, "Extraterrestrial Cause for the Cretaceous-Tertiary Extinction," in *Science* 208 (1980), pp. 1095–1108.

[2]J. C. Whitcomb and H. M. Morris, *The Genesis Flood* (Philadelphia: Presbyterian and Reformed, 1961).

[3]S. E. Nevins, "Stratigraphic Evidence of the Flood," in *Symposium on Creation III* (Grand Rapids: Baker, 1971), p. 37.

[4]Whitcomb and Morris, *Genesis Flood,* p. 157.

[5]Ibid., p. 158.

[6]M. Brongersma-Sanders, "Mass Mortality in the Sea," in *Treatise on Marine Ecology and Paleoecology* I (New York: Geological Society of America, 1957), pp. 941–1010.

[7]V. A. Krasilov, *Paleoecology of Terrestrial Plants* (New York: Halsted, 1975), pp. 61–62.

[8]M. Brongersma-Sanders, "Mass Mortality in the Sea," p. 972.

[9]Ibid.

[10]B. E. Northrup, "The Sisquoc Diatomite Fossil Beds," in G. E. Howe, ed., *Speak to the Earth* (Philadelphia: Presbyterian and Reformed, 1975), pp. 1–15.

[11]Ibid., p. 7.

[12]Ibid., p. 8.

[13]W. Schäfer, *Ecology and Paleoecology of Marine Environments* (Chicago: University of Chicago, 1972).

[14]Ibid., p. 58.

[15]Ibid.

[16]Ibid.

[17]Ibid., p. 59.

[18]Ibid., pp. 59–60.

[19]Ibid., pp. 60–61.

[20]Ibid., p. 51.

[21]Ibid., p. 60.

[22]Ibid.

[23]Ibid., p. 98.

[24]Ibid., pp. 98–99.

[25]Ibid., p. 99.

[26]Ibid.

[27]Ibid., pp. 33–37.

[28]Ibid., p. 23.

[29]See N. A. Rupke, "Prolegomena to a Study of Cataclysmal Sedimentation," in W. E. Lammerts, ed., *Why Not Creation?* (Philadelphia: Presbyterian and Reformed, 1970), pp. 141–79; H. M. Morris, "Sedimentation and the Fossil Record: A Study in Hydraulic Engineering," in *Why Not Creation?* pp. 114–37; and H. G. Coffin, "Research on Classic Joggins Petrified Trees," in *Speak to the Earth,* pp. 60–85.

[30]Rupke, "Cataclysmal Sedimentation," pp. 152–57.

[31]N. A. Rupke, "Sedimentary Evidence for the Allochthonous Origin of *Stigmaria,* Carboniferous, Nova Scotia," in *Geological Society of America Bulletin* 80 (1969), pp. 2109–14.

[32]Krasilov, *Paleoecology of Terrestrial Plants,* pp. 34–35.

[33]Ibid., p. 40.

[34]See Ager, *The Nature of the Stratigraphical Record.*

[35]S. E. Nevins, "A Scriptural Groundwork for Historical Geology," in *Symposium on Creation* II, pp. 96–99.

[36]Whitcomb and Morris, *Genesis Flood,* pp. 405–21.

[37]Ibid., p. 408.

[38]S. E. Nevins, "Is the Capitan Limestone a Fossil Reef?" in *Speak to the Earth,* pp. 16–59.

[39]H. Lowenstam, "Niagaran Reefs in the Great Lakes Area," in *Treatise on Marine Ecology and Paleoecology* II, pp. 215–48.

[40]Ibid., p. 224.

[41]J. W. Wells, "Coral Reefs," in *Treatise on Marine Ecology and Paleoecology* I, pp. 609–32.

[42]See the excellent discussion of the relationship between coral reefs and the age of the Earth in D. Wonderly, *God's Time-Records in Ancient Sediments* (Flint, MI: Crystal Press, 1977).

[43]Whitcomb and Morris, *Genesis Flood,* pp. 412–17.

[44]Nevins, "Stratigraphic Evidence of the Flood," pp. 53–54.

[45]Whitcomb and Morris, *Genesis Flood,* p. 412.

[46]Ibid., p. 417.

[47]See M. D. Picard and L. R. High, "Criteria for Recognizing Lacustrine Rocks," in *Recognition of Ancient Sedimentary Environments* (Tulsa: Society of Economic Paleontologists and Mineralogists, 1972), pp. 108–45.

[48]Authigenic minerals are those which grow directly from solutions in the pore spaces between mineral fragments in sediment deposits.

[49]Whitcomb and Morris, *Genesis Flood,* pp. 424–28.

[50]For example, Precambrian rocks in Ontario, Ordovician rocks in the Sahara, and Permian rocks in South Africa all show glacial characteristics.

[51]Whitcomb and Morris, *Genesis Flood,* pp. 245–49.

[52]W. Hamilton and D. H. Krinsley, "Upper Paleozoic Glacial Deposits of South Africa and Southern Australia," in *Geological Society of America Bulletin* 78 (1967), pp. 783–800.

[53]D. H. Krinsley and J. Donahue, "Environmental Interpretation of Sand Grain Surface textures by Electron Microscopy," in *Geological Society of America Bulletin* 79 (1968), pp. 743–48.

## Chapter Seven

[1]A negatively charged particle that orbits the nucleus of an atom.

[2]An electrically neutral particle that is present in the nuclei of most atoms.

[3]A positively charged particle that is present in the nuclei of all atoms. A chemical element is defined on the basis of the number of protons present in an atomic nucleus. For example, all oxygen atoms by definition have eight protons in their nuclei.

[4]The decay constant is defined mathematically as

$$\lambda = -\frac{1}{N}\frac{dN}{dt}$$

where $\lambda$ is the decay constant, N is the number of radioactive atoms of a particular kind in a sample at a given moment, and dN/dt is the rate of decay of those atoms at that moment.

[5]Halflife is the amount of time required for a large number of radioactive atoms of a particular kind in a sample to decay to half the original number. Halflife equals $0.693/\lambda$.

[6]Isotopes are different kinds of atoms of a given element. The difference is caused by varying numbers of neutrons in the nucleus. For example $^{85}Rb$ and $^{87}Rb$ are different isotopes of rubidium. $^{85}Rb$ has 37 protons and 48 neutrons. $^{87}Rb$ has 37 protons and 50 neutrons. $^{85}Rb$ is not radioactive whereas $^{87}Rb$ is.

[7]G. B. Dalrymple and M. A. Lanphere, *Potassium-Argon Dating* (San Francisco: W. H. Freeman, 1969), pp. 39–42.

[8]Ibid., p. 40.

[9]For example, H. S. Slusher, *Critique of Radiometric Dating* (San Diego: Institute for Creation Research, 1973), pp. 29–31.

[10]Dalrymple and Lanphere, *Potassium-Argon Dating,* p. 103.

[11]Ibid., p. 41.

[12]D. O. Acrey, "Problems in Absolute Age Determination," in W. E. Lammerts, ed., *Why Not Creation?* (Philadelphia: Presbyterian and Reformed, 1970), pp. 72–78.

[13]Slusher, *Critique of Radiometric Dating,* p. 30.

[14]R. L. Whitelaw, "Radiocarbon Confirms Biblical Creation (And So Does Potassium-Argon)," in *Why Not Creation?* pp. 90–100, and "Radiocarbon and Potassium-Argon Dating in the Light of New Discoveries in Cosmic Rays," in *Why Not Creation?* pp. 101–05.

[15]Whitelaw, "Radiocarbon Confirms Biblical Creation (And So Does Potassium-Argon)," p. 98.

[16]Ibid.

[17]Ibid., p. 99.

[18]S. P. Clementson, "A Critical Examination of Radioactive Dating of Rocks," in G. E. Howe, ed., *Speak to the Earth* (Philadelphia: Presbyterian and Reformed, 1975), pp. 365–75.

[19]Dalrymple and Lanphere, *Potassium-Argon Dating,* pp. 132–33.

[20]G. B. Dalrymple and J. G. Moore, "Argon 40: Excess in Submarine Pillow Basalts from Kilauea Volcano, Hawaii," in *Science* 161 (1968), pp. 1132–35.

[21]Slusher, *Critique of Radiometric Dating,* p. 32.

[22]Ibid.

[23]Ibid.

[24]M. L. Bottino and P. D. Fullagar, "The Effects of Weathering on Whole-Rock Rb-Sr Ages of Granitic Rocks," in *American Journal of Science* 266 (1968), pp. 661–70.

[25]S. R. Hart, "The Petrology and Isotopic-Mineral Age Relations of a Contact Zone in the Front Range, Colorado," in *Journal of Geology* 72 (1964), pp. 493–525.

[26]Slusher, *Critique of Radiometric Dating,* pp. 33–34.

[27]Ibid., p. 33.

[28]M. Cook, *Prehistory and Earth Models* (London: Max Parrish, 1966), pp. 63–64.

[29]D. W. Davis, J. Gray, G. L. Cumming, and H. Baadsgaard, "Determination of the $^{87}$Rb Decay Constant," in *Geochimica et Cosmochimica Acta* 41 (1977), pp. 1745–49, and W. Neumann and E. Huster, "Discussion of the $^{87}$Rb Half-Life Determined by Absolute Counting," in *Earth and Planetary Science Letters* 33 (1976), pp. 277–88.

[30]Slusher, *Critique of Radiometric Dating,* pp. 17–29.

[31]Ibid., p. 22.

[32]See the thorough discussion of concordia diagrams by Faure, *Principles of Isotope Geology* (New York: Wiley, 1977), pp. 207–16.

[33]Ibid., p. 206.

[34]Cook, *Prehistory and Earth Models,* pp. 23–62.

[35]H. Faul, *Nuclear Geology* (New York: John Wiley, 1954), pp. 270, 276.

[36]A. O. Nier, "The Isotopic Constitution of Radiogenic Leads and the Measurement of Geological Time, II," in *Physical Review* 55 (1939), pp. 153–63.

[37]Ibid., p. 156.

[38]Ibid., p. 155.

[39]Cook, *Prehistory and Earth Models,* p. 55.

[40]See the graph and table in Faure, *Principles of Isotope Geology,* pp. 204–05.

## Chapter Eight

[1]T. G. Barnes, "Decay of the Earth's Magnetic Moment and the Geochronological Implications," in G. E. Howe, ed., *Speak to the Earth* (Philadelphia: Presbyterian and Reformed, 1975), pp. 300–313.

[2]Mathematically the dipole moment is expressed as

$$M = \frac{4}{3}\pi a^3 J$$

where M is the dipole moment, a is the radius of the spherical magnet, and J is the intensity of the magnetic field. The intensity is the force required to rotate a magnet through a given angle.

[3]For a discussion of ancient magnetism see D. W. Strangway, *History of the Earth's Magnetic Field* (New York: McGraw-Hill, 1970).

[4]The Curie temperature of magnetite is 578°C and that of hematite is 675°C.

[5]Declination is the horizontal component of the Earth's magnetic field at a given point on Earth's surface. It is the direction in which a compass needle would point and is measured with reference to geographic north. Inclination is the angle between the horizontal and Earth's magnetic field. The angle may be measured by a magnetized dip needle. Polarity refers to location and possible "reversal" of north and south magnetic poles. For intensity see note 2.

[6]See especially the excellent review paper by P. J. Smith, "The Intensity of the Ancient Geomagnetic Field: a Review and Analysis," in *Geophysical Journal* 12 (1967), pp. 321–62.

## Chapter Nine

[1]J. C. Whitcomb and H. M. Morris, *The Genesis Flood* (Philadelphia: Presbyterian and Reformed, 1961), p. 382.

[2]See H. M. Morris, W. W. Boardman, Jr., and R. F. Koontz, *Science and Creation* (San Diego: Creation-Science Research Center, 1971), p. 78.

[3]B. Mason, *Principles of Geochemistry,* 3rd ed. (New York: John Wiley, 1966), p. 20.

[4]Whitcomb and Morris, *Genesis Flood,* pp. 379–80.

[5]H. Petterson, "Cosmic Spherules and Meteoritic Dust," in *Scientific American* 202 (1960), p. 132.

[6]There have been other estimates of meteoritic infall and not all yield rates of infall as great as those estimated by Petterson.

[7]Whitcomb and Morris, *Genesis Flood,* p. 380.

[8]The reader should consult the series of semi-popular reprints from *Scientific American* on plate tectonics, sea-floor spreading, and continental drift entitled *Continents Adrift and Continents Aground* (San Francisco: W. H. Freeman, 1976).

[9]S. E. Nevins, "Evolution: the Ocean Says No!" in *Symposium on Creation V* (Grand Rapids: Baker, 1975), pp. 77–83.

[10]Ibid., p. 78.

[11]Ibid., p. 80.

[12]Ibid., p. 81.

[13]Ibid.

[14]Ibid., p. 82.

[15]Ibid., p. 83.

[16]Ibid.

# Chapter Ten

[1]The sense in which I use the terms "uniformity" and "uniformitarianism" will become clearer through the chapter. There has been a great deal of discussion of the meaning of these and allied terms and of the statement, "the present is the key to the past" among geologists. No doubt many geologists would reject my using the terms "uniformity" and "uniformitarianism" as I do. But this is basically irrelevant because I am not so much interested in terms as I am in principles, and the principle I call uniformitarianism is one that is nearly unanimously agreed upon by geologists. For some interesting discussions of the idea of uniformitarianism see C. C. Simpson, "Uniformitarianism. An Inquiry into Principle, Theory, and Method in Geohistory and Biohistory," in *Essays in Evolution and Genetics in Honor of Theodosius Dobzhansky* (New York: Appleton-Century-Crofts, 1970), pp. 43–96; and also R. Hooykaas, "Catastrophism in Geology, its Scientific Character in Relation to Actualism and Uniformitarianism," *Koninklijke Nederlandse Akademie van Wetenschappen, afd. Letterkunde, Med.* (n.r.), 33 (1970), pp. 271–316. Both these papers have been reprinted in C. C. Albritton, Jr., ed., *Philosophy of Geohistory: 1785–1970* (Stroudsburg, Penn.: Dowden, Hutchinson, and Ross, 1975).

[2]For Northrup, "evolutionary macrochronological" is the same as "uniformitarian."

[3]B. E. Northrup, "Franciscan and Related Rocks, and Their Significance in the Geology of Western California: a book review," in G. E. Howe, ed., *Speak to the Earth,* (Philadelphia: Presbyterian and Reformed, 1975), p. 253.

[4]B. E. Northrup, "The Sisquoc Diatomite Fossil Beds," in *Speak to the Earth,* p. 3.

[5]H. M. Morris, "Sedimentation and the Fossil Record: a Study in Hydraulic Engineering," W. E. Lammerts, ed., *Why Not Creation?* (Philadelphia: Presbyterian and Reformed, 1970), p. 123.

[6]S. E. Nevins, "A Scriptural Groundwork for Historical Geology," in *Symposium on Creation II* (Grand Rapids: Baker, 1970), p. 97.

[7]L. C. Steinhauer, "Is Uniformity Meaningful?" in *Symposium on Creation V,* p. 89.

[8]J. C. Whitcomb and H. M. Morris, *Genesis Flood* (Philadelphia: Presbyterian and Reformed, 1961), p. 143.

[9]Ibid., p. 165.

[10]Ibid., p. 452.

[11]Those who hold to the gap theory also propose the existence of global catastrophes, but these are associated with the supposed judgment of Lucifer in Genesis 1 rather than with the flood of Noah.

[12]C. Burdick, "Streamlining Stratigraphy," in W. E. Lammerts, ed., *Scientific Studies in Special Creation* (Philadelphia: Presbyterian and Reformed, 1971), p. 125.

[13]N. A. Rupke, "Prolegomena to a Study of Cataclysmal Sedimentation," in *Why Not Creation?* p. 164.

[14]S. E. Nevins, "Stratigraphic Evidence of the Flood," in *Symposium on Creation III*, p. 60.

[15]Whitcomb and Morris, *Genesis Flood*, p. 408.

[16]See e.g., L. C. Steinhauer, "The Case for Global Catastrophism," in *Symposium on Creation V*, pp. 99-109.

[17]Steinhauer, "Is Uniformity Meaningful?" p. 85.

[18]Ibid., p. 90.

[19]Steinhauer, "The Case for Global Catastrophism," p. 106-7.

[20]Ibid., p. 107.

[21]Nevins, "A Scriptural Groundwork for Historical Geology," p. 80.

[22]Ibid., p. 81.

[23]S. J. Gould, "Is Uniformitarianism Necessary?" *American Journal of Science* 263 (1965), pp. 223-28.

[24]Nevins, "A Scriptural Groundwork for Historical Geology," p. 88.

[25]Ibid.

[26]Ibid., p. 90.

[27]Ibid., p. 99.

[28]Northrup, "The Sisquoc Diatomite Fossil Beds," pp. 7-8.

[29]Whitcomb and Morris, *Genesis Flood*, pp. 130-31.

[30]Ibid., pp. 136-37.

[31]Ibid., p. 137.

[32]Ibid., p. 200.

[33]A hard, compact sedimentary rock composed of very fine crystalline silica.

[34]Actually, an example of modern day chert precipitation has been reported. See M. N. A. Peterson and C. C. von der Borch, "Chert: Modern Inorganic Deposition in a Carbonate-precipitating Locality," *Science* 149 (1965), pp. 1501-03.

[35]Three recent introductory texts make this quite clear. See, for example, F. Press and R. Siever, *Earth* (San Francisco: W. H. Freeman, 1974), pp. 61-62. They say, "Uniformitarianism, as we understand it today, does not hold that the rates of all geological processes or their precise nature has to be the same." See also S. Judson, K. S. Deffeyes, and R. B. Hargraves, *Physical Geology* (Englewood Cliffs, N.J.: Prentice-Hall, 1976), pp. 18-19, and R. F. Flint and B. J. Skinner, *Physical Geology*, 2nd ed. (New York: John Wiley, 1977), pp. 84-85. The latter text says, "The more we learn of Earth's history, the more we must question whether the rates of all cycles have always been the same as they are now. The evidence seems against constancy, and some rates may once have been more rapid, others much slower."

[36]Just to see what a former colleague in a secular university would say, I asked him if he rejected the possibility of global catastrophes on a priori principial grounds. He said no. Then I said, "So then you would reject catastrophes because of the geological evidence." He replied that that was not true either, because he had seen many catastrophes. I said that those are only small-scale catastrophes. He then said that he thought anything was possible and that he thought there might have been great catastrophes in the past. For example, he thought the Earth passing through a comet's tail might have some devastating effects and thus be considered as a global catastrophe. This is hardly a rejection of catastrophes, and yet my colleague also thought of himself as a uniformitarian!

[37]Gould, "Is Uniformitarianism Necessary?"

[38]Naturally one could write at great length about the meaning of this statement. I do not mean to imply that *every* law is *everywhere* and *always* applicable. There are many situations where, for example, the ideal gas law does not pertain to the situation. All the statement intends to say is that God created a lawbound universe in which the laws of the past are continuous with those of the present. This could even mean that as the configuration of the

universe changes, some laws have systematically varied as a function of time just as some laws are a function of scale. But this only means that the law which is varying is dependent on a higher, more over-arching law.

[39] H. M. Morris, "Science versus Scientism in Historical Geology," in *Scientific Studies in Special Creation*, p. 109.

[40] Ibid., p. 111.

[41] Steinhauer, "Is Uniformity Meaningful?" p. 92.

[42] I have attempted to develop this point at great length in *Creation and the Flood*.

[43] An example of this is Patten's attempt to explain catastrophes in terms of errant movements of bodies within the solar system.

[44] Nevins, "Stratigraphic Evidence of the Flood," p. 37.

[45] Ibid., p. 43.

[46] Whitcomb and Morris, *Genesis Flood*, p. 417.

[47] See *Creation and the Flood*, chapter IX, and also R. O. Barnes, "Thermal Consequences of a Short Time Scale for Sea-Floor Spreading," in *Journal of the American Scientific Affiliation* 32 (1980), pp. 123–25.

[48] By no means does this mean that I necessarily do not think the Flood was global. It only means I reject the common catastrophist viewpoint which sees nearly all sedimentary rocks formed as a result of the Flood. In my judgment if the Flood truly were global then we ought to look for the evidence where we might expect to find it, namely, among Pleistocene or Recent deposits. Even then, I'm not sure how well we could recognize it.

## Chapter Eleven

[1] E.g., D. A. Young, *Creation and the Flood* (Grand Rapids: Baker, 1977), D. E. Wonderly, *God's Time-Records in Ancient Sediments* (Flint: Crystal, 1977), and numerous articles published over the years in *Journal of the American Scientific Affiliation*.

[2] R. L. Whitelaw, "Radiocarbon Confirms Biblical Creation (And So Does Potassium-Argon)," in W. E. Lammerts, ed., *Why Not Creation?* (Philadelphia: Presbyterian and Reformed, 1970), pp. 90–100.

[3] R. V. Gentry, "Giant Radioactive Halos: Indicators of Unknown Radioactivity," in *Science* 169 (1970), pp. 670–73, and "Radiohalos in a Radiochronological and Cosmological Perspective," in *Science* 184 (1974), pp. 62–66.

[4] Young, *Creation and the Flood*, pp. 81–89.

[5] Ibid.

[6] W. H. Green, "Primeval Chronology," in *Bibliotheca Sacra* 47 (1890), pp. 284–303.

[7] See the appendix in an article by A. C. Custance, "Flood Traditions of the World," in *Symposium on Creation IV* (Grand Rapids: Baker, 1972), pp. 9–44.

[8] I am not saying that theology is just a science like all the other sciences, nor am I saying that the Bible is merely a book of facts that need to be organized in a logical manner. Clearly theology has a religious-ethical end as well as an intellectual one. Theology should lead us closer to Christ. Yet theology does have a scientific character in that it is, and must be, based on biblical data.

[9] See J. D. Burchfield, *Lord Kelvin and the Age of the Earth* (New York: Science History Publications, 1975).

[10] H. M. Morris, *Studies in the Bible and Science* (Philadelphia: Presbyterian and Reformed, 1966), pp. 33–38.

[11] T. Lewis, *The Six Days of Creation* (Schenectady: Van Debogert, 1885), 1:1.

[12] See chapters 4 and 5 for a number of these theologians.

[13] The Chicago Statement on Inerrancy reflects the general essence of what I have in mind by the term *inerrant*.

# Indexes

# Index of Names

# Subject Index